CAREERS IN
PHOTOGRAPHY

By ART EVANS

Photograph by Jim Russi.

CAREERS IN PHOTOGRAPHY

By Art Evans

with contributions from Bill Alnes, Krisjan Carroll, Paul R. Comon, Tom Countryman, Chic Donchin, Harry M. Fleenor, Denine Gentilella, Mary Garand, Alice and Peter Gowland, Gerry Kopelow, Wesley Lambert, Randy Leffingwell, Dan Madden, Dennis Miller, Lieutenant Colonel Bart Oldenberg, Jim Russi, Robert Schlosser, Anne Sharp, Bob Shell, John Upton, James and Laura Weintraub, Pat Willits.

Library of Congress Catalog Card Number 91-67897

ISBN 0-9626508-3-8

Library of Congress Cataloging-in-Publication Data
Evans, Arthur G.
    Careers in photography / by Art Evans ; with essays by Bill Alnes . . . [et al.].
    p. cm.
    ISBN 0-9626508-3-8 : $19.95
    1. Photography—Vocational guidance. 1. Alnes, Bill. II Title.
TR154.E92 1992
770'.23'2—dc20   91-67897
                                                      CIP

Published by Photo Data Research
800-8 South Pacific Coast Highway, Redondo Beach, California 90277
Telephone (310) 543-1085, Fax (310) 540-8068

In cooperation with Patch Communications, Inc.

Manufactured in the United States of America

Cover design suggested by Krisjan Carroll. Cover photographs: upper left, Gerry Kopelow; upper center, Peter Gowland; upper right, John Schaer, courtesy of CNN; lower left, Art Evans; lower center, Gerry Kopelow; lower right, Bob Dunsmore, courtesy the Sports Car Club of America.

Design and layout by Lloyd Greenlund.

Photograph by Jim Russi.

CAREERS IN PHOTOGRAPHY

PREFACE

This book is volume one of a two volume set. The second book is titled, *Photo Business Careers.*

Originally, this project started out as one book. But very quickly, it became obvious that there was simply too much material for one book. And the material naturally divided itself into two distinct categories: being an employee and owning a photography business. The information in the two books is complementary. It is highly recommended that the second book be acquired. To order, see the last page of this book.

An interesting facet about writing and editing these books involved looking at the entire field of photography. To do this in an organized way, an outline was created. To put it more accurately, an outline evolved. As time went by, more and more specialties came to light and were included. And the outline was continually reorganized. Eventually, it became the basis for the contents for the books. But the outline itself is interesting enough to share with readers. So it is reproduced on the inside front cover. The outline communicates something of what is in the books.

One of the concepts of the books is to include the experiences and advice of professionals involved in various specializations. An interesting phenomenon came to light. Almost every successful professional is narrowly specialized. There seems to be very few generalists left.

There are many other activities that use photography which are not covered in this book simply because they do not require any special interest in or knowledge of any aspect of photography. A good example is copying, or to be more exact, xerography. One does not have to know anything about photography or xerography to operate a copy machine or, in fact, be aware that xerography is an off-shoot of photography.

Thanks are due to quite a number of people who were instrumental in bringing the books to life, in no particular order: John Upton, my friend and colleague at Orange Coast College; Stiles Wegener; Burt Reinhardt, Vice Chairman, Cable News Network and my former boss at Paramount; Alyssa Levy, Public Relations Manager., Turner Broadcasting System, Inc. News Division; Paul Comon whose advice and counsel is always valuable; Anne Sharp, without whom Photo Data Research wouldn't work; Blanka Kopecky at Imageland; Catherine Smith, Expansion Coordinator, Glamour Shots, Candid Color Systems; Staff Sergeant D. R. Livsey, Marine Corps Recruiting Service; Carol Fruik, Office of the Chief of Public Affairs, Department of the Army; Chief Ted Cook, Sergeant David J. Paroda and Identification Technician Nicole Whalley-Muller of the Culver City Police Department; Paula V. Druk, Public Relations, Princess Cruises; American Society of Camera Collectors president Gene Lester; Charles Evans, Marge Binks, Kay Kelly, Vice President, Sports Car Club of America; Nick Craw, President, Sports Car Club of America; Bob Shell, Editor, *Shutterbug* magazine and an important part of Photo Data Research; *Shutterbug* magazine; *PhotoPro* magazine; Rick Burns at Griffin Printing; Kiyoshi Suzuki, Asahi Photo and Video; Peter Jansen, Winnipeg Photo Limited; Dr. Robert Crum, Ms. Debra McMahan, Daniel Freeman Memorial Hospital; Michael Verbois, Vice President of Education, Brooks Institute of Photography; Gerry Kopelow, whose loyalty and hard work is much appreciated and Randy Leffingwell, a kindred soul in writing, photography and cars.

Essays by specialists are attributed to the contributors. All other materials in this book are by the author. While a large number helped, any errors are solely those of the author.

Photograph by Peter Burian.

CAREERS IN PHOTOGRAPHY

Table of Contents

Photograph by Bob Shell.

CAREERS IN PHOTOGRAPHY

Table of Contents (cont'd)

Photograph by Gerry Kopelow.

CAREERS IN PHOTOGRAPHY

Chapter 1

STRATEGY FOR A CAREER

If someone should ask, "Can you foretell the future?" you would undoubtedly answer, "Of course not." But this answer is not entirely true. With some reservations, you can foretell or plot your own future.

Okay, you answer. But how? First, think about these sayings: If you don't know where you are, how can you tell where you are going? And if you don't know where you are going, how do you know when you get there?

In order to foretell your future, you have to decide what that future is. In other words, what will your situation be when you get there? So before you can foretell your own future, you have to set a goal. This goal should be very specific. For example, you could say that you want to be a staff photographer on a major newspaper. Or you may want to own and operate your own portrait studio. Your's may be different from these two examples, but whatever it is, put the goal in specific terms. If you don't have a goal, you cannot foretell your career future. Remember, "If you don't know where you are going, how do you know when you get there?"

Once you have set a specific goal, part of the battle is already won. The next task in future foretelling is to analyze your own capabilities, resources and situation. In other words, where are you? (If you don't know where you are, how can you tell where you are going?) Then you have to determine the steps or processes necessary to achieve your goal. And finally, you estimate a reasonable time period in which to accomplish the necessary steps.

This may be difficult and may require some research. But after all, you are foretelling the future, and it's yours. Isn't it worth considerable time and trouble?

The final task in foretelling the future is to plan your strategy for getting there. This is somewhat easier than it sounds. Let's say that you have determined that it is reasonable and realistic for you to achieve your career goal in six years. If so, then analyze your situation and determine exactly what you will have to do, step-by-step. It's best to commit this to paper. Then, from an analysis of the steps, decide what you will have to do to get half way there, or in three years. Next decide what you will have to do each year

Photograph by Glen A. Derbyshire, courtesy Brooks Institute of Photography.

to achieve the interim three-year goal.

Now look at what you have to do the first year. Break the steps into 12 parts and determine what you have to do each month. Break the first month into four steps and determine what you will have to do each week. Now break the first week into 5 (6 or 7) steps and determine what you have to do each day. Tomorrow is the first day of your future. Get up in the morning and DO IT.

If you continue this process, you will achieve your goal and will indeed have foretold your own future. This is not to say, of course that the process is infallible. You could have an accident tomorrow and be blinded for life. This would probably put an end to your hopes for a career in photography! Why probably? Remember, one of the greatest composers of music who ever lived—Beethoven—was deaf when he composed some of his best music!

What should your strategy be for the development of a career in photography or in a related field? First, assess yourself and then assess the field.

The purpose of these books is to help you develop such a strategy. Study the different fields described in the books. Does any one appeal to you more than others? You may have said, "Yes, I want to be a director of photography in the feature film business." Then ask yourself, "How realistic is this goal?"

Certainly there will be some new directors of photography as time goes by. Those who are presently directors of photography will eventually retire or die. How many new slots will open up? Depending on your assessment of yourself, what are your chances of filling one of these new slots within the time period you have set for yourself?

After you have studied these books and settled on a field, the next step is to investigate it further. Go to the library and see if you can find other materials to read on the subject. If you are in college or plan to go, visit a counselor and instructors who are teaching the subject. Try to find and talk with others who are already working in the field. Pick out prospective employers and see if you can interview them.

Remember, you are only conducting an investigation at this point. You are not committed to anything. Once you go beyond the investigatory period, you will be investing considerable time and perhaps significant amounts of money.

Photograph by Dennis Miller.

CAREERS IN PHOTOGRAPHY

Take your time and do a good job of investigation. Would you like to be a year or even two down the road and then find out that the field you have selected is not for you?

If you are in high school or college (or in between), your immediate goal should be to go on to a degree (or certificate). For a young person interested in photography, enrollment in a community college may be a good course to pursue. You can achieve a major in photography in some community colleges and, at the same time, accumulate the credits necessary if you decide to go on to a four-year degree.

If you decide on this course, try to get a part-time job or enroll in a work-study course in the photographic specialty you are interested in. This is a good way to get exposed to the specialty without losing too much time should you discover later that it is not for you. Before you set out to try for a part-time job, research the possibilities in your area. Attempt to get employment or a work-study assignment with the very best.

While you are still in school, and particularly if you have a part-time job or work-study assignment, you can start to assemble a portfolio. At the same time you are working towards a particular specialty, you should take some courses outside that specialty. You may, in fact, achieve your goal in six years. Yet after fifteen or twenty years, you may want to change. You may not think you would want to now, but you cannot really tell now what your state of mind will be in fifteen or twenty years. The point is, while you should concentrate on your goal now, you should also keep an open mind. And while you are still in school, you should take courses in and gain some experience in the two fields related to photography that will in all probability stand you in good stead for the future: computers and writing.

Before you start working on a career strategy, read the rest of this book. The one you are now reading is only half the story of photography careers. There is a second volume called *Photo Business Careers*. This first book is directed more towards working as an employee while the second emphasizes starting and running your own business. To order the second volume, turn to the last page in this book.

Photograph by Gerry Kopelow.

STRATEGY FOR A CAREER

Chapter 2

EDUCATION and TRAINING

By John Upton

Prior to World War II, there was relatively little education available for aspiring photographers seeking careers in any field of photography. Most learned the fundamentals of professional photography by working for a professional photographer either in the capacity of paid assistants or, in many cases, as unpaid apprentices. Others were simply self-taught. A few trade schools and correspondence schools existed in large metropolitan areas. Very few colleges, universities or art schools offered courses in photography.

The situation changed dramatically after the war. Servicemen returning to civilian life had the benefit of government subsidized education under the GI Bill. Existing trade schools offering photography flourished and new programs were established to provide professional training for those seeking careers in a burgeoning media industry. The explosive growth of the television industry coupled with the extensive use of photography and motion pictures for reportage, advertising, public relations, education, science, entertainment and personal enrichment created what the communication theorist Marshall McLuhan called a "media environment." There was a realization that much of what we know of our social and physical world has been learned from electronic and photographic images. In the 1920's, the artist-educator Laszlo Moholy-Nagy prophesied the illiterate of the future would be the person ignorant of both pen and camera. The has become a fundamental truth of contemporary society.

By the 1960's, universities, colleges and art schools had developed comprehensive programs in still photography and cinema. A 1970 survey of American colleges and universities revealed that the enrollment in photography courses (including cinema and graphic arts) was 79,000. By 1978, the figure had increased to 162,000. The widespread entrance of photography into academia included not only the teaching of craft and skills, but it also encompassed the historical and

Photography by Glen A. Derbyshire. Courtesy Brooks Institute of Photography.

theoretical aspects of the medium. Most of these new programs were in the fine arts curriculums. However, enormous growth was also evident in cinema and professional photography programs.

Photography education in secondary schools has increased in recent years. Prior to 1970, only a few high schools had classroom instruction in photography. By 1978, 3000 of 25,000 American high schools offered elective courses in photography. Some innovative elementary school programs have been teaching children to use cameras to develop skills in communication and photography for personal expression. An underlying premise of these programs is to develop a visually literate society.

Today, the person interested in a career in photography has a rich array of educational opportunities in both private and public schools. For the person desiring beginning courses, there are classes in university extension programs, community colleges, adult schools, community sponsored programs and workshops in every region of the country. Enrolling in an introductory class will allow you to test your personal interest and aptitude. If you decide you would like advanced training to prepare for a career in some specialized field within photography, there are many choices.

However, before deciding on the college or program you wish to enter, you should research the profession itself. That is the purpose of the book you are now reading and the second volume, *Photo Business Careers*. While these two books survey the entire field, there are many specific occupational areas in photography which are the subjects of numerous other books. Visit your library. In addition, you should introduce yourself to photographers employed in the field in which you are interested. Their advice could prove invaluable in helping you make a decision about your career.

Generally, college-level photography education is found in three academic areas. Photojournalism is most often in a department of journalism or communications. Cinema may be in a combined television and motion picture program, or it may be included in a theater arts department. Fine arts photography is usually in the art of design department. However, it is important to carefully examine college catalogs because photography may be found in diverse areas such as industrial arts or some scientific discipline. Many colleges and universities offer only a few courses in photography. Their intention is to provide some photography training as an adjunct to a broader academic major. However, several colleges provide a broad range of courses in several areas of photography. These schools expect their graduates to enter the world of professional photography upon graduation. Your choice of educational institution should be based on careful research. Obtain the catalog of the institution you are considering. Visit the school and speak to a counselor within the department in which you will be enrolling. If possible, speak to graduates of the school to determine if the school will provide the education you will need to enter the field.

The three best-known professional programs of photography in the U.S. are at the Rochester Institute of Technology in Rochester, New York; the Art Center College of Design in Pasadena, California; and Brooks Institute of Photography in Santa Barbara, California. many of this country's most successful photographers are graduates of these institutions. All of them offer bachelors and masters degrees in a variety of specialization areas within the field of professional photography. However, all of these schools are private and therefore charge tuition.

Many universities, colleges and community colleges offer professional programs in photography. Generally, the tuition for state supported institutions is lower than private schools if you are a resident of the state. The least expensive professional training is available, in community colleges where the tuition is often considerably less than the four-year programs of state universities and colleges. Community college programs can usually be completed in two to three years. Two of the best-known community college photography programs are Orange Coast College in Costa Mesa, California and Daytona Beach Community College, Daytona Beach, Florida. An extensive listing of over one thousand college photography programs is available in Kodak Publication T-17, *A Survey of College Instruction in Photography*. Copies can be obtained by writing to the Eastman Kodak Company, 343 State Street, Rochester, New York 14650. Another reference is *The Photographer's Source* by Henry Horenstein published by Simon & Schuster in 1989.

For those more interested in photography as a fine art rather than as a commercial enterprise, there is an even greater choice of educational opportunities than in the field of professional photography. Art schools and the fine art or design departments of universities and colleges throughout North America include photography as a studio specialization along with painting, sculpture, printmaking and other more traditional art media. Often, students choose a particular program because of the reputations of the artist-photographers on the faculty. Besides learning the techniques of photography, students are expected to take courses in other studio arts, the history of art, art theory, criticism and other disciplines within the humanities. The primary objective of these programs is for the students to develop a personal vision. Although art programs do not usually teach photographers how to earn a livelihood, nevertheless many professional photographers have found art education to be valuable in providing them with an aesthetic understanding of how to inflict the meaning of their photographs. Most college-level fine arts programs offer course work leading to a bachelor of fine arts degree. Many art programs also accept graduate students seeking a master of fine arts.

If you are unable to enroll in a long-term educational program, there are other excellent possibilities for learning photography. Each year, hundreds of short-term workshops are offered by educational institutions, photography organizations and corporate sponsors. Workshops have the potential of providing intensive fine art or professional photography education in a relatively short period of time. Some workshops are taught by well-known figures in the field of photography. Other workshops may focus on photographic techniques or special processes. An example of the latter is the new Eastman Kodak Company's Center for Creative Imaging at Camden, Maine. Courses are offered year-round in digital imaging and computer graphics. Four of the most popular workshop centers with extensive programs are Anderson Ranch Arts Center at Snowmass Village, Colorado; Friends of Photography Workshops in San Francisco, California; The Maine Photographic Workshops at Rockport, Maine; and the International Center of Photography in New York City.

Another form of education that should be mentioned is working as a photographer's assistant or apprentice. For those who have learned the fundamentals of photography, this approach may provide the most direct route to a professional career. The advantage of learning while working is the experience gained by working directly with a practicing professional photographer. The disadvantage is that what you learn is limited by the knowledge and specialization of your employer. An ideal situation is to combine the experience of working as an assistant with the breadth of educations in a reputable school of photography.

If you decide to prepare for a career in photography, it is important to devote time and effort in research. Obtain catalogs and brochures from colleges and schools of photography. Survey the books in your library about the variety of opportunities in professional photography. Professional associations such as the Professional Photographers of America publish magazines and other information you may find helpful. Seek advice and counseling from successful photographers. It is important to realize that education must be a continuous process. In an age when continual retraining is an economic necessity, it is vital to realize that education is a lifelong activity.

Photograph courtesy Brooks Institute of Photography.

EDUCATION and TRAINING

CAREERS IN PHOTOGRAPHY

Chapter 3

AERIAL PHOTOGRAPHY

There are a number of specialties within the field of aerial photography. The one we are most familiar with is called oblique, because it is taken at an angle.

A second type is called photogrammetry, which is the process of making surveys and maps through the use of photography. In this case, the pictures are taken straight down; the lens axis is perpendicular to the ground.

Another sub-specialty within aerial photography is TV and motion pictures. Aerial footage is constantly used on TV news and by advertisers. Some companies in film-making centers specialize in this sort of work. Recently I saw a movie with a high-speed chase through the Grand Canyon, taken 20 feet above the water. Helicopters are often employed in making movies and TV shows. Some cinematographers specialize in aerial shooting.

OBLIQUE AERIAL PHOTOGRAPHY

By Bill Alnes

If you look, you will find aerial photographs in almost every publication. Newspapers use aerial photos almost every day. In magazines, these pictures are used to advertise real estate, leisure cruises and vacation locations to name but a few. Text books are full of them as are other types of books, calendars, posters and postcards.

This type of aerial photography is called "oblique" because it is taken at an angle. Oblique aerial photography can be accomplished with the sort of equipment most professionals and even advanced amateurs have. You simply load up, jump in your favorite flying machine and head for the job site. This is the sort of photography I do.

The unique aspect of aerial photography is that aerial

This shot of the Hermosa Beach Open Vollyball Tournament is an excellent example of oblique aerial photography. Photograph by Bill Alnes.

photographers get to go flying. This is the reason many become aerial photographers in the first place. It is an excellent excuse to go for a hop.

Starting a career in aerial photography is probably no harder than any other. You simply work, work, work until you are one! Someone has to do it; it might as well be you. Before you get into aerial photography, you have to master the art and craft of photography itself.

Oblique aerial photography is just like normal photography except that you look down more than you are used to. But it's the view that grabs you. The secret is to take just the right piece of it home with you.

Most aerial photographers I know or have heard of are accomplished fixed-wing pilots. Because of this, they know just how to get their cameras in the right position for the best possible shot. Flying skills and photographic skills go hand in hand.

A unique aspect of aerial photography is the range of landscape you can cover in a given amount of time. An airplane or helicopter affords you a freedom of movement and vantage point impossible to achieve from the ground. You don't necessarily need every pilot rating, but you do need to know the flight characteristics of the aircraft you are using.

The best plan is to find an aircraft you like and stick with it. If you don't know how to fly, you will also need a pilot you are comfortable with. Some flight instructors also do a lot of aerial photo work, so try to find such a person. The idea in aerial photography is to get the shot you envisioned in as little time as possible. This takes patience, practice and planning. Since there is a one-hour minimum for flying, if you finish quickly, you can spend the rest of the time shooting for stock.

A private pilot license for fixed-wing aircraft takes about 40 to 50 hours of flying with 20 hours of dual instruction. This is likely to cost between $3,000 and $4,000, but it's money well- spent. Hiring an instructor and airplane for a photo flight will cost you around $75 an hour with a one-hour minimum. An hour of helicopter time with pilot costs around $160 to $175 an hour. Airplanes and helicopters each have their own advantages and disadvantages. Helicopters can legally fly closer to the ground. But a fixed-wing is smoother and quieter.

Most aerial photographers I know about started as photographers first. My career started as a hobby that somehow got out of hand. I was a pilot for some years before I ever picked up a camera. I also have a full-time job involving heavy jet aircraft maintenance.

Some years ago, I finished rebuilding a fabric-covered airplane I had worked on for four years, a 1946 Aeronca 7 DC. I figured that aerial photography was a logical way to use my plane. I shot city scapes, large crowds, sailboats, other airplanes and anything else that looked exciting or interesting from the air.

After a year of this, I started participating in street fairs to generate some income and gain some exposure for my work. Now I have been doing this for some ten years. This method of marketing has worked well since aerial photography is a second career for me. Through selling aerial landscapes and local points of interest, I have made many valuable contacts and the activity has allowed me to continue to improve my craft and continue to fly.

Street and craft fairs are my main method of generating new business. I attend between 12 and 14 weekend events each year. My work is both black and white and color and I make all the prints in my own darkroom. I cut my own mats and do my own framing as well. When I started out, I bought prints from custom labs, but I changed to doing my own since the quality of the prints I make is better and the cost is lower. Through experience, I have found that in order to sell prints at fairs, the quality has to be really good and the price has to be reasonable.

I sell 8x10 color prints for $20 each, 11x14 for $40 and 16x20 for $70. The first fair I attended, I displayed about 25 framed prints and maybe 30 matted. The last show I went to this year, I took 70 framed prints and 1000 matted. I have sold as many as 80 prints on a good weekend.

The fairs also give me a chance to show my portfolio and pick up some assignment work. Contacts I have made at fairs have resulted in work from advertising agencies, major hotel chains, construction companies and several cities. When I do assignments, I bid the job by the picture. But it usually turns out to be between $250 and $400 an hour. This may seem like a lot, but remember, it includes the aircraft too.

Aerial photographs are not often found for sale at fairs. As a result, I usually draw a fairly large number of people. Some aren't quite sure what they are looking at. Some ask if I have a shot of Santa Monica. I ask, what part? When I show a selection, I have a sale. The next person asks if I have something of Catalina Island. I say sure, there is a box full.

Due to its nature, aerial photographers are able to collect relatively large sums for the sale of really good stock photos. There has never been a flight that could not produce at least a few good images. At present, I sell stock through my commercial contacts and from my ad in the yellow pages. Next year, I plan on making an arrangement with an agent. At the same time, I plan to take better advantage of my flights in order to add to my stock collection.

Recently I have noticed another type of aerial photography which seems to becoming more prevalent. Have you ever received a proof print in the mail of an aerial shot of your home or business? Along with the proof is a solicitation to order prints. Or sometimes, a salesperson will knock on your door with a matted 16x20. Different operations work differently, but the idea is that if anyone is offered a really good aerial, the chances are good this will result in print sales. With this sort of activity, someone up there is doing a lot of flying and picture taking. It might as well be me . . . or you.

PHOTOGRAMMETRY

By Bill Alnes

Photogrammetry requires specialized cameras mounted on the bottom of fixed-wing aircraft. The plane must fly at a predetermined altitude and must remain parallel to the ground at all times during picture taking. The cameras used are very different than those most of us are familiar with. In some, the film moves during exposure to compensate for the speed of the aircraft.

The sort of pictures which result from photogrammetry are used by map makers, land surveyors, developers and governments. In addition, photogrammetry is used for environmental studies and for legal purposes. These types of photographs are often used as evidence in court.

Some photogrammetry is done by companies rather than individuals. An example is Pacific Aerial Survey of Oakland, California which employs more than 60 people. There are also a few one-man survey outfits around. And, of course, the government, including the armed services, do extensive photogrammetry.

Pacific Land Survey bids government jobs by the linear mile. For survey work, they charge $460 per hour. This includes the aircraft and labor, but not photographic materials which are extra.

All work is done on a 9x9 film format. A contact print is $30 and enlargements are more.

If you are interested in photogrammetry, as opposed to oblique, one way to get started might be to investigate the training and positions offered in the armed services. Another way is to hang around airports and try to get work as an assistant or gofer.

Bill Alnes shooting from the cockpit of a small plane. Photograph by Bob Gemora.

AERIAL PHOTOGRAPHY

Chapter 4

AUDIO-VISUAL

What is audio-visual, or AV? In some ways, AV is a profession separate from photography. But it has its roots in photography and a good many of the skills necessary for AV are photographic in nature.

Audio-visual is an old term which goes back to the lantern slides of the last century. In those days before electricity, the audio was a live lecture illustrated by a succession of black and white glass slides projected with the light of a lantern.

The idea of AV then, as it is today, was to train, educate, communicate, amuse, illustrate, illuminate and persuade. But the profession has changed radically over the years, due not only to technological innovations but also to intellectual progress.

Today, audio-visual materials include a wide range of media: photographic prints, slides, filmstrips, motion pictures, overhead transparancies, charts, posters, models, realia, drawings, recordings, television, computers; almost anything mechanical or electronic that can be used to communicate.

There are a number of pursuits which fall under the umbrella of audio-visual. First, of course, media has to be created. The creators of audio-visual media include not only photographers, but also writers, editors, artists, model makers and many other skilled craftsmen.

But media creation is only part of the audio-visual lexicon. Many others are involved. Some professionals devote their careers to a function similar to librarians, i.e. purchasing, cataloging and distributing AV media. Others sell various media, while still others sell equipment and supplies. Some are involved in designing and setting-up facilities for presentations and training.

Entire volumes on the subject of audio-visual can be found in most libraries. This book provides only a brief overview of the employment possibilities.

It is interesting to note that "audio-visual" with a hyphen is the way *Websters Unabridged* (1989) spells it. Many writers, particularly those in the field, spell it "audiovisual," without a hyphen. Those in the field abbreviate it, "AV." In this book, we'll stick with *Websters*.

___

Photo courtesy of Eastman Kodak.

AUDIO-VISUAL PRESENTATIONS

There is a large industry built around industrial communications. Virtually all organizations have a continuing need for presentations of all sorts, both to individuals and groups. One kind of presentation is made in an auditorium, another at a booth in a trade show and still another on a desk. Take note of the use of the word organization rather than company. Yes, companies need AV, but so do governmental agencies, hospitals, charities, associations and clubs.

Those who put together these presentations work in the audio-visual profession. Some of them work in an audio-visual or photography department within an organization while others work for companies which offer audio-visual services. Both departments and companies come in all sizes from one-person operations to those with scores of specialists.

A group audio-visual presentation can consist of only one media or a combination of many. Even if the presentation consists of only a speech, AV personnel are often involved. The setting for a speech must be an organized affair, otherwise it is most likely doomed to failure. An AV specialist must have skills not only in the visual arts but also in the audio. A speech usually involves a microphone, but what kind? What kind of amplifier and speakers should be used? Where should be equipment be placed and how should the facility be arranged?

When other media are introduced, the job takes on complications requiring the use of additional AV skills. In the case of a speech, maybe it would be desirable to have large photographs placed in the presentation room. Or a slide sequence could illustrate part of the speech. AV specialists are involved in not only the use, but also the creation and the purchase of a multitude of different media.

Trade shows are important occasions for various industries to communicate with one another and with their customers. In the field of photography, for example, every year there is a trade show (called a convention) of the Photographic Marketing Association in Las Vegas. At PMA, new camera models and other photographic supplies and equipment are introduced by manufacturers to dealers. Every manufacturer who is seriously in business in the US has a booth at this show. The booths have to be designed to be attractive and to communicate what the manufacturer wants to get across. Often this involves not only the construction of the booth, but also the production of various media. At any one trade show you will likely see still photographs, models, slide sequences, film loops and videos. Some AV companies specialize only in trade shows.

Other sorts of presentations are made for individuals or small groups. These could involve a sequence of still photographs in a binder, a slide show in a small projector with a self-contained screen or a video. Usually these sorts of presentations are designed to help sell something. The use of the AV presentation allows the demonstration of products or services which cannot easily be shown in an office. Large earth-moving equipment is an obvious example. Or sometimes the presentation shows in a few minutes a process which might take days or weeks in real time.

Photograph courtesy Brooks Institute of Photography.

CAREERS IN PHOTOGRAPHY

Those who want to work in AV should be generalists. Most start out with photography, since almost all AV presentations are photography based. But in addition to knowing how to produce still photographs, the AV specialist needs to know something about motion pictures and video. The production side of AV is only half of the story, however. AV specialists have to know how to present the media too. This requires a familiarity with all sorts of projection and sound equipment.

Most AV specialists need to start out with a firm grounding in photography. Sometimes those who are already in a different field of photography gravitate to becoming AV specialists. This might happen when a commercial photographer is given the opportunity to produce a presentation for a client. Eventually, the discovery is made that there may be more money and more creative satisfaction in AV work than in straight photography.

Some photography students become interested in AV work while they are still in school. Since most schools utilize AV to one degree or another, there are often part-time, on-campus AV jobs available. Any student interested in AV should investigate these possibilities. Some schools have an AV club.

Most universities have audio-visual courses of one kind or another. These are usually found in departments of education. Those interested in the AV profession would do well to consider taking a few of these courses. The drawback, however, is that, for the most part, they are designed for classroom utilization rather than industrial.

While a number of AV professionals work as independent contractors, someone just starting out should look for an entry level job in the field. There is too much to learn and all of it cannot be learned in the classroom. Before you start looking for a job, assess your skills. Can you operate a motion picture projector? A slide projector? Remember, there are many makes and models. Can you set up a sound system? Can you shoot a slide sequence? These are some of the things you might be asked to do.

Those interested in becoming AV professionals should be creative. But they must also be goal oriented and have a measure of self-discipline. AV pros always have a goal. It is the presentation. Presentations are scheduled for certain dates and times. They cannot be late, incomplete or shoddy.

AV pros must be very quality oriented. In this day of automatic cameras, most people can take some kind of a recognizable picture. AV presentations are often viewed by the highest executives in an organization. So the work has to be excellent for the professional to survive as an employee or contractor.

Because of the multiple skills required, AV pros are often paid more than photographers. At the very least, an AV specialist will be at the high end of a photographic pay scale. And those who have their own AV companies are sometimes into big money, often taking home more than $100,000 a year.

INSTRUCTIONAL TECHNOLOGY

Today, all AV is not always even called AV. Another commonly used term is instructional technology, or IT. Actually IT is a separate profession which has grown enormously and now serves many vital functions in industry, education and government.

AV developed slowly until World War II. By 1941, electric bulbs had replaced lamps, celluloid replaced glass and color was introduced. The war caused an explosion in the AV field and the introduction of the concept of instructional technology.

WWII required the U.S. Armed Forces to expand rapidly and train millions of service personnel. The traditional method of training was person-to-person. But this was no longer sufficient because the peace-time forces of the thirties were too small. There were not enough trainers for the numbers of trainees. So AV was enlisted and the famous (or infamous) Army Training Film was born. A large number of Hollywood movie people were drafted or encouraged to join up. These film makers, among whose ranks was a future President, produced the training materials which enabled the U.S. to field citizen forces of the size necessary to defeat the traditionally-trained German and Japanese troops, a large number of whom were professional soldiers.

A Department of Audio-Visual at the University of Southern California began to study the psychological aspects as well as the technical components of AV. Largely through the leadership of Professor James D. Finn, a former Army Captain involved in wartime training, the department changed its name to instructional technology and a new profession was born. Or, to put it another way, an old profession in different clothing.

What was different about the new IT over the old AV was the application of the science of learning psychology to getting a message across via a medium. The original live-lecture slide show was joined by slides accompanied by recorded sound plus motion pictures, film strips, television, study prints, computers and programmed text. Laser-disc technology allows the combination of virtually all media.

There are many jobs in the IT field, and, since it is still growing, there will be many more in the future. As IT becomes more and more vital to industry, government and education, salaries and fees for both professionals and technicians will probably increase too.

Although lines may blur depending on various situations, the world of IT is divided between professionals and technicians with the professionals invariably paid more. This can perhaps best be illustrated by looking at the Army.

Suppose a presentation is necessary to illustrate or explain a process. An Instructional Technology Officer, usually a Captain or a Major, is assigned to the project and he (or she) studies the personnel to be affected and the results required. For example, new recruits will salute in a proper manner at the appropriate times. The IT officer determines the media or medium to create and its design. Then various enlisted personnel such as photographers, sound engineers, writers, artists and lab workers perform the necessary processes in order to produce what is required. The IT officer may also design a test to see how well the media function, both physically and psychologically.

The IT officer is the professional and the enlisted personnel are the technicians. How do these people get where they are in the Army (or Air Force, Navy, Marines, Coast Guard)? The officer was probably in the ROTC in college and probably majored in photography, cinema, communications, instructional technology or similar field. During his initial service after graduation, he evidenced a desire to pursue an Army IT career path. After initial training, he was probably sent to a civilian university to get a masters degree in IT.

While in college, the ROTC program helped pay for tuition, fees and books as well as a small cash allowance and summer employment (paid full-time training). The service paid for everything to do with the masters degree and provided a salary too. The current monthly pay for a Captain with 8 years service is $2738.10 and for a Major with 12 years, $3199.20. Added to this are rather generous allowances and benefits including full medical and 30 days paid vacation per year. After service, the officer is prepared for employment in industry, education or another part of the government as an instructional technologist.

The enlisted (EM) technician was probably interested in photography or a related field and may have taken photography courses in high school and worked on the yearbook or school newspaper. Upon enlisting (or even before), the EM evidenced an interest in the field. After completion of basic training, the EM was sent to a specialized school for Advanced Individual Training (AIT). After basic training, enlisted personnel earn $753.90 per month. Because of the skills involved, many of those in the field rise to higher ranks where the salary goes as high as $2910.60. In addition, enlisted personnel are supplied with food, housing, medical care and many other benefits.

Pensions are generous for both officers and enlisted and retirement is possible after only 20 years. Many who joined at age 17 retire at 37 and embark on a second career with the advantage of training and education paid for by Uncle Sam.

In the area of education, virtually all colleges, universities and public school districts employ at least one IT professional. These professionals have at least a masters degree and sometimes a doctorate in IT. Yearly salaries range from $30,000 to $70,000 and sometimes more.

The professional IT personnel provide much the same services as an IT officer in the Army. They are aided by various technicians (photographers, lab workers, etc.) who are usually called classified personnel (the equivalent of enlisted in the service). The classified people generally work by the hour and wages range from a low of around $10 to $40 or more plus benefits. A lab technician who processes film and makes prints would be hired at an entry level of $10 to $15 an hour. The new hire might have a community college degree or certificate in photography or equivalent training or experience.

The situation in industry is similar with salaries and wages probably somewhat higher and benefits lower.

A number of IT professionals have gone into business for themselves and established independent service organizations. They operate in much the same way as does a photography studio, but supply IT services and products instead of portraits. Many companies and other organizations are too small to have an in-house IT or AV department. So when a need arises, they turn to an independent contractor. Usually the contractor "bids" a job. First, the scope of what is required is examined. The costs are calculated and an amount for profit is added to make up the bid.

There are all sizes and kinds of organizations engaged in this sort of enterprise. They range from one-person efforts to those with extensive facilities and personnel. How much can be earned depends on a number of factors such as the quality of the work, business ability, salesmanship and public relations. Any established professional should be able to take home at least $30,000 and some net better than $100,000. An advantage of having your own business is that the company can usually be sold upon retirement.

In addition to those directly related to photography, there are a number of other skills associated with IT. Principle among these is an ability to write. Some professionals spend their careers analyzing commercially produced media and purchasing appropriate programs for their organizations. Others design, produce and market media with broad general applications. Many companies have professionals who work devising methods to train employees.

IT is interesting and rewarding. It involves helping people. Often there are products involved such as slides, films, overhead transparencies, recordings, TV programs and CAI (computer aided instruction). Anyone interested should try to acquire other skills in addition to photography. A photographer who cannot also do lab work, sound recording and TV production is rather one dimensional. In order to progress beyond the lower levels, writing skills are important. With the exception of the self-employed, advanced university degrees are necessary to reach the highest levels of the profession.

MULTIMEDIA

The word "multimedia" has been in professional use for some time; but recently it has taken on a new meaning. What was meant by the old and what is the new? (As an aside, *Webster's Encyclopedic Unabridged Dictionary* with a 1989 copyright does not list such a word while *Wedbter's Unabridged*, 1990 does.)

An audio-visualist might design and produce a multimedia presentation intended for a large audience. This means there are a number of elements working together in order to get a message across. For example, a typical multimedia presentation might include slides, live narration, sound recordings and short motion picture clips plus printed handouts.

The new meaning of multimedia relates to the use of computers together with the visual and aural media. In normal use, a multimedia program would be utilized by individuals. The idea is to use multimedia to promote a wider home use of computers. The software provides information systems that mix words, sounds and both moving and still images.

Multimedia is a group of technologies and programs hooked together. Of equal importance with the computer is the compact or laser disc. These discs have the capability of storing really huge amounts of data. The data can be in the form of computer programs, text, still pictures, motion pictures and sound.

A single disc can store an entire encyclopedia. An encyclopedia on a disc consists of the traditional words and still pictures, but it can also include moving pictures and sound. Access to a subject can be accomplished in microseconds. The information is displayed on a monitor screen, but can also be printed out.

A number of different companies have, or are in the process of developing multimedia systems. In late 1991, Philips Electronics introduced a system called Compact Disc Interactive (CDI). The machine sells in the $1000 range. Also launched in the fall of 1991 was a device called, Multimedia PC (MPC), by the Tandy Corporation (Radio Shack) and the Microsoft Corporation. This one sells for about $3000. Undoubtedly there will soon be additional systems from other companies.

A significant problem with the two systems already on the market (CDI and MPC), is that they are incompatible. An encyclopedia on a disc for CDI cannot be used on MPC. With these sorts of prices together with the compatibility problem, it could very well be that multimedia will not take the home market by storm the way CD audio has.

But regardless of the present state of the art, most experts feel that multimedia will eventually find its way into a very large number of homes and offices. This will create a tremendous demand for programs.

One of the significant characteristics of multimedia is that it will be used, in part, instead of printed materials such as books and magazines. Because of the increased storage capabilities, more photographs, both still and moving, will be required.

The need for programs will probably be filled by production companies who presently make motion pictures or computer software. Eventually, some organizations will specialize in the creation of multimedia programs. This will create a new source of employment for many workers, including photographers.

Philips has already established a subsidiary in Westwood, California called Philips Interactive Media with more than 125 permanent and many more temporary employees turning out programs for the Philips CDI system.

VIRTUAL REALITY

Virtual reality, like multimedia, is another new term all of us will soon become more familiar with. Virtual reality is an outgrowth of some of the same technology which has made multimedia possible. The important elements are computers with large memories and laser discs with large storage capabilities.

The idea is to place an individual in an environment wherein recorded sights and sounds seem to be almost real, virtually reality, as it were. The concept is not new. This is what aircraft trainers are all about. The student pilot is placed in a capsule which is a life-size model of a cockpit and motion pictures of flight situations with sound are displayed. The student learns how to handle the aircraft without putting actual passengers and planes at risk.

Video games are a step towards virtual reality too. An individual sees pictures on a screen and hears sounds to which he or she reacts by moving sticks, pressing buttons and turning wheels. Thus some of the experiences of warriors and race drivers are recreated, usually in conjunction with some sort of scoring system. The scoring heightens reality since battles and races are won or lost.

The more real a video game becomes, the more fascinating it is. Why not use stereophonic sound instead of monaural? How about stereo pictures too? This is better, but we are still looking at a screen which is a rectangular format surrounded by reality.

In order to put the participant further into the scene than can be accomplished with screens and speakers, special helmets have been developed. The front of the helmet becomes a personal screen which encompasses the entire range of sight in three dimensions. Earphones transmit the best possible stereo sound and even smells can be introduced within the confines of the helmet. Whatever situation is depicted becomes seemingly real. Some incorporate gloves to transmit feel and receive impulses.

The possibilities of these new systems for entertainment, education, training, information transmittal and even therapy are mindboggling. Some of the systems are interactive; that is, the participant can affect the progression of the program. Couch potatoes can become part of a soap opera. Students can be taken back and placed in the middle of the Battle of Gettysburg. Would you believe virtual sex?

Like multimedia, virtual reality will create an enormous demand for programming. It is possible to produce a virtual reality program with computer generated images. But these are not as believable as actual photography. And the important element in virtual reality is reality itself. Photography is unique among other art and information forms in having the ability to record images very close to reality.

So a large part of the programming for virtual reality will undoubtedly depend on photography. But, as the form develops, the sort of photography required could be very different from that as we know it now.

CAREERS IN PHOTOGRAPHY

Chapter 5

AUTOMOTIVE PHOTOGRAPHY

Automotive photography is a field in itself. Some—advertising, for example—falls into the category of commercial photography. Many pictures are taken for newspapers and magazines. These are photojournalism. And still others are portraits for their owners. Photography is also used as a scientific tool during the design process. So automotive photography spans a number of categories.

Automobiles are not just a means of transportation. They are part of our culture. A young man without a car is sometimes a young man without ready access to young women. Cars provide us with one of our cherished freedoms; we can pick up and go at a moment's notice. Vintage and antique cars have become valuable collectables. Some investors salt away significant amounts in their garages, claiming the appreciation is better than stocks or real estate.

Because of the significance, romance and mystique of the automobile, many photographers want to shoot cars. So the competition is sometimes fierce. Some of the very best photographers of our time—like Jesse Alexander, Art Eastman and Randy Leffingwell—have devoted themselves to the art of photographing automobiles. So unless you have the determination and ability to be among the very best, you probably should think twice before deciding to become a specialist in automotive photography.

AUTOMOBILE ADVERTISING PHOTOGRAPHY

By Randy Leffingwell

One ad you'll likely never see: HELP WANTED: PHOTOGRAPHER. Travel to exotic locations. Work eight hour days with six hour lunches between shoots. Produce two pictures per day. Salary up to $5,000 per day plus all expenses. Experienced photographers only need apply in strictest confidence to General Motors, Ford Motor Company, Chrysler Corporation, Toyota, Mercedes- Benz, et al.

What this ad doesn't say is that your hotel wake-up call comes at 3 AM, if you get to the hotel; that your expenses may exceed $5,000 per day and that you may have to wait 120 days for your check.

And, then of course, if you shoot automobiles in a studio, your days are longer. Much longer.

A conversation frequently overheard in Los Angeles' best color labs comes from the mouths of exhausted assistants comparing notes. They finish up their 20th straight 18 to 20-hour day, shooting one car, one view, 12 to 20 sheets of large-format view camera film, each day.

The photographs of automobiles published in the manufacturer's brochures are shot by the best car shooters in the world. These select shooters do charge $5,000 per day, do work 40, 50, 60 days straight without a day off. And they try to charge back every penny of their expenses.

In a tight year, the season is much shorter and a number of shooters have "adjusted" rates to accommodate tighter budgets. Manufacturers book fewer days or call for fewer shots in their brochures. Some high-end manufacturers go to black-and-white for their mailings.

The photographers' gross earnings, $500,000 or so at the top, gets eaten up quickly. A photographer without a studio of his own must rent space for $1,000 to $2,500 per day. Some discounts apply for rentals by the week or month. If the studio is the photographer's own, no discounts apply. That rent and those utilities must be paid every month, whether there are cars to be shot or not. More than half of their gross income is expenses. Those tired assistants constitute part of the overhead.

The summer of 1991, part of the Great Depression of 1991, saw a couple of car shooters go bankrupt. It saw several shooters do only several days all year. It saw some shooters do no work for two months. Two months with no income

Photograph by Randy Leffingwell.

makes it difficult to pay for the Maalox, let alone the rent—which itself may be $5,000 per month. It saw more than several shooters reduce their rates. Some came down to $5,000 per day.

Automobile photography is one of the most demanding specializations of all. Food, fashion, sports, travel and photojournalism all have their peculiar requirements and tricks. The details will kill you. But with automobile photography, most of your concerns have little to do with making pictures.

After looking at a recently published book, *American Muscle*, profiling a collection of cars, a successful real estate broker mused that she and the photographer were in the same business: "Location is everything," she commented.

As the photographer and author of that book, I spent an average of 12 hours per car searching for, finding and arranging the shooting locations I used. The book included 34 cars. That was more than 400 hours before a single exposure was made.

Complete freedom to choose my own settings gave me complete responsibility. I merely had to imagine a location where such an automobile might have appeared in the late 1960s, and then find it. I had to keep in mind whether, by its orientation to the sun, it was a morning or an evening location. Then I find someone in charge, introduce myself, explain what I was doing, explain what I wanted to do, and then complete the deal. This often meant applying for and completing the commercial photography permit for that community (or county or state), proving that I had general liability insurance in the amount they required (usually $1,000,000) and finally, paying the location fee. Oh yes, and in some cases, I had to pay the police officers' overtime when that was required by local law.

If you are shooting for a manufacturer, they generally have a theme in mind. That theme may be quite specific or quite vague. You must find the place they can seldom verbalize.

Then, arrange to get the car delivered to the location. Will it be driven or does it come on a transporter? Does the transporter stay through the shoot—and who pays his "waiting" time?—or does he return after sunrise or sunset to pick up the car? How does he know when to return? Are you paying or does the client? Will he take a check?

New car photography, on location or in a studio, requires one additional consideration. The car must be "prepped," prepared for photography. This does not mean spraying Armor-All protective solution on the tires. Car preparation is so specialized that in Los Angeles, several companies do only this task. This can mean anything from loading sandbags into the engine and trunk compartments to compress the shock and springs to the correct ride height, or taping the wire wheels closed from the back so no stray light shines through to outline odd shapes or otherwise distract.

And surely you have noticed and marvelled at the fact that so many new cars seem to be photographed just after a rainfall that somehow didn't soak the car. Many of the car preppers even operate water tanker trucks to wet down roads

or parking areas.

So, you have secured the location, your insurance certificate is on file, the film permit is pasted to your windshield to satisfy the one cop who will arrive precisely at the worst time. You have the car delivered. The art director and the manufacturer's rep have agreed the car has been correctly "prepped" (by looking at countless Polaroid test shots), and now you are ready to shoot.

Wait. Yes, of course, the cameras are loaded. The film has been pre-tested so you know what color the emulsion is to correct for what color their chrome will appear. Correction filters are over the lenses.

Wait. Yes, the meters are read. Film speed is checked. Shutters are closed, cocked. Sand bags weight the camera and tripod to the ground; forty pounds, sixty pounds, perhaps more.

Wait. The sun sets. It kisses the earth. Cracking on the edge of the world like a golden orange egg, it oozes across the horizon, distorting its shape momentarily. Everyone comments. Ooooh. Aaaah.

Wait. Wait for it. Now. Shoot. Frantically. One assistant cocks and rechecks the shutter, constantly checking the hand held light meter. One assistant retrieves and hands off film holders. You squeeze the shutter. You watch the light. You scrutinize the car like some proud parent at a first ballet recital. You see all. You miss nothing. You shoot like a maniac. Six times. Eight times. Twelve times.

No bracketing. There is no time. Twelve exposures is all you get. Now it's dark. Your exposures on 8x10 sheet film ranged from 15 to 60 seconds at f/45. In fifteen minutes of "golden light," even as the temperature dropped as many degrees, you break a sweat trying to shoot 12 pieces of film.

Now it's dark. Fire up the generators; turn on the work lights. Slip on the parka. Break down the equipment. One assistant, whose life and death responsibility is the film, is left alone to make notes on the holders. The holders then go into the ice chest for travel to the lab. He takes them. No one else touches them.

The equipment is packed up, the car loaded up or driven away and you stop for dinner. But you rarely dawdle. A normal sunrise shoot takes two or three hours of prep before the first light. So the alarm clock calls you at 3AM.

Where do you learn this? If you love sheet metal and really want to shoot cars, Brooks Institute in Santa Barbara and Art Center College of Design in Pasadena both offer education and training with a good emphasis on this particular area of commercial photography.

But, like virtually every other field within this profession, you learn mostly by doing and making mistakes. You learn by assisting.

Automobiles are shot on all film formats. Who the client is, and to some extent, who the photographer is, dictates the film size.

Most advertising, billboard and brochure photography is shot on 8x10, though an increasing amount is done on 4x5 film. The larger format used to be a necessity because of its ease in retouching. But with electronic engraving techniques, image enhancement and modification can be performed with excellent results on smaller formats. Now, you can electronically "retouch" the color of an entire car, changing a grey sedan to red, from 35mm Kodachrome originals.

Medium format, 2x2 or 6x7, is frequently preferred by the same manufacturers for their publicity photographs—those that run in the newspapers or magazines. This kind of work pays between $600 and $1,500 per day, depending on many variables.

Medium and small format is favored by the newspapers and magazines themselves. Many of the photographers shooting for *Automobile, Road & Track, Car & Driver, AutoWeek,* and any of the European publications, shoot 35mm. Medium format is generally left for covers. These publications pay between $150 and about $750 per day. Their prestige and your own will widely influence the rate.

But action photos, done from a moving car alongside the "hero" car, or from a stationary point as the car passes by, are nearly always done on 35mm. With extremely sharp lenses from all the manufacturers, and extremely sharp films—Eastman Kodak's Ektar color negative and Fuji's Velvia transparency film—the quality is very close to medium format. And the spontaneity is much greater. Manufacturers accept this more willingly, for PR and even national print advertising and billboards.

Another new technique complicates the situation greatly. During the past few years, car shooters have begun lighting cars in a studio style even though they're on location.

An easy way to recognize this is to look carefully at the car and at the sky. If the sky is glowing some rich deep color in the background and yet there are long slashes of highlights in pure white light along the side of the car you can see, it's pretty likely it was lit.

Lighting in the desert? Tricky. Complicated. Risky! It is done with an enormous—maybe 15 x 40 foot light box suspended over the car. Into this light box are placed a dozen or more powerful strobe heads, or "hot lights," (motion picture production-type 1,000 or 2,000 watt lights—known as 1Ks and 2Ks.) This creates a giant white "sky" over the car. This is either suspended from a crane (hired and driven to the location for $500 to $1,500 per day—as a package with the light box), or supported by four tall light stands which are thoroughly secured to the ground with cables and weights. Recognize the risk yet? You have suspended over a perhaps-irreplaceable one-of-a-kind prototype or classic car a 6,000 square foot sail which is loaded with 12 strobe heads ready to fire 4,800 watt/seconds each, all attached to a 2,000 amp portable generator on a trailer. For reference, that 6,000 square feet is about the area of your average America's Cup yacht spinnaker (parachute) sail.

One recent shoot in the desert required 500 pounds of ballast on each corner—in the form of concrete bags. When someone asked the lighting director what would happen if it rained, he smiled and suggested they might have a monument.

It didn't rain and when the light evening breezes blew, the giant soft box didn't move.

Expenses for that shoot nearly matched the magical $5,000 shooting fees quoted earlier. Rigging time ran far longer, and required many more than two assistants.

So, if "location is everything" and lighting is everything else, the successful car photograph adds up to about 200% of its ingredients. It's that second ingredient that is subject to so much interpretation.

Car shooters seem to shoot under two kinds of light. Some shoot when the sun is over their shoulder, rather high in the sky. With enough polarization via filters, the color saturation is good, the exposures are short, you get little star-burst highlights on the car, and you can sleep later and go to dinner earlier.

The other light also wants the sun over the photographer's shoulder, but waits for it to be below the horizon. This generally requires little or no filtration, gives good color saturation, requires much longer exposures, and gives you softer, flowing "liquid light" highlights which are not dots but curves. Breakfast is from a thermos bottle; sometimes dinner is too.

There is beautiful work produced from both disciplines. It is a matter of photographer's style and client's preference.

A brief word is necessary here to those interested in auto racing photography. Getting started is tremendously difficult. The field is extremely competitive. The work is physically demanding, the pay generally inadequate, the hours long, the working conditions filled with hassles. There are too many photographers willing to shoot for no pay in order to get the pass, and there are too many clients who do not recognize that you get what you pay for.

John Mecom, one of the wealthiest participants in motor racing, is author of one of its greatest quotes: "I know there is a lot of money in auto racing. I put it there."

The beginning motor racing photographer will feel like he or she took lessons from Mecom. Virtually no one shooting motor racing in the United States makes their entire living from it. Yet it is exciting, there is an element of glamour in it, and, quite frankly, there are stunning photographs to be made.

What is the future of automobile photography? What is the future of the automobile? Because Ford Motor Company, Porsche, Toyota, Volvo and all the rest want to sell cars, they will need photographs to tantalize customers. Because cars are such an integral element of the American society, the enthusiast magazines will continue to test and evaluate the developments and show the results. The magazine art directors are usually willing to look at new talent. These outlets become excellent showcases and provide the foundation of the portfolio which may get you PR work from the major manufacturers. A good eye will advance you from there.

And when you get to the top, where location is everything, remember, summer sunrise in the desert is 5:30 AM. Don't forget to set your alarm.

Chapter 6

COMMERCIAL PHOTOGRAPHY

EMPLOYMENT OPPORTUNITIES IN COMMERCIAL PHOTOGRAPHY

by Gerry Kopelow

Commercial photography is the production (for a fee) of photographs which are used to support or sell some sort of product, personality, or service. Anyone who makes a living by producing such photographs is a commercial photographer. The range of work is very wide and includes such specialized areas as advertising illustration, corporate and institutional photography, architectural photography, food photography, and much more.

Commercial photography is a demanding business and busy photographers need a lot of backup support. Competent assistants should be well versed in all technical and esthetic matters. Studio managers must have a grasp of modern business practices and how they fit with professional photography. Darkroom staff are expected to be reliable perfectionists. In some operations, all these roles are juggled by one trusted employee who might eventually end up a full partner in the business. For any prospective employee, training, experience, and motivation are key factors in breaking-in and succeeding.

It helps if the initial steps are taken early. Various opportunities arise in high school, camera clubs or school papers, for example. Photography has a universal appeal and is very thoroughly explored in many fine magazines, books and videos, so any young person with initiative can master the fundamentals. Many high schools offer photography courses, and career-oriented students can supplement their academic activities with part-time work in neighborhood studios or camera stores. In larger centers, commercial photographers can be located through the yellow pages and persuaded to give simple jobs such as sweeping the studio, running errands, painting sets, etc.

Most universities offer photographic courses, usually through a faculty or department of fine arts, which emphasize style and personal expression, while de-emphasizing the sophisticated technical skills and equipment typically required for the actual practice of commercial photography. More practically minded post-secondary students should consider technical schools or private institutions dedicated to photography.

When preparing for employment in the commercial photography business, it is worth remembering that mastering only photographic skills might not be enough. Accounting, management and marketing savvy will widen your horizons. However, before committing to an intensive (and possibly expensive) educational program, I recommend that you seek the advice of practicing professional photographers to see what they require their employees to know. You will find that most professionals are willing to give a few minutes of their time to students. Write a straightforward letter requesting an interview and include a reference from a trusted teacher or someone you know who is already well-established in some aspect the photography business.

It is interesting to note that entry into the field is not limited only to people with formal training. Those who have mastered the basics on their own and are willing and physically able to work long hours for very little pay will usually find some sort of position. Persistence, cheerfulness and self-motivation are the most sought-after characteristics. The ability to learn on the job is crucial and doing a variety of work is almost always a necessity. Be adaptable and accommodating. It is the accomplished generalist who will do well in the shadow of the successful shooters. Also note that those who will prosper as an assistant, studio manager or business partner to a commercial photographer must have an affinity for the intense personal relationships which inevitably accompany photographic work at this level.

Consider a typical career path. Probably the first stirrings will occur early on, possibly with the encouragement and

---

This photograph of the Heritage Building in Winnipeg is an excellent example of exterior architectural photography. Photograph by Gerry Kopelow.

guidance of a teacher or parent. A 35mm camera, a basic black and white darkroom at home or school, plus a subscription to a photography magazine will inspire and instruct. A couple of photography courses in high school and a couple of years at a technical school or college will complement a continuing commitment to personal development. Part-time positions in areas related to photography—sales, processing, assisting established photographers—will point the way to more specific training. An important consideration is that a basic university education in non-photographic areas will stimulate the intellectual development so necessary for satisfying and productive interactions with professionals in both photographic and non-photographic fields later on.

After school, a one, two, or three year period of apprenticeship will result in a more thorough understanding of real-world photographic and business practices, but just as it is impossible to learn all the necessary skills in an academic setting, it is not sufficient to simply watch someone else work, as in an apprenticeship situation. The most effective learning is accomplished by doing; by trial and error. Hard workers will be given more and more responsibilities as they progress. Five or six years of experience at a managerial level in a big studio should make one employable in virtually any city in the western world.

The commercial photography business can be very lucrative. Beginners can expect to receive the minimum wage at first, but substantial five figure incomes are possible later on. There are also less tangible rewards such as the opportunity to work closely with other high achievers. A prosperous photographer's client list might include clever entrepreneurs, upwardly mobile corporate types, influential politicians, community leaders, active cultural organizations and performing artists, together with designers and art directors working in the advertising industry. The are some of the most stimulating and intelligent individuals urban society has to offer.

This portrait of Gerry Kopelow, taken by his assistant, is an example of another kind of photograph often required by the clients of commercial photographers. Photograph by Michael Holder.

PRODUCT PHOTOGRAPHY

By Randy Leffingwell

So long as mankind continues to invent, modify, perfect, restore, repair, design, redesign, improve, mark down, put on sale and reinvent everything from the wheel to a better mouse trap, the producers, (or their marketing and advertising departments) will need their products photographed. The future of product photography, in short, seems secure.

A product photographer may be asked one day to shoot computers, the next to shoot park benches, packaging for fast food chain hamburgers on the next and an automobile with a model to promote a new car wax the day after that.

Training, as with the other areas of specialization, might begin with a commercial photography-oriented school, such as Brooks Institute in California, Rochester Institute in New York, or any other similarly oriented school. From there, you can begin your career assisting an established photographer or, with adequate backing, open your own studio.

Unless you can develop both a potential client list and a distinct photographic style while you are in school, the more prudent path to follow is to work for and with an existing shooter. As sharp as you may be, there are many photographic tricks and many business-management techniques which can be elusive in your early years, but which you can eventually acquire while still earning a modest wage as an assistant.

Product photography has many potential buyers. You may shoot an object for the producers themselves at the very beginning, for their patent applications. In this case, artistry is neither required nor desired. Following that shoot, you may reshoot the same product for its packaging—the box or bag in which the product is sold. Another use may be for public relations releases which are sent to appropriate magazines, newspapers and trade organizations. The next use might be for advertising, and depending on the importance of the product and the wealth of the client, that may include uses as lavish as outdoor billboards.

If it seems as though the product photographer is a jack of all trades, be sure to understand that this same photographer must be a master of them as well. Products can be shot on any film format from 35mm up to 8x10 sheet film, black and white or color, transparency or negative. Exceptional versatility and imagination in lighting is a given. The ability to manage reflections—to keep them when necessary and eliminate them when not wanted—is part of your stock in trade.

If you have already completed school and spent a year or two assisting an established studio shooter, you may be ready to set out on your own. Because you have worked with your boss' equipment, you know what you need. Because you can read your own check book balance, you also know how little of that you can afford. But you also learned from your boss that when you don't have what you need or you only need it once, you rent it.

This can save you a fortune as you get started. You can even rent the studio in which you shoot. A studio large enough to shoot an automobile in Los Angeles rents for $1,000 per day including a fair assortment of lighting. Smaller spaces can be had for as little as $75 for a half day. And, as you worked for a shrewd businessman, you learned that you can charge these expenses back to the client.

Well, not all of them. Clients, whether inventors seeking patent photos or an award-winning international advertising agency expect the photographers they hire to have a basic "kit" included as part of the day rate. This usually includes the camera and a few lenses in the format normally used, some minimal amount of lighting equipment and stands and a few accessories such as a tripod, ladder and other such basics. The camera format normally used means either 2 1/4 or 4x5 if that is the kind of work this agency usually requires, or 35mm and 2 1/4 if that is their usual need. This means that if, historically, you have shot jobs for them and similar clients on 35mm and 2 1/4, and they ask you to shoot on 4x5 film for a particular job, you can charge back to them the 4x5 camera rental.

Likewise, if they ask you for a specific kind of lighting and you have to rent a particular piece of equipment for it, you can charge that back as well. And, as you learned from your boss, film, Polaroid film and film processing charges naturally are billed. Further, you will have learned from your first working experience what the normal procedure in your area is regarding charging for first, second and additional assistants.

Some photographers include the first assistant in their studio day rate; others add it as a separate "line" expense. If this is confusing—intimidating even—to those of you who have not assisted an established photographer, it is important to understand one more thing. It is every bit as important for a product photographer to be a sharp business man as it is to be a lighting genius. In fact, there are many more clients who will accept uninspired studio product photography than there are who demand spectacular work. And you must remain in business to keep working, no matter how brilliant is your work.

The point is, if you are still in school, add an accounting class and business-management courses to your curriculum. There is plenty of time for artistry when you are out on your own so long as you can continue to pay your bills.

If you are still in school or just starting out, this is a good time to talk about paying bills. You will quickly learn that few clients believe they really get what they pay for in photography. As a beginner, and even later on, you will find yourself "bidding" for a job against some client's "uncle who has a camera." When you shoot the job, the client will, probably, love your work. However, when you submit your bill, you will likely wait 60, 90, even 120 days to be paid. This is especially the case with major clients and agencies.

Meanwhile, you have your rent, your assistant, your equipment rentals, your film supplier, your processing lab, your car/van/truck payment, your insurance payment and

Photograph by Gerry Kopelow.

countless other studio expenses to meet. And, of course, you want to eat something.

By now, you may be thinking that you are reading the wrong chapter, that you wanted to know about product photography; that you weren't interested in a business seminar.

As a product photographer with a studio—even if it is just your garage at home—if you are NOT interested in a business seminar, then you are a hobbyist. Which is perfect, because

about the time you are bored shooting computers, crystal decanters, silver tea services, ball-point pens, hydraulic fittings, toilet seat covers and diamond brooches, you'll be broke.

It has been said that a boat is a hole in the water, surrounded by (take your choice) wood/fiberglass/steel, into which you pour money. But a boat for most people is a hobby. Your studio should not be the same.

The importance of business acumen cannot possibly be

overestimated. Fortunately, there are some guides which make the bewildering business world more approachable and understandable. The ASMP (American Society of Magazine Photographers, an organization much broader in scope than only magazine photographers) publishes a business practices and a stock photography hand book. These are compiled by their working membership and give good solid figures on what rates should be as well as photographic ownership rights.

The APA (Advertising Photographers of America) and the PPA (Professional Photographers of America) produce newsletters, professional guide books and also sponsor frequent seminars on business practices, copyright and photographic rights ownership plus the more common equipment trade shows. And a number of companies are now producing software for computers which will help you operate your studio and your business profitably. Finally, the monthly magazine *Photo District News* runs frequent articles on studio management and business matters.

But what about the aesthetics? That is wide open. Personal shooting styles exist and are definitely sought after by the bigger budget agencies and clients. Pete Turner in New York, Dennis Manarchy in Chicago, and Hosemaster (TM) inventor Aaron Jones in New Mexico have photographic styles as distinctive—and different from each other—as possible. Yet each is busy and well-rewarded for his skills.

Rates at the top, where these three operate, can exceed $10,000 per day plus expenses. For that, you get the shooter, an assistant and studio time. Everything else is expenses. At the bottom of the product photography food chain, you find photographers in small towns shooting products for local clients for $35 per picture. But in the major metropolitan areas, day rates usually range between $1,500 and $3,000, with uses of the photographs having an additional impact on fees. A one-time use for a black-and-white PR release is a very much less expensive shoot for the client than is the national advertising campaign in color for mass circulation magazines and billboards. In those cases, a single image can bring $25,000 and more, especially if the client must "own" the image; that is, buy all rights.

Photo usage is another thorny issue confronting product photographers. Nearly as much has been written about it and nearly as many seminars have been launched about it as there have been for business issues. A stunning image shot for a client may promote its own uses: billboards, magazine advertising, packaging, point-of-purchase displays. The client, not wanting to risk seeing "their" image used in any other way, will want to "buy out" all rights. Expect ample reward. In one case, a photograph sold to a European cosmetic chain yielded the shooter a new Porsche. And when he visited Europe months later on another shoot, he saw his image everywhere.

It is not possible to discuss equipment in this chapter because it is both a personal and budgetary matter. There are many good 35mm, 2 1/4 and view cameras available; many good strobes manufactured and countless studio accessories.

But if you want to shoot products and you are already out of school, your best bet is to scour the monthly popular magazines. As a new student, pick out the images that appeal to you and, in your garage or living room—or your studio— try to duplicate them. Study them very carefully to determine where the light is coming from and whether it is soft light from a light box or specular light from a spotlight source. Watch the reflections, play with reflectors, experiment, experiment, experiment. You need not have an 8x10 Sinar P to learn. So save your money for film and processing.

Then, when you have a number of images you are satisfied with, you can begin to promote yourself. You can use one of two time-proven techniques. Hire a representative with whom you split the proceeds of the work they bring in, or produce a postcard promotion piece. When you get firmly into the middle ranks, do both and also take out a studio advertisement in any of the annual photography reviews such as the *American Showcase*. A full page ad in color is costly—more than $4,000—so make sure business merits it.

Near the top of the product-shooter hierarchy, you will find photographers spending $20,000 and more per year on promotion. And, since they are still in business, you can be assured it pays off. Many of the world's most influential art directors look over these annual sample books to discover new talent.

But it's at the top that it's the most interesting. Those photographers with their distinctive styles and proven performance records of imaginative, inventive and creative work don't need to advertise.

By the time they get to that point, they've added one more element to the business contract with their clients: "Photo credit is mandatory." So the client is not only paying, but also promoting them. And that's very good business.

FOOD PHOTOGRAPHY

By Randy Leffingwell

The blow torch slid gently across the goose. Little pockets of fat in the skin sparked as they popped from the 2,000 degree flame. In less than 15 seconds, it was ready.

In the dim light of the studio strobe modeling lights, the stylist backed out of the set. A metallic clunk signaled that the "Hosemaster (TM)" shutter had solenoided open. The metronome tone began, beep, beep, once a second.

A nearly blinding flash of light set down the base exposure on 4x5 film. Then the photographer moved in with the "hose;" the fiber-optic cable attached to an intense light source. The "Hosemaster (TM)" and others like it allow the photographer to "paint" light on the scene before the lens.

Playing over the holiday feast with concentrated light, he added highlights and contours in the style of Italian Renaissance painters. With this technique, light could come from a thousand suns, even appearing to illuminate some objects from within. The metronome beep reminded the photographer of his exposures and that the camera shutter was still open.

Another metallic clunk and the solenoid shut the auxiliary shutter, an assistant closed the view camera lens shutter and a piece of film was shot. Total exposure time was about two minutes following a 2,000 watt-second initial blast.

The film holder was flipped, the stylist stepped back in and caressed her goose with her blow torch once again, tightening up the skin and enhancing the juicy, golden-brown appearance. A quick baste of the vegetables with a small paint brush of vegetable oil and water and everyone was ready for the second sheet of film.

The usual comment by non-photographers about food photography is, "At least you can eat the food when you are done!" After staring at it through a view finder for hours, after watching the stylists poke, prod, baste, torch, slather or repair the food, many food shooters just call Domino's Pizza for a delivery.

Food photography is a highly collaborative craft. The photographer is one of many key players in the shoot, which usually includes an art director charged with planning the look of the picture; a prop stylist hired to locate and bring to the studio all the tables, dishes, accessories, flowers, cloths, and other props which appear in the picture; a food stylist who is responsible for making the food look perfect; and a variety of assistants to the photographer and stylists. An editorial assignment—newspaper, magazine or cookbook—will also include the writer or editor of the section or book.

This example of food photography was taken for Manco Dairy. Photograph by Gerry Kopelow.

The assignment to the photographer usually comes from the art director or editor who often leaves the choice of food stylist and prop stylist up to the photographer. All of them bill the editor or art director independently for their services and expenses. Top food photographers charge in the neighborhood of $2,000 per day and in that 12-hour (sometimes longer) day will produce two or three finished images. Their expenses include Polaroid, film, processing and usually their second and third assistants if the shoot is big and complex (the first assistant is included in the day rate.)

The best food and prop stylists in the country charge between $400 and $600 per day. The food stylist gets a "grocery" list from the editor or art director and spends the day before the shoot gathering up the most beautiful, perfect samples of everything on the list. Any fragile food, such as fruit and vegetables, are often bought in quantities ten times as large as the shot calls for in order to have the perfect flawless examples for the final, or "hero" setup. Other ingredients are usually sufficient to make two or three examples in case of failure or damage under the lights. The groceries and a food-preparation assistant are all billable expenses for the food stylist.

The prop stylist can often borrow items from stores. For editorial purposes, usually photo credit is offered in exchange for the loan: Dishes courtesy of The Broadway, for example. But in advertising and cookbooks, credit is not given and so props must be rented. In addition, in Los Angeles where so many motion pictures are shot, there are "prop houses," giant warehouses filled with wonderful objects which can be rented for use in still photos as well as the movies. But all rentals are very costly. A rental budget of $400 to $500 per shoot is barely adequate. The best stylists are hired because of their ability to stretch the rental dollar and wheedle and cajole friends and relatives into loaning family treasures and heirlooms. Prop stylists bill their prop search time at full rate as well as shoot days and a prop-return day. Billable expenses include fresh flowers, rentals and any disposables bought which have only a one-time use such as paper for shooting surfaces and props.

Food photographers shoot everything from lavish table setups to individual bags of french fries or individual bowls of ice cream. Their shooting fees are high because of the overhead of having and maintaining a full commercial kitchen to prepare the food in the studio. But even the best equipped kitchens sometimes need more. For a french fried potato shoot for a fast food chain, one photographer rented several deep fryers; and then had to fumigate his studio to get the aroma out of the walls. Another photographer rented three enormous freezer chests and two frozen yogurt machines to meet the needs of an ice cream company's introduction. These rentals, too, are billable.

As with most photography at the advanced level of $2,000 per day, photographers learn by doing and by testing and experimenting. But the basics can be learned at any school which offers courses in product and "table-top" photography. There are certain principals which apply whether you are shooting sugar beets or baseballs. An eye for composition is essential, but the critical element is the lighting. Once the food is prepared and the set is propped by skilled, talented stylists, it is the lighting that makes or breaks a good food photograph. The student would be well advised to study the same way the working pros do; by constantly looking at monthly food magazines and glancing through new cook books.

In California, an excellent education is offered at Brooks Institute in Santa Barbara and Art Center College of Design in Pasadena. Both are expensive. Supplementing photo classes with design classes in the art or painting department, and art history classes—especially of painting and sculpture— would be valuable.

Your education will never be complete, but the next major step would be to work for an established photographer as an assistant. The pay varies. In Los Angeles and New York, first assistants make between $85 and $150 per day. The days are long, the wages not the best, but the assistants probably get all the pizza they can eat.

INDUSTRIAL PHOTOGRAPHY

By Randy Leffingwell

The biggest challenge which confronts many industrial photographers is the color of the light on location; most of the time it is the wrong color and the rest of the time there is no color. Industrial plants and manufacturing facilities are rarely lit by pure light sources. And the subjects—human or machine—are usually monochromatic.

Industrial photography is a combination of product photography and photojournalism. The industrial product may be a small silicon computer chip which must be photographed in a studio for a public relations release or a 400-ton steel stamping machine which must be shot for a company's annual report. Or the subject may be a piece of computerized electronics which must be multiple-exposed to show all of its significant features as well as to make it seem like a real-life spin-off from a Steven Spielberg film. Sometimes people must be in the pictures, either to give the object a sense of scale or merely to provide "human interest." Other times, because the operation being photographed is so risky, no one ever touches it and yet the photographer still must make it exciting.

The industrial photographer must first "clean up" the light; that is, bring the color balance of short duration mercury vapor, sodium vapor, quartz halide or other energy-efficient-but-weird- color light sources back to daylight. This is done by placing color correction filters over the lenses since changing the lighting fixture is usually too expensive and too physically difficult.

The next step however, is even more challenging. Factory

This industrial photograph was used to document the condition of a factory prior to demolition. Photograph by Randy Leffingwell.

walls are often industrial green or yellow. Machines are frequently industrial yellow or green, or sometimes gray. If everything is not completely stainless steel! Worker uniforms are generally solid colors, usually dark and often not too bright. Injecting color back into the photograph is the creative part, done with theatrical-lighting color gels over strobe heads.

Of course, the third challenge is really the most difficult. The industrial photographer seldom gets to work with professional models who are comfortable in front of a camera and who take direction. The photographer must use officers of the company and hourly-wage employees who are ill at ease under the best of circumstances. (Frequently too, their colleagues stand just outside of the camera viewing area and

tease the subjects about their new "stardom.")

Industrial photography demands excellent photographic technique, a very quick and creative imagination and the director's skills of a Cecil B. DeMille. The rewards for these combined abilities can reach $7,500 per day if you are one of the dozen or so top industrial shooters producing the best corporate annual reports.

Training for this comes from a good photographic education. Rochester Institute of Technology in New York and Brooks Institute in California offer excellent training. From the technical standpoint of simply getting the image on film, the industrial photographer should know both photographic chemistry and the physics and theories of light. But industrial photography involves so many other disciplines that a good

CAREERS IN PHOTOGRAPHY

liberal education might be a bonus. The ambitious student may want a minor degree in theater and he may want to work as a lighting director in order to get hands-on experience with what one color does with another. Lastly, classes in human behavior, psychology or even stage direction could also prove beneficial.

Industrial photography is costly to the client in ways far beyond the potential $7,500 per day shooting fee. Even for a $500 public relations shoot, when a photographer shoots in a manufacturing facility, production is interrupted. The hourly-wage machinery operators stand around and the machines are idle. The work which pays for the plant and pays for the photography is not being done.

The industrial photographer is usually presented with two options. There is either a 50-minute time window allowed during the employee lunch break or the shots can be made on weekends or at the end of the day. In the first, equipment set up takes place around the workings of forklifts and hoists and manufacturing. Final adjustments are done during the employee lunch break. Final Polaroids are shot when the "models" return from lunch. Film is shot and then equipment is broken down again amidst the manufacturing activities.

The second option offers a double-edged sword. Set up can be done at a more leisurely pace with no interruption from moving machinery. However, if employees are needed in the shots, many companies are reluctant to keep an employee on overtime just to be a model. Executives can rarely be enticed to appear for a 10PM or 2AM shoot.

With these considerations in mind, it is easy to understand why few companies will risk hiring an unproven industrial photographer. Too much money is at stake, even if the pay is only marginal. For the beginner, it is necessary to assist an established shooter. This allows the assistant the benefit of furthering a practical education while earning some money. It also exposes the assistant to potential customers.

A practical education cannot be over-stressed. In this kind of commercial photography, unlike any other, there are physical risks which may result in serious injury or in badly-damaged equipment. The Occupational Safety and Health Administration (OSHA) has done much to ensure that work places are much safer and much less risky than they were even ten years ago. But accidents can happen, especially to visitors unfamiliar with machinery and locations.

Chemical processes in manufacturing also pose risks. In some locations, the use of flash is impossible. Lighting must be done with "hot" lights: motion picture type lighting. In any factory, the availability of 110v power is questionable. Most heavy machinery operates on 220v or even 440v current. The 220v is perfect if you are using hot lights of 5,000w and 10,000w (5Ks and 10Ks.) or some extremely powerful strobes. But smaller lights, and most strobes require 110v. This may call for hundreds of feet of extension cords to bring power from the executive offices. It may require the photographer's own generator.

Industrial photography is shot on every format. Some annual reports are shot on 35mm, some on 8x10. Public relations release photography is usually done on 2 1/4. The amount of equipment which is brought into some industrial sites rivals the biggest motion picture location shoots. In fact, they are quite similar.

Large factory scenes absorb light the way black velvet does. Many factories with a patina of years of grease and dust simply reflect no light. A million watts would provide barely enough. Other modern electronics manufacturers work in bright, white "clean rooms" and minimal light produces beautiful photographs. Whenever possible, industrial photographers scout their locations prior to the shoot date at the same time of day they plan to shoot.

Industrial photography has many clients. Technical trade magazines and the business magazines such as *Forbes*, *Business Week*, *Fortune* and others often hire photographers to produce pictures for a story on a company. Advertising agencies for trade journals, technical publications and even general consumer magazines also hire industrial shooters. And of course the cream of the crop are the design studios who produce corporate annual reports.

Because industrial photography is most often done on site, studios are not a regular requirement. When individual products must be shot, studios can be rented. Industrial photographers and their assistants haul their large assortment of equipment around in vans. The lighting equipment and even generators are bulky.

When it comes to getting the green out of the light, a three-color, color temperature meter is essential. Minolta and Broncolor make reliable meters which are sensitive to strange light sources even in low-light levels. These meters range in price from roughly $700 to more than $1,000. But like something else green, most industrial shooters won't leave home without them.

ARCHITECTURAL PHOTOGRAPHY

By Randy Leffingwell

Between 1980 and 1990, the prevailing styles of architectural photography changed drastically. Until 1980, architectural photographers were as much theatrical lighting directors as documentarians. The light inside rooms matched the outside. There were no deep shadows; every detail was recorded in breath-taking sharpness. Every object was spot lit for drama.

Then a generation changed. Younger photographers, impatient with the amount of equipment and time necessary to light every nook and cranny and suspicious of the artificiality such lighting created, began shooting with less and less encumbrance.

Sunlight, a former problem for interior shooters, was embraced by the new breed. The honest look of the room became the goal. Brilliant swaths of light across floors and furniture, plunging other areas into deep dramatic shadows, taxed films and magazine reproduction to the maximum. Pictures were published which showed only a limited range of detail; the highest highlights and the deepest shadows were lost. But the effect caught the eyes of influential art directors and editors. The new style was referred to as "the gasp you have when you first walk into a room."

Architects and designers, pleased to have their work shown in magazines, were less than pleased when their subtle efforts disappeared in reproduction limitations. For them, the details were still important.

The next significant evolutionary step occurred when photographers switched to smaller cameras and even to faster films. Interior photographs no longer absolutely worshiped the non-convergent vertical lines, no longer needed every horizon to be absolutely horizontal and no longer banished grainy photos to the art work on the walls. Magazines published fuzzy pictures. Smaller cameras allowed photographers to relocate the view from eye-level to waist level. Instead of looking at the furniture, the camera got into the furniture. The "feel" of the room was most important.

As with any artistic revolution, once the pendulum has swung full the other way, the result is visual growth. Today, architectural photography has grown much more than 10 years from the old style. Current work is filled with subtle detail and yet is visually exciting. The representation is there, but so is the "gasp."

Architects will quickly state that the best architectural photographers were former architects or are photographers who studied architecture. They cannot explain precisely why, but they all agree that there is a sensitivity to "space" that non-architecture-trained photographers cannot seem to match. Designers agree with this preference, but less vigorously. To them, a good eye, a very good sense of light and a brilliant sense of composition are the elements they require. A degree in architecture is less important.

Architectural photographers are loathe to talk about earnings. Where one knows fashion shooters who reportedly earn $10,000 in a day, or car shooters at $5,000 and food shooters working for $2,000, the annual earnings of the busiest, best architectural photographers is a closely guarded secret. It must be assumed they are in the same league as their colleagues in the other disciplines. Because certainly the design and architecture magazines are filled with advertisements for new windows and furniture and bathroom fixtures which have to be shot by someone.

Training? Education? Consider this: if you go through college as an architecture major, you are in school with all your potential customers. When you graduate, so do they. As another architect, you are a competitor; as a photographer, you are an ally. Architects and designers need photography to show their work to potential clients who may not have the time to spend a day visiting other buildings and homes. Architects and designers constantly compete against each other in national and international contests. The judges cannot travel, so the entrants must send photos.

Any university with an architecture sequence which also offers a photo sequence could be the best bet. Architecture now is a five-year program and as a photographer, you really don't need that degree; only the education and the contacts. Following school, as with many other commercial photographic disciplines, you should work for several years as an assistant. The tricks you learn and the contacts you make more than balance the barely adequate pay and long hours.

Each photographic profession has its benefits. There are unique benefits to architectural photography. One is that there is little need for a studio (unless you specialize in furniture, and you shoot in North Carolina for that.

But perhaps the greatest benefit comes a few years down the road. If you shoot news, you know the cops. If you shoot cars, you can borrow the newest sports car from the manufacturers. If you shoot food, the chefs whose cookbooks you shoot will make you memorable meals. But after you've achieved your success as an architectural photographer, when you're ready to build your own home, you know whose work you like. And it is always possible to trade your photographic work for their custom designs.

Photograph by Gerry Kopelow.

CAREERS IN PHOTOGRAPHY

Chapter 7

FASHION PHOTOGRAPHY

by Bob Shell

Although I work as a magazine editor these days, I came up through the ranks as a working photographer and have done just about every sort of photography at one time or another. One of the specialties I developed was fashion, because I have always had an interest in the fashion image and consider some of the work done in fashion as among the best of contemporary photography.

Work in fashion photography requires a very well-developed sense of style. Many of the best fashion photographers are also painters or designers. An art background makes a lot of sense to the aspiring fashion photographer. In my case I studied art formally, but photography is totally self-taught. I am, honestly, not all that impressed with most photography courses taught in school. I meet far too many graduates who haven't learned the first thing about photography. Photography schooling probably won't do you any harm, but it is far from a necessity.

Most fashion photographers start out as assistants to other well-established photographers, working as general gofers in the studio at first, then graduating to setup and finally to camera work. After a year or two of this training, they usually go out on their own and start their own studio. I interviewed a number of prominent fashion photographers in preparation for this book, and every one of them recommended starting out in fashion photography by assisting. They recommended this even though many of them did not come up through this route, because they see it as an easier way to gain the necessary knowledge.

Fashion photography requires a detailed knowledge of every aspect of photography, from the simple nuts and bolts of how the camera works to the esoteric little details which are learned only by observation and experience. This does not mean that you have to be a techie, just the reverse; you must know the technical details well enough that they become so automatic that you don't have to think about them while working. Just as a musician must practice scales before learning to play with feeling, the photographer must master the basic operations of photography so that they are so sublimated that the creativity necessary to good work can flow unimpeded.

In a recent conversation with top fashion photographer, Robert Farber, he emphasized that he considers the aesthetic aspect of photography far more important than the technical. He learned the technical stuff well enough to be able to produce the sort of images he wanted, worked until it became second nature, and then began to work toward the feeling he wanted his images to convey. Now he mentions technical details like types of lighting, filtration, lenses and cameras, merely in passing; he knows them, but they are not obtrusive on his thought processes when planning and executing a shoot. When asked for details, he seems surprised at just how much technical knowledge his answers reveal. If you want to start a career in fashion photography outside of the major fashion districts of the big cities, you can probably get your foot in the door more easily. There are fewer jobs, but far fewer people scrambling for them, and it is not as likely to be so cutthroat. Also, lets face it, standards will be a little lower as well, and when you are first starting, your work might not be up to the demands of the big-city clients.

The first thing to do is to put together a camera outfit appropriate to fashion shooting. These days nearly all fashion is shot with 35mm cameras in the U.S., and only occasionally with medium format or view cameras. I have found, however, that overseas clients still tend to prefer larger transparencies. Nearly all of it is shot on transparency film, as well.

A basic outfit for fashion shooting would include at least two camera bodies (cameras do break down, and at the worst times), a 24mm, 28mm, possibly 50mm, 85mm and often longer telephotos. If you want, you can cover the 28—80 range with a good, modern zoom lens. Many fashion photographers prefer the compressed perspective of long telephotos and their ability to completely blur out a background. My friend Todd Ferrin, who shoots many catalog shots for Ujena swim wear, sportswear and athletic wear, nearly always shoots outdoors with 300 and 400mm telephoto lenses. Fashion clients are picky about sharpness, so buy the best lenses you can afford and always use the longer ones on a sturdy tripod. Because even the best in-camera meters can be fooled by unusual lighting, one of the most important pieces of

Photograph by Jim Russi.

equipment is a good incident light meter. You will find that use of such a meter will greatly improve the overall exposure quality of your transparencies. And remember that transparency films have the least exposure latitude of any films. If you do use a medium-format camera, the most important accessory is a Polaroid film back. Determining exposure with Polaroid is tricky, but it will show contrast range, composition and flaws quickly and will help you to spot a malfunctioning piece of equipment, such as a fill-flash which is not firing, or a shutter with problems. Unless you are working with a client or art director who understands the differences between Polaroid's rendition and that of the film

you are shooting, it is dangerous to let them see the Polaroid proofs. They may expect to see results exactly duplicating the Polaroid, and that is impossible.

Before going out in search of fashion clients, you will need some sort of portfolio. Initially, you may want to work with friends to produce some fashion-type images for this purpose, but be sure that the friend you ask to model at least looks like a fashion model. To learn what types of photography are in at the time, look at the major fashion magazines such as *Vogue*, *Mirabella* and *Elle*. You will also be able to get posing ideas from viewing a number of issues of these magazines. Just remember that these magazines represent the big-city esthetic. If you are working in a small town, you may have to tone things down a bit to fit regional tastes.

Once you have a basic portfolio of fashion-type shots, you can start looking for clients. Anyone involved with fashion selling is a potential client. Everyone who sells fashion goods and accessories needs photos of their products to sell them, so the market is very large. Don't waste your time with local outlets of national chains at first. They nearly always do all of their photography through an agency in one of the larger cities. Visit the locally-owned clothing shops, and make courtesy visits to local advertising agencies and get to know their art directors and photo buyers. Whether you personally like these people or not, it is important to get on their good sides. Spending hours in idle conversation (which seems like a total waste of time) can lead to big sales down the road. This art of carrying on conversations with industry people as though you are interested, buttering them up for later sales, is referred to in the business as schmoozing. Learn to be a master at it.

You will be surprised to find that in almost every part of the country there are clients for good fashion photography for newspaper advertising. If you can develop a rapport with several of these clients, you will be on your way. Produce the best possible work, settle for nothing less than

Photograph by Jim Britt.

perfection in your images, and always go above and beyond the requirements of the job; it is your reputation you are building. Don't expect to get rich at this stage. You may even have to work at some other "regular" job while you are becoming established.

Once you have established yourself with newspaper ads, you can set your sights higher. Look for regional companies which produce national wholesale or mail-order fashion catalogs. There are hundreds of them, often in the most unexpected locations. Labor costs for manufacturing textiles and textile products are lower in rural areas, and this is where the factories are found, with the managerial offices often in the same place. I live in a relatively small town surrounded by farming country, but there are no less than a dozen small fashion-goods manufacturers in my area. They all need photography.

While you may be satisfied to become the "big fish in a small pond" and stick with local accounts, there is no reason you can't go after national accounts, regardless of where you are located. Talk to ad agencies for the companies you would like to work for. You may be surprised and find that you have just happened to call when they are looking for a new photographer and a new look for their advertising. It has happened to me as well as other photographers I know. It could be the stepping stone to the top, which in the fashion field is almost unlimited. The top photographers in this field earn incredible amounts of money and travel the world.

One question which people getting started in fashion photography will always ask is, "How much can I make?" You will have to determine this based on the overall economy of the market in which you are working. Perhaps the best way is to try and find out what other photographers doing similar work are charging. Don't try to establish yourself in the market by undercutting everyone else on price. Then you will only establish a reputation as being the "cheap guy." Once you have gotten stuck with this reputation, it is almost impossible to raise your prices. In smaller markets, you will have to do the necessary research, but I'd say that beginning fashion photographers ought to be able to charge somewhere in the $20 to $50 per hour range, excluding film and processing, model's and stylist's fees, location fees and transportation. Intermediate level photographers should be charging $100 to $200 per hour, and top people should be well above that. Don't give your work away. $20 per hour may sound like a lot to some people, but you have to figure in the costs of doing business. And after you do that, it is really very little. These price ranges are for photos produced for one-time-only use. If the client wants an "all rights" contract, the price should be considerably higher, particularly if the photo will be used in national ads, promotional posters, and so on. It is impossible in a book such as this to give definite prices for all situations, so do your homework and set your prices and standards to meet the competition.

Another important point is that your work is your calling card. No matter how insignificant you consider the job or the client, do your very best work. Don't let anything out which is not up to your own personal best standards. Since word of mouth will be your primary means of advertising, you need for that word and your reputation to be that you will only produce the very best. All too often I have heard a photographer say, as justification for shoddy work, "Well, that job just didn't pay enough to motivate me." Maybe not, but who knows how many people will see the shoddy job and not hire that photographer as a result.

No matter where you are located, it is important to keep up with fashion trends and fashion photography trends. Robert Farber emphasized just how important this is. His advice is to read all of the major fashion magazines on a regular basis, paying particular attention to the editorial photography, since it tends to be the trend-setting work, and to read not just the American but also the European fashion magazines. This will help you keep up with trends and changes in trends. Robert emphasizes that fashion is a very trendy business. What is in today is out tomorrow, and that goes for photography as well as design. If you have one sharply defined style, and come in at the right time, you can quickly move to the top. But unless you are a chameleon in your ability to follow trends, don't plan to stay there. The few at the top are in a constant shuffle, with the same names coming into vogue, passing out, and later coming back in again.

Fashion photography is the most experimental of all types of photography. If you plan to make a big success in it, you must learn to work with non-traditional techniques and develop a reputation as a master of them. Not long ago I bumped into David Stetson, a top fashion shooter, in Tokyo. David was there on a six-month "dream assignment" from a Japanese fashion magazine called *Bacchus*. The editors really liked his work and his experimental style, so they gave him carte blanche to shoot for them for six months. He was shooting the whole time with 35mm Nikon gear and was using Polaroid's instant process black and white PolaPan for all the photos, a film which Robert Farber has also used extensively for advertising and personal photography. The magazines love it.

New York photographer Danny Gonzalez is another great fan of PolaPan, having used it for many fashion projects for major clients. Danny also has experimented with a technique favored by many of the avant-garde fashion photographers: cross processing film. What this means is that a film designed for transparency processing in E-6 chemistry is instead processed in C-41 color negative chemicals. This reverses the colors and produces strange tonalities, much of which cannot be predicted by the photographer. Likewise, color negative films may be processed in E-6 chemicals for another unusual look. Standard Polaroid pack films are also being manipulated in a number of ways by many fashion shooters.

The secrets of fashion photography, then, can be summed up in knowing fashion and its trends, knowing photography, knowing your market and producing your best work.

48

Chapter 8

GLAMOUR PHOTOGRAPHY

By Alice Gowland

The question most aspiring glamour photographers ask is, "How do I get started?" There is no pat answer, no book of instructions. Every photographer's story is different.

I can only relate what happened to Peter and me. In doing so, you will see that many of the things we have experienced are probably valid for others.

When I first met Peter Gowland, he was an extra in the motion picture business in Hollywood. Photography was a sideline. He lived in a California bungalow and had converted one bedroom into a darkroom. A friend introduced us. I was impressed with a beautiful black and white photograph of a child that hung over his fireplace. My friend asked Peter to make a portrait of me. I was coaxed into agreeing. He took the pictures in a part of his living room that had no furniture.

The first thing that surprised me was that Peter had me lie on a white, goat-skin rug on the floor. He told me to lie on my stomach and then he asked that I pull the neckline of my dress low so that it exposed my shoulders. I felt quite naughty because that was daring in 1941. Then he asked me to take all the bobby pins out of my hair and let it hang loosely around my face. He used spot lights and was careful in positioning them just so. I felt like a movie star. When I saw the results, my ego soared. I had never looked so glamourous! Naturally, I decided to marry this person who could make such magic with his camera.

We had been married only a month or two when I realized that Peter's talent was wasted on being an extra. I was amazed at how much he knew about every phase of photography. He was familiar with various cameras, lighting equipment and printing. He told me that art was his favorite subject in high school, but that he had learned everything else by reading photography magazines and asking questions of a successful

---

Great photographers develop an individual and recognizable style. Any expert would not have to be told that this is a photograph by Peter Gowland. The model is Amy Whittaker. Peter is one of the world's best-known glamour photographers. Photograph by Peter Gowland.

portrait photographer he knew. And he learned by practicing. So here is your first clue. Be avid about learning technical details about photography before you jump into the ring.

I quit my job as a secretary at Lockheed Aircraft and we started taking pictures of young, aspiring actors and actresses who had little money and quite often didn't pay us. I learned to assist Peter by moving a light here or there and attending to the subject's hair or straightening a collar. We bought a typewriter and I made the sitting official by presenting the clients with typed invoices.

While Peter was still working as an extra, I learned to develop and proof black and white pictures. Peter already had a neat filing system. Negatives were not tossed recklessly into drawers. Even today, we can track down a picture taken more than 40 years ago. It only takes a minute. So here's another clue. Keep good records and files.

We were able to supplement Peter's income by making portraits. After our beautiful daughter was born, we decided to try color which was then becoming more available. We photographed her eating a cookie or watching a kitten drink milk or just in the bathtub with bubbles all around. I found the name of a calendar company on the back of a calendar and sent these pictures to them. They were on 4x5 Kodachrome. When the calendar company bought the first one and sent us a check for $150, we both knew that photography was the direction we would take. This brings me to another clue. Marry or acquire a partner who is eager to help and willing to share in building a successful career.

A GI loan enabled us to build our first studio in 1947. I'm not sure if the same option is available today, at least in our area (Santa Monica, California) with such high real estate prices. But in glamour, because you concentrate on the beauty of a person rather than the entire scene, it is possible to use a living room or bedroom for portraits, boudoir or nude subjects and to use the great outdoors for bikini and fashion. We took any job we could get in our first studio. We photographed babies, animals, portraits, weddings and architecture. So here's the next clue: Don't shun any kind of photographic job. Everything you do will add to your expertise and help pay the bills.

We are beach enthusiasts. On weekends, we would head for the sea shore and combine business with pleasure. Initially, I was sometimes jealous when Peter would shoot another woman. But I got over it after I was able to sell two covers to *See* magazine. These were shots of a young woman friend Peter had photographed on his last day before going overseas in the service. At first I was furious. But seeing the covers and the name credit changed me into a scout. I would point out girls I thought would make good subjects. We had no money to pay a model fee, but offered prints and a percentage of any sales.

We do the same thing today with aspiring young models who need pictures. In order to keep our stock file supplied, we depend on models who are new to the field and need photographs for their portfolios. They are willing to pose for less money because we provide them with pictures plus a modest fee, usually $100 to $200 for a session, not by the hour. Stock photographs do not bring in as much income as an assignment does. Calendars, trade journals and some magazines provide an outlet for stock sales. The pay is almost never more than $500 and many times it is less. So it isn't possible to pay a model a day rate of $1200 when you may only get one or two $300 sales. Model agencies want to insist on the day rate. They prefer photographers to make "test" photographs which cannot be sold. This is okay if you have a client who needs to see recent pictures. But to spend a day or a half day and then not be able to sell the pictures is not financially productive.

In the years after World War II, magazine stands were filled with publications that featured covers and articles about young women. They did not have to be famous, just pretty. Today those markets are still there, but are much different in content. Magazines such as *Playboy*, *Penthouse* and *Hustler* contain very explicit photographs. The work we used to do for *Adam*, *Man* and *Playboy* appears tame in comparison with today's standards. Even so, it was often difficult to find models who would pose in the semi-nude or for artistic nudes. We mainly concentrated on the "California Girl" look; the healthy, outdoor type with a pretty face as well as a great figure. One of our first subjects was a girl named Pat Hall. She had sent us a snapshot of herself posing in a two-piece bathing suit. I contacted her and we ended up photographing her many times. Most of her pictures were sold for covers. *Popular Photography* used one and Peter's name was prominently displayed.

Young women began to call us, eager to model. After a few years, we were able to give up the portraiture and wedding part of our business and concentrate on glamour. We made photographs of women at the beach, in negligees and artistic nudes, all sold to magazines or calendar companies.

Eventually, we learned that the real money was made in doing assignments for companies that wanted to use a pretty girl for advertising or publicity. We never made the rounds of agencies, portfolio in hand. It wasn't necessary because we always insisted on picture credits, even if it meant less money for the use of Peter's photographs. It paid off when advertisers began to seek him out, giving us an edge. And that's another clue, isn't it? Always insist on credits. Some of our best clients came to us from seeing one of our stock pictures in a trade journal or on a calendar.

In today's glamour market, many of the techniques Peter and I have used over the years to gain sales still apply. In years past, only a few professional photographers were concentrating on the specialty. But today there are many more, all going after clients.

There are scores of magazines featuring glamour photographs published every month. Each uses a large number of pictures. Publishers continually look for new faces and figures.

My advice to anyone interested in glamour photography is to first of all seek excellence in technique. Know what you are doing. Serious amateurs often send us pictures and ask for comments. I can't believe some of them! I see unflattering lighting, backgrounds that swallow up the model, bad posing and poor attention to detail. The technical aspects of photography are never easy; it's not something that happens automatically. Today, after 50 years of photographing women, we still study each situation on its own, calculate shutter speeds and apertures, use meters, measure flash distances and take Polaroids to make sure we have the correct lighting and exposure. We know that bushes and trees are the least flattering backdrops, that backgrounds and props must frame rather than overpower a model. Having a subject face the sun, unless it is very early in the morning, will cause squinty expressions. It is preferable to use back-lighting with flash the main source of light.

Most important is the selection of the subject. That's the key element that the sale of a glamour picture hinges on. The most successful glamour photographers look at faces first and are not tempted to use models with less than perfect facial features because of an excellent figure or a pleasing personality. At times, when working on speculation, we find ourselves doing this because we are taken by a model's personality. But, sadly, in the end, these pictures usually stay in the file and are never sold. Those who live in small towns have an advantage because there is an opportunity to discover new model talent. Here in Hollywood, that is next to impossible. There are so many scouts about that any girl over the age of 12 with exceptional features is snatched up by model agencies.

When we work for a client, we interview models from agencies. While our opinion is taken into consideration, the final decision is usually up to the client.

Today, we are often hired by large companies and we are able to charge considerably more than $300 a picture. But we still like to shoot for our stock collection because when we do, we are not limited by a clients's opinion. We can do what we wish. When we are asked to quote a job, we first have to know exactly what is entailed. We never blurt out a quote off the top of our heads. First we find out all of the details of what is required. Every job we do has a different price based on the amount of time and effort that goes into it. We have a number in mind that represents how much we want to net as profit. Every professional photographer has such a figure. It may differ depending on circumstances. The amount invested in the business has to be taken into consideration as well as overhead and expenses. If you are just starting out, your circumstance could be quite different than ours or someone else's.

But at first, don't worry about how much money you are going to make. Worry about doing the absolutely, positively, very best job every single time you pick up your camera or go into the darkroom. In today's market, nothing short of excellence has any sort of chance. This is my last and most important clue.

BOUDOIR PHOTOGRAPHY

By Krisjan Carroll

There is a new and different kind of photography gaining more and more popularity. Some call it glamour portraiture, but it is more generally known as "boudoir." *Webster* defines boudoir as "a lady's bedroom or intimate sitting room." And indeed, this more or less defines the sets usually used in boudoir photography.

Actually glamour portraiture has been around for a long time. This is the sort of photography often used by Hollywood studios to publicize beautiful stars. But the difference is that boudoir photography is applied to all clients, not just models or stars.

And herein lies the artistry and the elements which make boudoir a distinct specialization.

By definition, models and stars are beautiful and glamourous. Most have perfect complexions, regular features and ultra-slim physiques. But few of us ordinary folk qualify. Probably due to such factors as diet, smoking and lack of exercise, many American women are overweight with a complexion in need of help.

But at the same time, most women have a secret wish to be a glamourous model. Of course this is an impossible

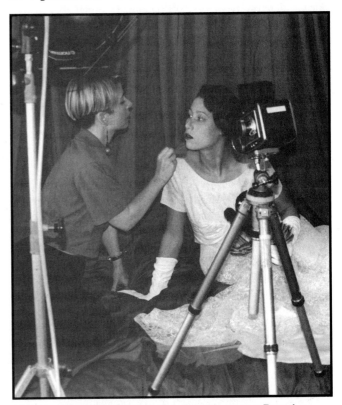

Krisjan Carroll (left) at work in her Hermosa Beach, California studio. In boudoir photography, preparing the client may take more than two hours while the shoot itself might last only a few minutes.

This is an advertisment from a company called, Glamour Shots. The company has a number of studios all over the U.S. Most of them are located in shopping malls. Ad courtesy of Glamour Shots.

dream for most, but with the with the proper preparation and techniques, almost anyone can be made to photograph like one.

I first got into photography through my interest in art. My father is a graphic designer, so possibly this is inherited. At any rate, I studied at the California Institute of the Arts in Valencia. As I studied art and design, I began to use a camera as a tool. Eventually I found that I was more interested in photography than art.

After I left school, I got a job in a commercial still lab in Hollywood. Without any experience, the only position I was able to get was as a delivery driver. But I was working for a photographic company. Eventually, I got to know the other personnel and finally graduated into the lab itself. I learned to process and print both black and white and color. If I have any advice to give someone about to start on a career in photography, I think it would be to first get a job in a professional lab.

After a few years, I decided I didn't want to spend my life in the dark. Besides, I wanted to be taking pictures, not just working on images others had created. Because a lot of the negatives and transparencies I worked on in the lab were glamour shots of stars, I became interested in this specialty.

At first, what I wanted to do was shoot models and stars. But the fact is that there are very few jobs in Hollywood for still photographers in comparison with the number who want these jobs. Even with the connections I made in the lab, I couldn't even get started.

At the same time I decided I wanted to get out of the lab and start shooting, the new type of portraiture called boudoir was becoming popular. Small studios were opening in mall locations, so I quit the lab and got a job in a mall studio. With my lab experience and college training, getting the job wasn't hard. It didn't pay much, but it was a start and I learned a lot.

The boudoir specialty has more or less sorted itself out into two camps: high end and low end. The mall studios are, for the most part, low end. By low end, I mean they are organized to process the largest number of clients in as short a time as possible. Everything is done by formula and the actual shooting only takes a few minutes. Clients are brought in with low advertised prices.

For instance, I have an ad from a chain with eight mall locations in Southern California. They are advertising "2 sittings for only $29.50." In small print, it says, "prints are additional." The studio I worked for advertised a similar low price, but the makeup and hair styling was extra. And without very specialized makeup and hair styling, boudoir photographs are not possible!

These chains and mall shops employ lots of people, but for relatively low wages. Many also employ those who are inexperienced and train them. By low wages, I mean anything from the minimum wage to two or at most three times the minimum. For atmosphere, they like to hire young, good-looking people. Women have just as much chance to be hired as men.

If you are going to school or just starting out, this could be a great place to work. For someone interested in photography, it is a lot better than working at a fast-food outlet. Because of the long mall hours, part-time jobs are often available. To get a job, just go to a mall and ask. If you have had any education in photography, this will be a plus.

After I had been with the mall studio for a year or so, I was hired away by a nearby competitor for more money. I stayed at this second studio for another year, but I soon became unhappy with the rigid formulization of what I was doing. Everything was like an assembly line. In the meantime, I had become friends with a co-worker and we eventually decided to quit and start our own business.

We decided to go into the high end of boudoir, mostly because we were tired of the low end. By the way, I don't have anything against mall studios. They provide a service for a lot of women who can't afford what we are doing now.

My partner, Pamela Peterson, and I opened our own studio a little over a year ago. We are both in our late twenties, but we have both had considerable experience, not only in photography, but also in our specialty of boudoir. Even so, the first year was difficult. In addition to desire and experience, it takes some capital to start a business. I understand from the Small Business Administration that a majority of new businesses fail in the first year. As I write this, our country seems to be going into its second year of recession. So we seem to have started out at just the wrong time.

But even so, we have survived. Just recently, we moved a block from our original location to a facility with more space. We are doing some advertising, so business is coming. Also, we get quite a few referrals as a result of previous clients.

Do we make a lot of money? Not yet, but we have hopes. Here's how we work. At our high end of the business, we take between two and three hours for a sitting. Each client is treated as a unique individual. We spend a lot of time in planning and preparation. Wardrobe, makeup, lighting and accessories are very important to the final effect. Since none of our clients are professional models, we have to analyze their good and bad features and take the pictures accordingly. From a photographic standpoint, this involves very specific techniques.

At present, we charge $300 for a sitting which includes three prints in a leather folder suitable for a gift. (Virtually all of our clients are giving pictures to their husbands or boyfriends.) Working this way, we can do two, or at most, three sittings a day. Sometimes we work on weekends too.

This may seem like a lot of money, but unfortunately, we don't have our own darkroom, so we have to have all our processing and printing done out. In order to maintain quality, we shoot medium format, so our film and developing are not cheap. Then there is our rent, telephone, advertising and other overhead. And, of course, there are two of us to divide the profit.

I don't think I'll ever get rich this way, but then I understand very few photographers get rich taking pictures. But we are doing what we love to do—photography—and we are doing it our own way.

If I have any advice for someone interested in our specialty, remember, portraiture is a people business. A lot of photographers I know are all involved in equipment and technology. But our most important element is the individual women we work with. You have to like people and have the ability to develop a rapport with many different personalities.

I'm lucky in having a partner. I emphasize the artistic and photographic parts and Pamela is in charge of business end. Not everyone will be this lucky, so if you want to get into business for yourself, you had better learn something about business in addition to photography.

This is a typical boudoir photograph. The clients are posed very carefully in order to emphasize their good points and hide the others. Camera angles, lighting and lens selection are also important in order to achieve a glamourous result. Photograph by Krisjan Carroll.

CAREERS IN PHOTOGRAPHY

Chapter 9

GRAPHIC ARTS

Graphic arts includes the science, art and technique of copying an original. Usually this refers to copying in order to produce an image capable of being printed.

Today, almost all printed materials are produced with a method called photo lithography or just lithography. Litho, for short. In lithography, a photographic image is "burned" onto a metal plate. The image is composed of grease. This plate is then installed in a printing press, curved around a drum. As the drum spins, a dilute solution of liquid soap is washed over the plate. Then the plate is rolled against an inked roller. The ink sticks to the grease image and does not adhere to the parts of the plate without grease. The plate is then rolled against another roller which is rolled against paper and the image is reproduced.

So almost all printing, not just printed photographs, is based on photography. The lithographic method is faster and less expensive than other methods of printing. In many instances, it is also of higher quality. The book you are now reading was printed using the lithographic method. Without photography, printed materials would be less accessible and more expensive.

Those involved in the printing trades make the plates. It is not necessary to be trained or skilled in photography in order to "burn" a plate. The grease image on the litho plate is a positive. This image is created from a film negative.

Here's how it works. The words you are now reading were originally typed into a computer and then printed on paper with a laser printer. The paper with type was then photographed with a special camera called a "process" camera using special film made for lithography. The film was then developed, fixed, washed and dried in the normal manner. The resultant negative was then contact printed (or "burned") onto a special photosensitive metal plate.

This is the famous shot of the Chinese student standing in front of a tank in Tiananmen Square. The top picture shows the image as it was received at CNN headquarters in Atlanta. The bottom picture is the same image after it had been manipulated in a computer. Note that the static lines are gone and the image appears sharper. Photograph by John Schaer, courtesy Cable News Network.

In order to print photographs, a special screened negative has to be taken. Look at a photograph in this book with a magnifying glass. You will see that the image is composed of tiny dots. This is because ink cannot create different shades and tones as can a silver photograph. The creation of these screened negatives is not only a science, but also an art. The quality of a printed image is, in large part, a result of the skill of the cameraman.

So graphic arts is basically copying. But it includes a number of other specialties. Sometimes, an image just needs to be copied. Perhaps the original negative has been lost.

The processes of retouching and restoration are also often included among the graphic arts. Most of these processes are being affected by the capabilities of computers. Many of the steps which were formerly done by hand can now be performed using a computer.

Since many photographs end up on a printed page, anyone interested in photographic careers should also become familiar with graphic arts. Today, this also involves computers and other devices such as laser printers, color copiers and scanners.

ELECTRONIC IMAGING

The decade of the nineties will likely see a multitude of technological developments. New products will be introduced in a possibly bewildering quantity and variety. A revolution in photography looms over the horizon and its name is electronic imaging. Anyone contemplating a career in photography or a related field should be well aware of the changes taking place.

One of the most famous news photographs of the recent past is the picture of the Chinese student facing a tank in Tiananmen Square in 1989. The photograph was taken by John Schaer of Cable News Network. You would expect that Schaer used a Nikon or maybe a Canon. But what he did use was a version of the Sony Promavica, an electronic camera which recorded the image on magnetic media. This allowed the photograph to be transmitted back to the U.S. by telephone shortly after it was taken. There was no film, developer, darkroom or silver print.

This example illustrates an innovation already with us which directly affects the field of photojournalism. Today, not every photojournalist uses an electronic camera; probably a relative few are in use. But in the competition for immediacy among news gathering organizations, their use will surely increase.

Electronic imaging is a marriage of photography and computers. In order to understand this, it is necessary to examine the nature of an image itself.

A conventional photograph is composed of tiny dots of silver halide. A computer and a printer can make a picture too. The picture created by a computer is also made up of tiny dots. Those in the computer field call these dots, "pixels."

At the present time, a silver halide image has 250 times more dots or pixels in a given area than does a computer image. For this reason, a conventional photograph has much higher quality. The forms appear sharper and there are more shades of black and white or color.

But an electronic image has some very real advantages over the silver halide one. It can be manipulated and transmitted in a variety of ways. In the example of the Chinese student, the photographer was able to go to a telephone immediately after the shot was taken and transmit the image to CNN headquarters in Atlanta in a few seconds.

Compare this with the conventional process. After the shot was taken, the film would have had to be developed, fixed and washed. It could have been printed while the film was still wet and the print could have been processed in a machine. But, counting travel to the darkroom facility, at least an hour had to have gone by before a print was available. After the print was made, to get it to Atlanta, it would have had to be transmitted by wire photo requiring sophisticated machinery.

When an image is in digital form in the memory of a computer and when appropriate software is utilized, the picture can be manipulated in almost unlimited ways. We are all familiar with the images from space which appear fuzzy until they have been "enhanced" in a computer. For anyone who has ever taken an out-of-focus photograph, the transformation is almost miraculous. Virtually anything that can be done in a darkroom or through retouching can be done in a computer. And the results are immediately available.

The changes taking place through the technology of electronic imaging will affect not only professional applications but also the amateur market. $16 billion a year in the U.S. is now spent on cameras, equipment, film, paper and services. Most of this is by amateurs.

Many of those who pursue one or another field of photography for their livelihood do so in connection with the amateur market. So as this market is affected by electronic imaging, changes will take place for those who work in it.

Some manufacturers have already tried to attack the amateur still-camera market with electronic cameras. The best known are the Sony Mavica, the Canon Xapshot and the Fuji Fujix. But the problem with these cameras, aside from their hefty prices, is that the pictures they create are crude in comparison with those from a film camera. The reason goes to the number of dots or pixels which create the images. So these initial forays have been far from commercially successful.

An area where electronic imaging has been successful, however, is in amateur movies. In just a few short years, camcorders have driven 8mm film cameras from the market. And this is in spite of poor quality when compared to a projected silver halide image. The question manufacturers are asking themselves is why has the public accepted camcorders for movies and not electronic images for stills?

The answer to the question is probably multifaceted. We are already used to the image on a TV screen and the latest camcorders produce excellent TV image quality. Cost is undoubtedly a factor too. And it's easier to produce an acceptable movie with a camcorder than with a film camera. Finally, image quality or lack of it is much less apparent in a motion picture than in a still picture. We watch the motion rather than contemplate details.

So the problem faced by manufacturers is, how much more quality is necessary before electronic imaging takes over the still picture field the way camcorders did amateur movies? No one knows exactly, but some experts think the transition could take as much as 20 years. Others believe it will never happen. Maybe the answer is somewhere in between.

The experience of Polaroid is interesting when considering the future of electronic imaging in the future of still photography. For quite a few years, sales of Polaroid cameras and film have been relatively flat. During these same years, sales of 35mm cameras and film has soared.

But the Polaroid picture is immediate! Why are most of us content to wait an hour or a day or two to get our prints? I don't pretend to know the answer, but I know my own reactions. I own the best Polaroid camera available plus a Polaroid back for my 4x5 camera. Additionally, I own a number of high-quality 35mm, medium format and point-and-shoot cameras. Only rarely do I choose Polaroid. Why?

The answer for me is that I am not satisfied with Polaroid quality from a Polaroid camera. I can obtain high quality if I use my 4x5, but this is not very handy. So if I want to take some snap shots of the family, I use a point-and-shoot or my Nikon and go to the nearby one-hour processor.

So it may be that electronic imaging will not take over the amateur market anytime very soon. It would seem to me that an electronic still picture has to be at least within the quality and price range of Polaroid in order to make a significant impact on the amateur snap-shot market.

This is not to say, however, that electronic imaging will not have an effect on other fields of photography. At least in the example of the Chinese student, it already has for photojournalism. It is already being used extensively in commercial graphics and advertising.

Other areas are exploring the possibilities made available through electronic imaging. A rather recent and interesting application is in photo restoration. The usual process to restore an old photograph has a number of steps and it takes some time. First a negative is made of the original. Then the negative is retouched. A print is made from the retouched negative and the print is retouched. Finally a negative is made of the retouched print and then multiple prints of different sizes can be made.

In electronic restoration, a scanner transmits the image from the original photograph to the memory of a computer, usually a hard disc. It takes about 20 megabytes to store a photograph. Then, using appropriate software, the computer operator can manipulate the image in virtually unlimited ways. When the manipulation is complete, the image can be printed using a laser printer. Those who doubt the quality of a laser print should take a small color print to a shopping-mall copy center and order an enlargement. Electronically, a restoration can be produced much more rapidly and the results are equal to or sometimes better than can be done using conventional methods.

One innovation which will likely come very soon is the video or laser disc. These are presently used widely in the recorded music market. But most experts think that video discs will take over a good part of the videotape market. Videodiscs produce images of noticeably better quality than tape and they have much longer lives. After a videotape has been rented a number of times, it begins to pick up static and lose image quality. A laser disc will probably last a lifetime.

Laser discs can do a lot more than provide more durable and higher quality rental movies. A tremendous amount of information can be stored on a single disc; an entire encyclopedia, for example. And, using a computer with a disc player, data can be accessed very rapidly. Laser discs can be interactive too. This holds all sorts of interesting possibilities and not just for new video games. Teaching and training can become truly individualized and self-paced.

As more and more technological changes take place, our ideas of what is a photograph and what is photography may have to expand. Many of us will have to enlarge our capabilities into other related fields. Any present photographer-in-training would do well to at least become computer literate.

GRAPHIC DESIGN

Look at the front cover of this book. You are looking at a graphic design. This particular cover is a combination of six different photographs plus the lettering which is called typography. This particular cover was designed with the use of a computer and a laser color copier. The cover was done in this way in order to provide an illustration of electronic imaging.

Here at the offices of Photo Data Research, we do not have the equipment necessary to perform a task like this. The equipment is very expensive and, considering the number of books we publish, purchasing would not be cost effective.

So we utilized the services of a company called Imageland which is located in Westwood, California, about a half hour away by freeway (but not at rush hour). Imageland has a number of computers and color copiers plus some technicians to help in the process. The technician assigned to us was Miss Blanka Kopecky. She had recently graduated from the University of California at Los Angeles, which is across the street from Imageland. After obtaining her degree in graphic design, she went to work for Imageland and had been there for more than a year at the time of our visit.

The concept behind graphic design using electronic imaging is to load all of the various individual elements into the memory of the computer, to create some other elements using various programs and to perform the designing on-screen with a program made for the purpose and then to print out the results on paper. The equipment used for this job was a MacIntosh computer and a Canon Laser Copier 500. The computer must have a large memory. When the design was complete, our cover job consisted of 19 megabytes.

The elements of this job consisted of the six photographs plus the type. When we called to make the appointment, we were told that Imageland had the type and so we need not bring our own. The pictures included two black & white 8x10 prints, an 8x10 color print and a color transparency of the Eifel Tower, the Gowland Calendar, the *Sports Car* magazine and a 35mm slide supplied to us by CNN.

The first task was to load all of these pictures into the computer. This took about half an hour. Imageland did not have the capability to scan the Eifel Tower transparency because it was larger than 35mm, so the print had to be used. The CNN slide had to be manipulated because the original electronic picture is a horizontal format. When the image was cropped to the vertical, the CNN logo was in the wrong place. So Blanca cut it out with some electronic scissors and pasted it in at the location where it is now. She also retouched the slide. The results and a discussion are included in the section on retouching and restoration.

Next Blanca created a black page with 8 1/2" X 11" dimensions, the size of this book. After cropping 5 pictures

Blanka Kopecky working on a preliminary version of the cover for this book at Imageland.

(the magazine cover didn't need cropping), she reduced each in size to fit the six-frame design. Then she typed in the wording, "Careers in Photography," selecting from typefaces on hand. While we could see the pictures with great clarity on the screen, this was not also true of the type. We could not tell exactly what the type would look like until the job was printed on paper by the Canon. We also directed her to have the computer program reverse out the type onto a black background and draw white lines around each picture. The total time consumed in doing the on-screen designing was one and a half hours.

Now we were ready to load the design into the Canon. Because of the size of the job, we were told this would take some considerable time. When we asked how long, she said anywhere from 15 to 45 minutes, but she could not tell in advance. Unfortunately, during the down-loading, the program displayed an error message on the screen. This meant something was not working properly. She tried again two times, but each time there was an error message. No one there seemed to know why it would not work, so we returned to our office.

The next morning, Blanca called the company that designed the program and received instructions. By about 1 P.M. that day, she was able to get a satisfactory print from the Canon. But there were a few problems. The type was not what we had wanted and Imageland could not supply our requirement. Also, the quality of the reproduction, while possibly acceptable, was not as good as can be obtained using traditional photographic methods.

The total cost of the job was $319.34. This included scanning 6 pictures at $15 each, 90 minutes of computer (design) time, 1 print-out to the Canon and 5 additional copies. The California sales tax was $29.34. If it had not been for the glitch in sending the job to the copier, we could have come away with an almost acceptable cover in about 3 hours total time.

This allowed us to evaluate the cover design in a way we never could before. Some of our distributors want to see covers in advance and this allowed us, for the first time, to send them a cover long before the book was actually printed.

We could have used this computer-imaged cover to make separations from which our printer could have produced the final books. Unfortunately, the quality was not acceptable by our standards. Upon close examination, we could see that the edges of the type are breaking up. And the Canon was unable to render the background to the dancers black enough. But this electronically imaged cover, even at $300, was valuable to us in the process of producing this book. And it is very likely that in the near future, we can perform the entire process with electronic imaging.

Just as this book was going to press, we received a newsletter from the Photo Marketing Association which announced that the Meisel Photographic Corporation had just opened a facility in Texas similar to Imageland called the ImageCenter. Imageland itself has another facility in Chicago. Undoubtedly more and more of these types of services will become available.

RETOUCHING and RESTORATION

By Mary Garand

Correction, enhancement, highlighting, erasing, glamorizing, remaking, restoring, rebuilding, creating illusion and coloring are just some the things a photographic artist does. A photographic artist works with a photographer to create a perfect image in order to preserve a moment or a mood.

Retouching can be very simple or extremely complex. At the simplest level, a few specs of dust may have been on the negative when a print was made. The image of the dust can be removed from the print by retouching. This is usually called spotting and most professional photographers can do this themselves.

But when a task of more complexity arises, the great majority of photographers cannot handle it. They turn to a specialist who is called a retoucher or a photographic artist. Few photographers want to acknowledge the existence of this specialty. Because of this, the career of photographic artist is a well-kept secret. Photographic artists are relatively rare. The job takes a special combination of talents and temperaments to be successful.

Photographic artists usually come from a background in a photo lab which specializes in doing work for professionals. These kinds of labs have an art department where such things as negative retouching, spotting, blending, enhancing and air brushing are performed. Each of these involves various levels of expertise. Most of the work in a lab, however, is rather tedious. Consequently some photographic artists are not content to continue for very long in a lab. Many strike out and set up their own businesses.

Not all photographic artists come from labs. Commercial photography studios have a continual need for photographic art services. Some, of course, have them performed at a professional lab. Others find someone on their staff with a combination of photography skills and art training and establish a position of photographic artist. Often the staff person is not well trained enough in art and has to be encouraged to seek more schooling.

The two best-known schools for instruction in photographic art are Orange Coast College in California and the Veronica Cass Academy in Florida. Orange Coast offers evening courses in negative and print retouching, air brushing and restoration. The Veronica Cass has full-time courses which last from two to eight weeks, depending on the subject matter. In addition, there are occasional seminars and workshops given by various professional photography associations.

If you are interested in being in business for yourself, you will first need a portfolio with which you can show prospective clients what you can do. Even after you have received some training, it is necessary to do a lot of practicing before you will be able to make an acceptable portfolio.

To get started, you have to market your services. Start out with professional and custom laboratories and professional photographers. Make calls, visit and show them your work. Even though the work may be tedious, a pro lab is really the best place to begin. This is because a lab will have the volume and variety of work necessary for you to become proficient and efficient. It is an excellent atmosphere in which to understand and experience all aspects of the photographic process and the roll of the photographic artist.

Because there are not many photographic artists, jobs are not difficult to get. During the time you are working in a lab on a salary, you can start building up your portfolio. You may have an opportunity to meet directly with clients. This is very valuable experience.

Eventually, some photographic artists set off and become independent contractors. It is even possible to do this work out of a home. Others work out of a commercial location. Actually, it does not take a lot of space to do the work and the necessary equipment can be acquired for a few hundred dollars.

One of the problems with the specialty is that photographic artists have traditionally been undervalued as to the importance of their services. Laboratories pay as little as $5 an hour to trainees. Beginners in a lab are always put to work spotting. After learning how to do more complex tasks, the salary goes to $7 or $8 an hour with a top of $10. Those who learn to air brush earn up to $15 in a lab. Admittedly this is not a lot of money. But there are some compensations. Most labs will employ on a part-time basis as well as full-time. And, as I mentioned previously, it is great experience.

How much can you earn if you are in business for yourself? First of all, it should be understood that anyone with the training and talent can go into business with a very small investment. A few hundred dollars will buy a drawing board, a light table, an air brush and some supplies. Additionally, the work can be performed almost anywhere, so there may not even be any additional rent to pay.

Spotting a print or retouching a negative are the simplest tasks. This usually takes between ten and thirty minutes and you can charge $15 each. Depending on how fast you work, you can make between $30 and $45 an hour. To do air brushing, I charge $50 an hour. To retouch the portrait example in this book, I would charge $100. Some restorations are difficult and complex and the fee often runs into the hundreds.

Much of Mary Garand's work consists of retouching portraits. This is a print of a portrait without retouching.

This is what the same portrait looks like after it has been retouched by Mary Garand.

Chapter 10

LEGAL PHOTOGRAPHY

Photography is used extensively in matters having to do with the law. Basically this usage falls into three categories: forensic, security and liability or tort law.

Forensic photography is the science of using photography as evidence in criminal law. Most police officers are trained in simple photography. Medium-size and large police departments have photography sections which employ both officer-photographers and civilian photographers plus lab personnel.

Security photography has to do with using photography (and video) in order to increase the security of installations and facilities. Banks, for instance, often have cameras which record sequential pictures of customers. When the customer turns out to be a bank robber, the resultant images can help in the apprehension of the criminal and the possible return of the funds. Photography is also used to record insured inventories. This provides a positive record in the event a claim is made due to damage or loss of an item. For example, the companies which insure collectible automobiles invariably require photographs of the cars. Home and commercial building insurance also requires photographs.

Liability photography is possibly less-known than forensic and security. In this instance, photographs are used by attorneys as evidence in tort cases. A tort is a civil (as opposed to a criminal) wrong. Your neighbor's child throws a ball which breaks a window in your house. You have been wronged or damaged and are due money to replace the window. Maybe you have to sue to recover the money. In this case, a photograph of the broken window could be used as evidence.

FORENSIC PHOTOGRAPHY

by Gerry Kopelow

How many TV murder mysteries begin with an unfortunate corpse dramatically illuminated by the bright pop from the flash of a cigar-chomping photographer? Must be thousands . . . yet the popular view of a police photographer as a hard-bitten, world-weary stereotype is somewhat dated.

I interviewed James Adlard, photographer at the Forensic Laboratory of the Royal Canadian Mounted Police in Winnipeg, Canada, and he told me that in all his years with the force, he has never photographed a body or an actual crime scene. In fact, Adlard's work, and the work of his colleagues in eight RCMP labs across Canada, involves painstakingly accurate scientific photo-documentation of various kinds of evidence: weapons, bullets, documents, paint samples and

Jim Adlard, RCMP Forensic Photographer, works with a Leitz scientific close-up camera. The tube in Mr. Adlard's right hand provides light via fiber optics. Photograph by Gerry Kopelow.

more. In most Canadian police forces, uniformed officers (the "Ident" squad) are trained to shoot basic flash-on-camera pictures in the field, but the real forensic photography goes on in well-equipped studios run by specialists.

Now nearing retirement age, Jim Adlard admits he is possibly the last of the forensic photographers who entered the profession as a self-taught photo enthusiast. He began with a home darkroom and didn't use his photographic skills professionally until after he had left a seventeen year stint as a member of the Canadian National Railroad Police. He saw an advertisement placed by the Mounties, and his amateur experience combined with his work for the CNR was sufficient qualification to secure the post. Jim brought himself up to the required technical level by studying textbooks dealing with the preparation of photographic evidence followed by trial and error experimentation. He also attended a number of conferences, seminars and courses to hone his skills. These days, he says, most forensic photographers have a thorough technical-school photographic education. In Canada there is only one technical school (in Edmonton, Alberta) that teaches forensic photography technique. Students in other places study traditional commercial photography.

Duties at the Forensic Lab include processing and printing film produced by peace officers, but most of the work is much more technical. The various branches of the RCMP crime lab require different kinds of photographic support. The documents section needs black and white, color, infrared and ultraviolet photos of altered or damaged documents, checks, bank notes and lottery tickets. The physical evidence section requires very detailed shots of weapons, bullets, hair, fiber, footwear, wood splinters and other kinds of objects and samples gathered at the scene of a crime. The chemical investigation section needs shots of blood and paint stains, paint chips, gun powder patterns and various kinds of microscopic marks and striations on collected materials.

RCMP forensic photographers are not usually required to give evidence in court. They are required, however, to prepare photographic prints and displays to be used as evidence. In the U.S. the services of forensic photographers are often required at crime scenes as well as in the lab.

Some public or private police or security experience is a real advantage when searching for a job. Since forensic photography is a quasi-scientific enterprise, the main characteristics for anyone interested in this work are patience and a very meticulous working style. Applicants will be required to undergo security checks and IQ tests. There are also various civil-service exams specific to particular departments.

Photographers with the RCMP are paid between $33,000 and $37,500 per year depending on education, experience and performance on the job. Forensic photographers are civilians, not police officers. Nevertheless, these positions are part of government service, so benefits and job security are very good. Photographers can rise through the ranks to the administrative level. Some science advisors, as they are called, earn up to $50,000. To reach this level, they have to obtain a university science degree.

An apprenticeship program, which can take from four to twenty-four months, offers a starting salary of $33,000 per year to trainees. Some experienced photographers without formal education are still accepted after very thorough evaluation of their skills.

LIABILITY PHOTOGRAPHY

There are a large number of civil law suits in the United States. There are also many such law suits in other countries, although the U.S. leads in this area. A civil suit has to do with a dispute between parties. There are many types of suits, but one category has to do with something lawyers call "torts."

A tort is a civil wrong as opposed to a criminal wrong. A criminal wrong is a crime committed against all of us and we are represented by the state or government entity. When a crime is committed and a suspect identified, the state sues. When a tort is committed, an individual may sue.

One element of a tort is that the person wronged, the plaintiff, must have suffered damages. These damages have to be able to be expressed in monetary values. An act can be both a tort and a crime. A drunk crashes into your car. The state prosecutes for drunk driving, takes away the driver's license, exacts a fine and possibly a prison sentence. But the

state gets the fine money. This does not fix your car. So you sue to recover damages, the cost of fixing your car plus maybe lost income, car rental and attorney fees. These are two separate actions in court.

When you go to court, you must prove your case. In order to do so, you present witnesses and evidence. The other side, the defendant, will try to negate your allegations. Photographs are often important evidence in tort cases. Both defendants and plaintiffs use them frequently.

There are two types of photographs presented as evidence. One type is taken during or just after an occurrence has taken place. Police commonly take photographs of crime scenes. These pictures are forensic in nature. But others, including participants, bystanders and professional photographers sometimes take pictures. The second type of pictures are taken well after the occurrence. In tort cases, it's common to re-create an incident and photograph it for presentation in court. These second types of pictures are almost always taken by professional photographers.

The reason for this is that not only the photographs, but also the authenticity of the photographs is an issue. Often the photographer must testify under oath as to the circumstances of taking the pictures. He or she must demonstrate that the pictures introduced as evidence do, in fact, represent an accurate record. Photographers who do this sort of work usually specialize in it. One reason for this is that not everyone makes a good and credible witness. Photographers who do this must not only be excellent at their craft, they must also be able to substantiate their professional credentials and be good on the witness stand.

The photographs must be technically excellent, otherwise the other side may be able to challenge their validity. Photographs and photographers are used by attorneys for both plaintiffs and defendants.

The tort or liability system in the United States is such that there is often a lot of money at stake. In many cases, there are no limits on liability as there are in most other countries. This means that a plaintiff can be awarded a large amount. Some are in the millions. Often, a tort defendant is defended by an insurance company. The other side, the plaintiff is usually represented by an attorney who is speculating on the chance of getting a large share of any money award.

With large amounts of money at stake, both sides will go to great lengths with regard to producing evidence. Accident recreations are sometimes very elaborate. Photographers who specialize in this work are paid well. Hourly rates are normally in the $100 an hour range plus expenses. And the fees are paid while testifying, conferring and waiting as well as while shooting.

It would be unusual for a photographer with no experience in this field to be employed by liability attorneys. Photographers who do this work most often have a continuing relationship with attorneys. A relationship can be established by first being an assistant to a photographer who specializes. Photographers work for police departments, as officers, civilian employees and as independent contractors. This is another avenue for gaining experience and contacts.

POLICE PHOTOGRAPHY

Police forces come in all sizes and so do their photography departments. Regardless of the size of the department, however, photography is a very important element in police work.

There are a few departments—such as New York, Chicago and Los Angeles—with large photographic units, elaborate equipment and highly trained specialists. Many departments are medium-size and have a small photography section. And some departments are so small that they have no specialized photographic capabilities. In these latter cases, small departments depend on larger nearby departments such as services from the county sheriff's office or the state police.

The department of a mid-size city contrasts with the RCMP in the previous essay. The city chosen was Culver City, California, one of the many municipalities in Los Angeles County. The section which performs photographic services is headed by a police sergeant and has three civilian employees. The sergeant is really an administrator; the civilian employees are the shooters (photographic, that is).

Photography in Culver City is really on three levels. Police personnel who are investigators carry mid-level point-and-shoot cameras. They receive periodic instruction in how to take the required photographs, but they are not photographers, they are policemen. When an accident or crime scene requires more than the most cursory coverage, one of the three civilian photographers is sent out. These people are equipped with sophisticated 35mm SLR equipment and lights. When there is a truly horrendous happening, Culver City calls in the Los Angeles County Sheriff's photographic unit. With the advent of one-hour labs, Culver City shut down its own laboratory and sends out all processing. Most of the shooting is on 35mm negative color. All of the work is sent to a single lab in the city. The lab has a contract with the police department and the work is strictly controlled so that the "chain of evidence" is not broken. A great deal of the fingerprint photography is done with specialized Polaroid equipment. Culver City has found it less expensive to send out for processing and printing than doing it themselves.

The civilian photographers are hired based on a civil service examination. The exam has two parts: written and oral. Most applicants have some community college photography education. One of the present photographers studied at San Jose State University, one of the leading forensic institutions in the U.S. Another came from a similar unit in a nearby city. Culver City has no provisions for interns or work-study programs in police or forensic photography.

Civilian photographers in Culver City are in a "dead-end" position. They are all on the same level; there is no "head" photographer and their supervisor is a police officer. The starting salary in 1992 was in the $16 an hour range. They receive periodic raises until they reach the highest possible level which is between $3000 and $3500 a month. The personnel are represented by a union of all city workers and there are periodic cost-of-living raises too. All three are full-time; there is no provision for part-time personnel. In addition to the salary, there are excellent fringe benefits including full medical and dental coverage plus life insurance.

Culver City was chosen as an example because it is typical of the great majority of medium-size cities in the U.S. While the very large police departments and the FBI receive most of the press attention, the fact is that there are more police officers in departments this size than any other. There are very probably photography opportunities in most of these departments.

There are also employment opportunities in larger organizations such as big-city departments, county sheriff's offices and state police forces. Work in these larger organizations is, for the most part, much more specialized than that found in Culver City. So the requirements for getting a job are most often more stringent insofar as photographic education, training and experience is concerned.

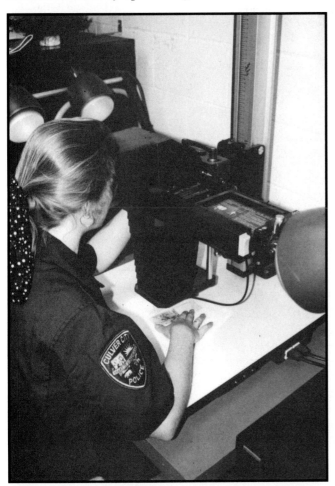

Nicole Whalley-Muller works at a specialized Polaroid copy camera photographing fingerprints. Nicole is one of the three photographers, called an "Identification Technician," in the Culver City Police Department. The three technicians are supervised by Sergeant David Paroda.

64

Chapter 11

MILITARY PHOTOGRAPHY

Free training, guaranteed apprenticeship and a chance for excellent experience and foreign travel; these are some of the benefits the military can provide for young people interested in photography. Each of the military services—Army, Navy, Air Force and the Marines—train and employ many photographers. With a range of jobs from public relations to the White House to combat, the assignments can vary from boring to death defying.

While the specifics vary from service to service, there are two basic alternatives: officer or enlisted person. It is possible to receive training and assignments as a Photographic Officer, but there are no guarantees. You can, however, be guaranteed training and assignments as an enlisted person. Officers, generally, are paid more.

As you continue to read this chapter, you should be aware that there are variations from service to service. And conditions change from time to time. As this is being written, all of the services are undergoing significant reorganizations which include severe reductions in force levels due to the end of the Cold War. If you are interested in the opportunities offered by any of the armed forces, after reading this, you should spend considerable time and effort investigating. As a first step, visit a nearby recruiting office. Offices are listed in both white and yellow pages of the phone book.

PHOTOGRAPHIC OFFICER

By Lieutenant Colonel Bart Oldenburg

Let's look at the different alternatives. If you plan to go to college or you are just beginning your college career, the Reserve Officers Training Corps (ROTC) is something you may want to investigate. The ROTC program provides officers for the various services in both reserve and active-duty status. Active duty means you work for the government full-time while reservists have what amounts to a part-time job.

To participate in the ROTC program, you must also be enrolled (or about to enroll) in a college or university. Certain colleges have ROTC programs on campus. Your college registrar can tell you if there is such a program at yours. If your college does not have an ROTC unit, you can probably participate at a nearby college which does have one, and still maintain your present enrollment. To investigate, first call a recruiting office to find out where the nearest ROTC unit is located. Then make an appointment to visit and talk with the Professor of Military Science and Tactics (the officer in charge) or one of the assistants.

Official U.S. Air Force Photo

The ROTC program consists of a number of courses—usually one each semester—you take during each school year. They are courses like military history, military procedures and other things you will need to know as an officer. These courses carry unit credit which you can apply towards your degree. Some colleges accept some of these courses in lieu of physical education. You need not major in military science; you can choose any major you wish. During part of your summer vacations, you will train on a full-time basis at a military base. During these times, you will be paid and receive food, housing and travel.

Almost any college student can join the ROTC during the freshman and sophomore years. After your first two years, if you wish to continue, you must take a series of medical, mental and physical tests plus pass a security check. These tests are more stringent that those for enlisted personnel. If you pass, you can continue into the Senior ROTC program which is for college juniors and seniors. During your last two years, you will receive a stipend of $100 per month and the government will pay for all of your college fees, tuition and books. Additionally, the ROTC has a number of scholarships to award.

When you graduate and complete your ROTC training, you are "commissioned" (appointed) a second lieutenant (or Navy ensign), the lowest commissioned officer rank. Each ROTC graduate "owes" the government a certain period of service, either active-duty, reserve or a combination. At times in the past, when our armed forces were larger, most, if not all new ROTC graduates were put on active duty for a period of time. But the military has other sources for active-duty officers: the US Military Academies (West Point, Annapolis, the Air Force Academy) and the Officer Candidate Schools. Today, most ROTC graduates serve in a reserve status.

At this point, it should be noted that there is another avenue to a service officer career. I have just mentioned the military academies. But graduates of these institutions will not be assigned to photographic training or duties. However, a graduate of an Officer Candidate School could. Officer Candidate Schools are for people who are already in the service as enlisted people. If you are presently in the service, you already know how to receive counseling about OCS. The problem is to get photography-related assignments and additional photographic training after graduation. If you are not now in the service, a recruiter can tell you about OCS.

As an ROTC cadet about to graduate, if you want to serve on active-duty (full-time), you must request it. There is no guarantee you will be selected, since the government employs ROTC officers on a need basis. Top ROTC graduates have a better chance of getting active duty than others. Top does not necessarily mean those who have the best college grades, but rather those who have excelled in the ROTC program.

New officers, whether active-duty or reserve, are assigned to a "branch." Military personnel specialize and the branches represent military specializations. In the Army, the branch which supplies photographic services is the Signal Corps. So if you are interested in photography, you must first attempt to be assigned to the Signal Corps. For the most part, new officers are allowed to choose their branch, but there is no guarantee. The service assigns officers on a need basis. Those who did better in their ROTC training are more likely to receive their first choice.

After you have been assigned to a branch, you will receive additional training. If you were selected for the Signal Corps, you will go to a base near Atlanta, Georgia to be trained as a general-purpose Signal Corps officer. After this, you will receive more schooling in photography.

When your training is complete, you will receive your first assignment. If you are in luck, it will be photography related. But remember, if you selected the officer route, there are no guarantees. The priority for commissioned officers is, "For the good of the service." This means that you may be trained in a specialty, but never have much use for that training if the military does not have an appropriate requirement.

If you have made it through ROTC or OCS, the Officer Basic Course and additional photographic training, you may look forward to a number of challenging assignments. Large units (Divisions with 15,000+ personnel) have Public Information Officers. Or, you may become a Platoon Leader, an officer in charge of a team of enlisted photographers and technicians. You could end up as an assistant motion picture or television director.

The author of this section served as an assistant motion picture director in New York City, a training officer in Colorado, the commanding officer of a Combat Photography Company in Vietnam and as an Instructional Technology Officer. This was the good part. But I also spent my share of non-photographic assignments as a Communications Officer in Germany, a supervisor of food service, a contract administrator and a legal officer.

ENLISTED SERVICE

As you can see, to become a service photographic officer can be difficult. Even if you are successful, the types of assignments are usually more in the nature of management rather than hands-on photography. You tend to supervise the enlisted people who do the actual work. But of course, supervisory experience is valuable when you go to apply for work in the civilian world. If, however, you want to get involved more directly with photography, perhaps you should explore the possibilities open to enlisted personnel.

An enlisted person is a technician. They are the technical experts who actually perform the assigned tasks. (Officers tell enlisted who to point at and enlisted pull the trigger.) Some senior enlisted personnel perform supervisory duties in addition to officers.

When you become an enlisted person, it is possible to be guaranteed the type of training you will receive plus your first assignment. The service can also provide you with considerable advanced training and valuable on-the-job experience. Training in the military is usually designed to extract immediate results. You will often learn a skill one day and apply it the next.

If you want to explore enlisted career possibilities, your first step is to contact a service recruiter. You may already have a preference as to which service: Army, Navy, Air Force, Marines. If not, there are some recruiting offices with representatives of all of them in one place.

You should also remember that recruiters are there to counsel young people regarding not only active duty but also reserve service. The reserves and National Guard employ many photographic specialists on a part-time basis. Reservists often receive the same training as active-duty personnel and many of the same benefits.

A recruiter—usually a senior enlisted person—will explain all of your options in detail. If you decide to join, first you will take a test (called ASVAB) similar to the SAT. This same test is used by all four services. The purpose of the test is to determine if you are mentally qualified. It takes about an hour. If you are truly interested, you should go ahead and take it since, if you are not qualified, you would be wasting you time to pursue the matter further.

Of course there are other qualifications in addition to the ASVAB test. There are age limitations and limitations with regard to a criminal record, if any. A service person must be physically fit too.

Assuming you are qualified, the next step is the guarantee.

Ask the recruiter if there are any photo related slots (jobs) available. He or she will be able to check this very rapidly with a computer. If there are, you may be offered a contract. This means that you agree to serve for a certain number of years and the service agrees to train and assign you to a specialty. Be very sure that the written contract is what you wish to agree to.

You should remember that the contract is binding on you. Unlike a civilian job, you cannot quit before the end of the term. If you do, you will be considered to be absent-without-leave or a deserter. You would then become a fugitive from justice and subject to arrest, trial and imprisonment. So becoming a member of the service is a serious commitment.

Before you sign, think about it. The military is a way of life, even for those who serve only a few years. In part, it is even a way of life for reservists. You will not be the same person you are now and, for better or worse, the experience will affect the rest of your life. If you now have problems with alcohol or drugs, the military is not for you. Additionally, if you have criminal problems or lean towards an alternative sex life, don't join. In spite of a growing public acceptance of alternative life styles, there is no present tolerance within the military and you will be in for some very unpleasant experiences.

If you are qualified and if you have been offered an acceptable contract, you will take a physical and be sworn in. Regardless of your ultimate assignment, you will first go to basic training or boot camp. Here you will learn the skills required of every soldier, sailor, airman or marine. This initial training lasts three or four months.

After basic or boot training, you will begin your photographic training. In the Army, this takes place at Fort Gordon near Atlanta, Georgia. Regardless of your previous civilian experience, you will begin with the basics: how to take, develop and print still b&w and color photographs. You may also learn motion picture photography and video production.

As you near the end of your photographic training, you will receive final confirmation of your initial assignment. The location could be almost anywhere in the U.S. or in other countries where there is an American military presence such as Germany, Japan or South Korea.

You should keep in mind that every person in the service is required to perform as ordered. A combat photographer may have to shoot and kill. Enlisted photographic personnel can be asked to perform non-photographic tasks. Before you go any farther than reading this chapter, you should try to see the movie "Private Benjamin." While the film is a spoof, parts of it are very real. It is usually available for rental on videotape.

After the conclusion of the war in Vietnam, the American military services eliminated the draft. Now all personnel are volunteers. In order to get and keep quality people, the Congress has had to offer a level of salaries and benefits which make military service attractive.

The following will give you some idea of the present pay levels. A private in basic (boot) training gets $697.20 a month. After completion of the first 16 weeks of training, the rate is $753.90. After 3 years, a sergeant makes $1140.60. After 20 years of service, a master sergeant makes 2209.20. A second lieutenant or Navy ensign just starting out makes $1444.20. A captain with 6 years service makes $2643.30.

Reservists and National Guardsmen train for two days and are paid for four days each month. Additionally, they serve on active duty for 15 days each year, usually in the summer. Employers are required by law to give reservists time to serve in addition to their normal vacation time. A private in the reserve after completion of initial training is paid $100.52 per month. A sergeant with 3 years service, $152.08. A master sergeant with 20 years, $294.56. A beginning second lieutenant or ensign makes $192.56 and a captain with 6 years, $352.44.

Remember that in addition to pay, there are loads of benefits not available in the civilian job market. Many of these most of us know about. Enlisted people eat for free and are provided with clothing and living accommodations. Those who are married or live off-the-post receive payments in addition to their salaries. While officers have to pay for their meals and uniforms, the amounts are relatively small. And there are all sorts of lesser-known benefits like free or inexpensive life insurance, free medical and dental care and free travel. There are inexpensive resorts, even in the Alps, for service people and their families. There is a very inexpensive luxury hotel on the beach in Waikiki. There are camping sites on the coast of California. The Air Force even has its own community college. Officers can get insurance (through USAA) at about half rate. And there is retirement after only 20 years of service. You can even buy cameras and film at a store on a military base without paying tax and at a price near cost.

According to the latest edition of a book called the *Military Career Guide*, published by the U.S. Military Entrance Processing Command, there are a total of about 2,500 enlisted photographers in all of the armed services. There is a need for about 240 new photographers each year. There are about 1,500 motion picture camera operators and the yearly need is 170. There are 1,600 audio-visual production specialists and a need for 170 new ones each year. There are more than 3,600 photographic equipment repair personnel and a need for almost 400 more every year. There are more than 1,800 photo lab technicians and there is a need for about 220 new ones each year.

The military isn't for everyone, but for some, it provides a career in photography. And many others get their start in the military and go on to successful civilian careers. Burt Reinhardt, formerly the President and now the Vice Chairman of Cable News Network was instrumental in making the CNN picture on the cover of this book available to us. Master Sergeant Reinhardt served in the U.S. Army Pictorial Service as an cinematographer and was in the first group to arrive in Japan after WWII. After leaving the Army, Burt has pursued a distinguished career in photography, journalism and communications.

Chapter 12

MOTION PICTURES

The ability to make a motion picture is not only an art, it is also a trade and a science. Except for amateur productions, the making of a film usually involves quite a number of people. So there are many jobs connected with such an enterprise.

When one thinks of motion pictures, the first thing that comes to mind is the entertainment business: feature films, TV shows and TV commercials. But in actuality, this aspect of film making is small in comparison to other sorts of motion picture productions.

Being involved in making a motion picture can be a wonderful and rewarding experience. All sorts of arts, crafts and sciences are combined to create a unique entity. Movies are an art form all their own. They entertain us, but they also perform all sorts of other functions. They are used in business, science, industry, education, government and the military. So there are many jobs involving motion pictures outside the bounds of feature film making.

INDUSTRIAL MOTION PICTURES

By Tom Countryman

Before we look at the industrial motion picture field, maybe we should decide just what is an industrial motion picture. While it is easy to identify a theatrical film, sometimes people confuse documentary films with industrial ones.

A documentary producer is pretty much his own guy. He doesn't have anyone to answer to other than himself. He usually writes it, shoots it, directs it. A documentary film is intended to be shown in a theater or on TV the same as a theatrical film.

An industrial film, on the other hand, is made by or for

Tom Countryman operates a 16mm Arriflex, the workhorse of the non-theatrical motion picture industry.

an organization whose purpose is other than making films. Often the organization is a company. But many governmental agencies make films as do charities, associations and unions. An industrial motion picture explains a process or tells a story that the sponsoring organization wants told.

Why would a company want an industrial film made? It could be an analysis of how a machine works. Sometimes this is done with high speed cinematography. Maybe it's a marketing film to promote the company's operations or the products they make.

One of my biggest clients was the Minnesota Mining and Manufacturing (3M). I have made films for 3M for over 20 years. I originally got started with them because the Reflective Products Division was having problems. They had a photography department, but they were having trouble shooting a reflective material called "Scotch Lite." I took the time on my own to make all kinds of tests. I tried different kinds of light and different kinds of film. I shot for a couple of weeks. When I got what I thought was pretty good, I took it over to show them and they loved it. From then on, I did every film made for that division.

I started as a one-man operation. I got together enough money to buy an Arriflex and just started to film. In those days, local TV commercials were filmed on 16mm. I went around and sold local advertisers. 3M was my first big account and so I got into industrial films that way.

I think a good way for someone who is interested in motion pictures to get started is to first learn still photography. That way you can learn the process from the ground up. That's the way I started. I was a Signal Corps (still) photographer in the Army. This gave me a solid grounding in the basics.

When I got out of the Army, I went to the University of Oklahoma and studied journalism and photography. At first I thought I wanted to be a press photographer. I had already learned the photography part in the Army, so I thought I had better learn the journalism part before looking for a job. Besides, I had the GI bill.

A buddy of mine and I started out shooting fraternity and sorority parties. That same thing could be done today with video. Most production companies today shoot video as well as film. And many start out with just video because it is cheaper and easier to get into.

In my company, in the past, we have had as many as 17 permanent employees. In those days, you couldn't pick up a phone and get trained and experienced specialists at the drop of a hat. But in later years, we hired the necessary staff on a temporary basis just for that project. Every day we had people coming in looking for work. We kept a record of those we thought would work out. Then, when we started a production, we assembled a crew. Sometimes we hired a few interns from the University. I know the TV stations here do that too.

The last film I produced was for the American Automobile Association on driving safety. We shot with a relatively small crew. The cameraman got $450 a day, the sound man with his own Nagra and mikes got $250. Then I had two drivers, one on the camera car, for $200 a day. I also had a production assistant at $125. Some of the time we had two additional cameras, so I hired two assistant cameramen to operate at $250 a day. I was the director and the production (shooting) part of the job took three weeks.

Everyone in the film industry today is hired by reputation. I hire people I have worked with before because I like the way they work. The old story is that you are only as good as your last job. Today, most everyone is a freelancer, working on a specific job and then going on to another one. They hear about jobs by word of mouth.

Another source of work is the state film commission. Each state wants to promote making motion pictures in their state. Here in Minnesota, the State Film Commission puts out a "Film Book" which lists all kinds of qualified people who are available to work along with their credits. A qualified person can get in this book by contacting the state government. Because I am listed in the phone book as a producer, the state sends me a copy of this book whenever a new edition is printed.

Most untrained people start out as production assistants. People who are interested in getting started usually know someone in the business. Sometimes it's luck. They happen to call a producer at just the right time when help is needed.

Today it is preferable for someone starting out to get a university education. Many colleges have both a film and a communications department. The communications department usually is concerned with TV. I would suggest that everyone be familiar with both film and the electronic media. So it would be a good idea to take courses in both departments.

You need a background in both film and TV. But there is a big difference between the two. A lot of industrial films are shot on tape, but when you need the best quality, you shoot on film. You get noticeably better results shooting on film and then transferring to tape than shooting on tape.

The gray scale on film is about 10 times that of tape. Obviously there are advantages to shooting on tape since you can take a look at what you have right away. But a good film cameraman knows what he has; he doesn't have to see it right away.

I don't think a person starting out today should assume that all of the future will be electronic. I believe he or she should have experience and training in film. If I were designing a course, I would say take art and take photography. You have to know composition as well as lenses, exposure, emulsions and what cameras are capable of. It's too easy today to give someone a little video camera and say, "go be a producer." But without training and experience, that person isn't going to be able to make something for which anyone would pay very much.

THE MOVIES

By Art Evans

The movies. Hollywood! Oh, the glamour, the excitement, the stars, the money. Maybe most would-be photographers have an idea in the back of their minds that this just might be the job for them.

There is no doubt that cinematography is a career option. There are many ways that motion pictures are used, not only for entertainment, but also as tools. Many of these require specializations beyond that of photography and the cinema.

But let's look at the entertainment industry, "the business" as it's called in the trade. Is a career as a feature film cinematographer a realistic goal for an aspiring photographer? Well, yes and no.

Obviously there are photographers employed shooting feature films and television shows. And just as obviously, as time goes by, these photographers retire or die and are replaced. But the problem for someone trying to break into the business is that there are not a great number of working photographers employed and it is very difficult to get started.

Films made in the United States are made in Hollywood or are made mostly by crews from Hollywood. Why? It costs a lot of money to make a feature film. Hundreds of thousands and often millions are spent. Producers and directors don't want to take chances. A day or even a few lost hours costs big bucks. Therefore only experienced personnel are employed. So if you want to make it in films, you will probably have to live in LA. Yes, some film work is done in New York, Chicago and Miami. But, in comparison, very little.

If you want to get into film work, how should you prepare yourself from an educational standpoint? In the motion picture industry, college degrees mean nothing unless you want to be the staff nurse. This is not to say that you can't learn to make films in school. It just means that your school will not help you get work.

There are two well-known film schools in the Los Angeles area: UCLA and USC. In the main, UCLA is staffed by professors who are career teachers, not film makers. USC, on the other hand, employs mostly working professionals. With some exceptions, such as Francis Ford Coppola, few feature film professionals have come out of UCLA. Quite a number, on the other hand, have come from USC. UCLA (the

University of California at Los Angeles) is a part of the California University system and is a state college. USC (the University of Southern California) is a private institution. It costs quite a bit more to go to USC than UCLA. And neither are especially easy to get into.

If I were counseling a young person who wanted a career as a cinematographer in feature films, would I recommend USC, UCLA or NYU? I suppose I would since if you don't make it in the movies, at least you have a college education and could go on, perhaps better prepared, to something else. Additionally, there are many other opportunities in film making outside the entertainment business. But graduation from one of these will not get you one hour's work on a feature.

Virtually all features are made with union crews. In Hollywood, if you don't belong to the union, you can't get a

Art Evans (second from the right) directs a scene at Paramount with the late actor Godfrey Cambridge (seated). The cameraman takes a incident light reading while assistant Barbara Buce looks on. Mrs. Buce is now the Director of Programming for Paramount domestic television, a high executive position. Photograph by Carlos Chiri, courtesy Paramount Pictures.

job. And if you don't have a job, you can't join the union. Catch 22!

The photographic chores on a motion picture are performed by a number of individuals. One person does not shoot a film by him or herself. On the top of the heap, of course, is the director. The director may or may not know much about photography, but most do. And those who do not invariably work with a director of photography who does.

Here's how most films are shot. The director decides (often in consultation with the director of photography) where to put the camera and how to move it. The director of photography decides how to light the scene. (In motion pictures, even most outdoor scenes are illuminated with artificial lights.) The cameraman operates the camera turning it on and off as ordered by the director. The assistant cameraman pulls focus (refocuses the lens as the camera or subject moves) and performs other such chores. A loader inserts unexposed film and removes exposed film from the magazines. A gaffer and assistants take care of the lights.

Two facts of life make it hard for new blood to move in. First, a great many of those already employed tend to continue to work long after those in other fields are retired. This is particularly true of directors of photography. Secondly, there is a lot of nepotism. Just read the credits on a film! How often do you see the same last names? This is hardly a coincidence. Nepotism sometimes goes deeper than is apparent. People change their names so that everyone on a crew won't have the same last name.

Here's the way film folks get work. Usually a producer selects the director. The director selects a director of photography who then hires his own crew. If a son or daughter wants to get started, guess who gets the job? A director doesn't just look in the phone book to find a director of photography. They are not listed anyway. There is no such thing as an inexperienced director since all directors come to their work from related fields, such as director of photography, editor or actor. So a director will hire a director of photography with whom he has worked before or one he has heard about or met in the course of doing business. Many directors of photography always work with the same cameramen and assistants.

The situation in Hollywood is such that there are always more workers than there is work. After all, the jobs pay a lot and they are glamorous and fun. Being cute and 22 and being able to call out, "It's a wrap," is better than a good orgasm. So the system is designed to keep outsiders out and new blood within the family.

Of course every new hire isn't a relative and occasionally outsiders become insiders. How? There isn't any one path to take or everyone would be taking it. The first thing is to try to get some kind of a job on a crew. Entry-level positions are in the nature of "gofers." A gofer goes for this and goes for that, run and fetch, as it were. How do you get such a job? I don't know for sure and no one else does unless he or she is in a position to hire today (in which case Aunt Hilda's second cousin's kid comes first). In my personal experience, I hired one from UCLA (a mistake), one from USC (not a mistake) and the rest I knew from working with them or from others who worked with them. I suppose the best way is to just try to get any sort of a job where you can meet people and start to build up a network of relationships.

For the most part, my best advice for someone who has the feeling that he or she wants to get into the business is to lie down and wait for the feeling to go away. For those of you who are very talented, very bright, very lucky and very determined, a few will make it. But the odds are in the nature of college football players making it to the pros.

How much can you expect to make if you should be lucky enough to get employment? There are union and non-union pictures. The union most film employees belong to is the IATSE (pronounced eeatsea, the International Alliance of Stage and Theatrical Employees). If it is a union picture, there is a scale, or minimum wage. After August 1, 1991, the daily studio scale for a director of photography was $447.52; for a cameraman (called an operator), $273.95; for a first assistant cameraman, $198.24; for a second assistant, $182.24; for a film loader, $155.60. Pay is about 20 percent more when the work is on a distant location. After 8 hours a day, pay is time and a half; on weekends and holidays, double time. The printed scale is somewhat misleading. For various reasons, most make more; often much more.

The following essay is by my good friend Chic Donchin who I have known for many years through our work in the Hollywood film industry. His story is interesting because it illustrates what a slim chance a photographer has to get on in the business and how important is the element of luck.

MOVIE STILLS

By Chic Donchin

In contrast to all the other members of a union motion picture camera crew, the still photographer is the only one whose work background is not specifically prescribed by the IATSE union. A still photographer may enter the industry from both traditional and unconventional backgrounds.

The only conventional route for a still photographer from the ranks of the camera crew is from the position of motion picture camera operator. Having risen through the ranks of film loader, second assistant and first assistant, a direct change in classification to still photographer is permitted. The hourly rates are equivalent. To my knowledge only two still photographers now active have taken this route. There are 150 still photographers in Local 659 (Hollywood). Every other still person entered this field through other areas, from set lighting gaffer to script person; but most from non-motion picture areas.

In my case, the route was quite circuitous. By 1955, I had finished a stint in Korea as a Combat Photo Officer and thereafter earned a masters degree from Ohio University in fine arts with an emphasis on photography. I found myself in Rome doing freelance photography for U.S. publications. I had subleased a small apartment from another American photographer, Leo Fuchs, who planned to be away in Portugal for a couple of months covering a film called "Lisbon." We kept in touch. It was not long after Leo came back that we both returned to Los Angeles. Leo landed a most unique position with Universal Studios as a nonunion still photographer doing special projects. I opened a small photo studio on Sunset Boulevard next to the Hollywood Palladium. Leo, who was not big on lighting, would occasionally bring in a big star, such as Rock Hudson. I would do the lighting and Leo would take the pictures.

One day Leo approached me with a proposition. Universal wanted him to do some special group shots of David Niven, Shirley Jones and Marlon Brando in connection with their latest film, "Bedtime Story." Because of a special bounce-strobe system that I used in my studio, which was a departure at that time from the usual, Leo asked me if I would come to Universal with my entire setup and light the group shot. My monetary compensation from Leo was minuscule in comparison to what happened next.

Leo's film went to the Universal photo lab where Glenn Adams, then in charge of all still photography on the Universal lot, saw the photos from the "Bedtime Story" shoot. He was familiar with Leo's work and immediately put out the word to find the photographer who did the lighting. When I met with Glenn, he asked me if I would be interested in becoming a member of the union. At that time, Local 659 was taking in about three new still photographers a year. Of course I was overjoyed with the offer and after a few days covering an assortment of TV shows, Glenn put me on a big feature staring Marlon Brando. I was on my way!

Photograph by Chic Donchin.

CAREERS IN PHOTOGRAPHY

Chapter 13

PERFORMING ARTS PHOTOGRAPHY

By Randy Leffingwell

Perhaps more than any other photographic area, if you choose to specialize in the performing arts, you must truly care for your subject. This is because you will accept some percentage of your pay from aesthetic and cultural enrichment. No theater, no opera promoter, no dance company has enough money to support itself adequately. Photography, which they all recognize is essential to promote their performances, can only be a small budget item. The sole exception is popular music, rock and country; however, there are other considerations which balance the scales even in these more lucrative areas.

Performing arts photography offers some of the craft's most daunting challenges. The payoff is an unmatched opportunity to see, through the viewfinder, some of the most spectacular musical performances, some of the greatest dance, some of the most exciting live drama and comedy of modern times. But a love for performing arts is essential. That is because the limitations and restrictions on how and when the photographer can shoot, the expensive and specialized equipment required and the general lack of big clients with big photo budgets can easily match the pleasure obtained from photographing an extraordinary performance or concert.

Performing arts photography is normally done at three times during the life of any performance. One opportunity is at full dress rehearsal (for theater, opera, dance and some orchestra-with-chorale presentations), a second opportunity is during a specially arranged "photo call," and last is during the opening night performance.

During a dress rehearsal, you will see the performance as it will be presented to the paying public. Costumes and sets will be finished (usually!) and the only thing not at full performance level will be performers' voices. Photographers shoot from the audience seats and shoot as if it was an actual performance. The shooters may not be able to work from the center of the house because the various directors are seated there with their headsets and control panels watching the final run-through. You will need tripods and usually medium-long lenses are required in large theaters—such as 135mm and 180mm lenses for full figures; much longer for faces.

One benefit of shooting dress rehearsals is that occasionally the performance is stopped and restarted, giving the photographer a second opportunity to shoot a scene. But the shooter has no influence over the lighting or composition. If two players in a drama are on opposite sides of the stage for the most dramatic scene, that is all that is possible—two small figures with a vast stage between them.

Dress rehearsals exist as a photo opportunity because performers must be paid. Small companies may not be able to afford an additional day's pay for a separate photo call. Larger companies with vast casts and crew may not be willing to bring in all the union personnel needed to light up the stage and move the sets.

To shoot dress rehearsals, in addition to a tripod and long lenses, a spot-reading light meter is very helpful to determine the light on an actor's or performer's face. Many times the light reading changes frequently and drastically during a show and the faces can be much brighter than the surroundings, which can catastrophically confuse behind-the-lens meters. In addition, a small focusing flash-light will help you reload cameras or follow the show in the playbill to identify important cast members.

Another opportunity is the "photo call." This is specifically planned for photographers and allows you to work right on the stage and to have much more control. Stage lights can be turned up to full brightness and actors can be relocated on the stage for tighter composition. Photo calls are always done in full costume with a fully "dressed" set, meaning all the props and scenery are in place just as for an actual performance. But the shooter is really in charge and scenes can be shot with one lens and then re-shot with another to get a different perspective. The actors run through their lines and action, in slow motion if needed, to get into their characters and the photos, especially if done with a wide-angle lens such as a 24mm or even a 20mm, give an intimacy to the scene that puts the viewer INTO the show.

Jan Latham-Koenig directs the Los Angeles Philharmonic Orchestra at the Hollywood Bowl. Photograph by Randy Leffingwell, courtesy the *Los Angeles Times*.

If a photo call is made available, it is better for the photographer to arrive early than late. Again, for the financial reasons outlined earlier, the company manager and director may be more willing to let you try another variation or setup if you have not kept expensive talent waiting your arrival in the first place.

A tripod is normally not needed at a photo call and the light can be read with a normal hand-held meter or the meter in the camera. Be aware, however, that the human eye is easily tricked by theatrical stage lighting and what appears evenly lit across an entire stage may vary by two stops or more, plunging one actor into the dark while another will appear burned up. Careful metering and even relocation of the actors may be necessary.

The last opportunity to shoot is during an actual performance. This is the most difficult. You are never allowed to shoot in the "house," that is, inside the theater, with one notable exception! For theatrical performances—drama, comedy and opera—the shooter must work from the lighting booth at the back of the auditorium. Sometimes this is on the ground, or orchestra, level; other times it is above the highest balcony. Tripods and long lenses are an absolute necessity, as is a spot meter.

Two other serious considerations can affect the quality of the photos. From very high positions, the photographer shoots down on the performance. This is sometimes valuable for dance, but it makes it difficult to clearly show how high the lead dancers really soar. And, for dramatic theatrical presentations, you end up shooting the tops of heads.

But the most serious problem is the quality of the glass through which the photographer must shoot. Most theaters have "optical" glass in place or normal window glass. Optical glass does not bend the light waves and shooters get clear undistorted images. However, this glass is very expensive and it may only be installed in front of their own projectors. These projectors are frequently carbon-arc type machines which are very heavy and critically aligned to a screen hundreds of feet away which cannot be moved. So you must wedge your equipment in any where possible. Some gymnastic positions necessary to see through the camera become excruciating after a two-hour performance. Shooting through standard window glass gives you unsharp images. You will discover this sooner or later. Either the image seems never to come into focus through the lens or, worse, it appears reasonably sharp in the finder (a distinct possibility in darkly-lit performances) and will be definitely unsharp in finished prints or transparencies.

For classical music performances, it is frequently possible to shoot from the stage wings. But it is only possible to do this if the you have a "blimp." This is a sound-proof covering for the camera. Soft blimps are available directly from some camera manufacturers; Nikon, for example, makes their own; and it retails for something like $125. However, this soft, bag-like accessory will not totally silence the camera and will not be acceptable during any but the loudest parts of a classical music concert.

The only fool-proof solution is a hard blimp such as those manufactured by Mark Jacobson, of Jacobson Photographic Instruments in Hollywood. This box fully encloses a motor-driven camera—photographer's choice—and has peep holes to view the film counter and viewfinder. A large hole in front accepts the camera's interchangeable lenses and lens tubes are fitted over them. An electric shutter release fires the camera from outside the box. It can even be operated remotely with a cord.

Jacobson's blimps silence the cameras to such an extent that they are acceptable even on motion picture sets during actual filming—when the sound recording engineer rules all! But Jacobson's silence is golden. A hard blimp for a Nikon F4 or 8008S runs $500 each; and lens tubes range from $125 up to $275 for each lens. A blimp for Canon's EOS is $600. These usually can be rented in major metropolitan areas for around $25 per day, and the major rental houses will ship them anywhere in the country.

Setting a camera to its automatic exposure function can betray the shooter who is hoping to avoid cracking open the blimp. Because principal performers can be brightly spotlit while surroundings are much darker, this will throw off the reading.

The hard blimps are a mixed blessing. They can be cumbersome to operate, especially at first. The photographer must open them to change exposure and film and must nearly dismantle them to change lenses. And lens tubes for long, fast telephotos such as a 300mm f2.8 are custom orders, very expensive and a handful to use. Yet, they may simply be the only way to get the photos.

In Costa Mesa, California, the stunning new Performing Arts Center was constructed without any spare space in the sound, lighting and projection areas for photographers to work. They must stand inside the auditorium to shoot. It is one of the most difficult venues to shoot. The photographers feel uncomfortable and obvious and the paying customers must literally scramble past tripods, camera bags and self-conscious photographers to get to their seats or to the exits. Even worse, concert patrons have been known to complain about the noise of a fully hard-blimped camera. In truth, a shooter with an eye to the viewfinder can barely hear it, but some people are never happy unless they can find fault.

All these considerations change when dealing with rock concerts or jazz or country-western music festivals. Live popular music is loud enough to mask the noise of any camera. Photographers shoot opening night performances, usually from an area immediately in front of the stage. Here, instead of requiring a blimp to silence the camera, ear plugs are recommended to save the photographer's hearing.

Instead of critical exposure-reading with a spot-meter, setting the camera to auto-exposure is frequently a safe bet. As computer-controlled light shows send backlight spotlights swaying madly across the stage and through the audience, the subject is likely one instant to be blindingly backlit and the next to be spectacularly side or rim-lit. Stunning performance photos are possible. Quick reflexes are essential.

Here, instead of critical focusing through blimps and

optical glass, some photographers resort to autofocus for some of the more athletic performers. Short lenses and medium teles are all that are needed; a 300mm would fill the frame with only part of a face! The wild gyrations, the dancing with side players, guitars and microphone stands that are part of so many performances would simply be lost.

Most popular music performers, however, allow photographers in the auditorium to shoot only the first three—or sometimes only two (or one!)—songs the band plays. On balance, these are most often well-lit and are frequently long versions of their most popular works. Two or three songs can amount to between fifteen and twenty minutes of performance time. Shooters working for the pop music magazines can frequently burn twenty rolls of color film in that period.

Some of these photographers use fill-flash during the concerts to balance weird stage performance lighting to obtain a color image which can reproduce on any paper stock. Many performers, distracted by the flash, have begun to demand no flashes. Shooting medium-speed color transparency film is more difficult but the best shooters still get exciting, technically satisfactory images.

Audiences are audiences, however. Whether the performance is Michael Jackson or Michael Tillson Thomas conducting Mahler, or Mikhail Baryshnikov dancing with the Bolshoi, they resent photographers being in front of their $4, $40 or $140 seats. At the opera and the symphony they are well behaved. At rock concerts, though, it is important to remind them that all the photographers must leave after three songs. Reassure them that the best stuff happens after you leave (it always does!). And hope they accept it at that.

If the concert promoters offer you a seat in the house after the performance, it may be tacit approval to shoot more—with a long lens, very discretely. Be careful. It may be only a courtesy and more shooting could result in something less pleasant. Some performers take real exception to "unauthorized" photography.

Some performers go further; they try to control the images photographers produce. At many rock venues around Los Angeles, shooters are required to sign agreements which give the performer first-right-of-approval of the pictures. This means that you agree, in exchange for the right to shoot three songs, to show the performer and their PR people all the images you shot and to accept their veto. Many of these agreements also try to limit the markets to which your photos can be sold. It may constitute restraint-of-fair-trade, but the performers have a captive market. Normally the photographers want to shoot the concert more than they want to sit home that night or to fight a legal battle over rights.

That brings this chapter around to the matter of the real payback for performing arts photography. The income from popular music publications can be lucrative. A creative, energetic photographer with a good eye and a vivid imagination may be hired to shoot an album cover based on the performance pictures they have taken. That may pay as much as $5,000 for a single shot.

In classical music and legitimate theater, life is less lucrative. Dance, theater and opera companies need photography for their posters, program covers, playbills and publicity. But as mentioned at the beginning of this chapter, these same companies are constantly fighting budgets constrained by tight economies and dwindling or canceled federal grants.

There is one form of reward that will not go far towards paying your bills. It is simply the joy and thrill of witnessing some of the finest performances, whether it's Jimmy Hendrix playing guitar with his teeth or Joan Sutherland piercing the opera house air with an electrifying solo. And the benefit to the photographer is almost private. While still photographs can eloquently capture the energy and excitement of a live performance, they cannot capture the sound. That is left for the ears of the paying patrons and the working performing-arts photographers.

The San Francisco Ballet featuring Wendy Van dyck dancing the Queen of the Snow in Tchaikovsky's *The Nutcracker*. Photograph by Randy Leffingwell, courtesy the *Los Angeles Times*.

PERFORMING ARTS PHOTOGRAPHY

CAREERS IN PHOTOGRAPHY

Chapter 14

PHOTO EQUIPMENT

There are many jobs associated with photographic equipment. Each product has to be designed, engineered, manufactured, advertised, marketed and sold. Additionally, many are employed in the rental and repair of equipment.

Photography in all its ramifications is a big business. And the hobby is one of the world's most popular pastimes. This means that the total number of employees and the employment opportunities are very significant.

Of course, everyone employed in every phase of the photographic equipment business doesn't have to be trained in photography or even interested, for that matter. But many are, even those who do non-photographic jobs such as receptionist and bookkeeper.

In the past, the manufacture of photographic equipment was significant in North America. Unfortunately, however, that is no longer true. The vast majority of cameras produced today are made in Japan. Some are made in Korea, a few in Taiwan; some are made in Europe such as Rollei in Germany and Hasselblad in Sweden.

Even though most equipment is not made in North America, there is still significant employment in other aspects: distribution, rental and repair.

DISTRIBUTION

(This essay is based, in part, on an interview with Mr. Carmen Porto, Marketing Representative for the Consumer Products Group of the Olympus Corporation.)

Mr. Porto has had a life-long love of photography. When he was seven years old, he was given an old box Brownie and he has been an avid amateur photographer ever since.

All through school, Carmen took pictures. He shot sports in grade school, took pictures all through high school and served on the yearbook in college. At Youngstown State College, he majored in theater and psychology, but his continuing interest was photography.

Paul Comon of Paul's Photo in Torrance, California stands amid an array of photography equipment.

Porto has worked virtually his entire career—which spans more than 20 years—in the distribution end of photographic products. Before coming to Olympus, he was with Mamiya.

His official title with the Olympus Corporation is Marketing Representative. The job entails selling Olympus merchandise to retail camera stores. He covers the Los Angeles and Orange County area. In some other companies, the title is Sales Representative. Probably 80 percent of all cameras sold are produced by five companies: Canon, Minolta, Nikon, Olympus and Pentax. Each of these companies have large operations in North America.

Olympus has divided the U.S. into four geographic regions. Each region has between six and ten marketing representatives. Some other companies divide the country differently with more or fewer regions.

A marketing career with Olympus involves much more than just selling cameras. It is important for the company to be responsive to their dealers. So one of the jobs of the marketing representatives is to try to forecast what products and in what quantity will be needed. Part of the company's success depends on being able to deliver the products the dealers want when they order them and, at the same time, not having a lot of items on hand which are not sold.

Another part of the sales and marketing job is to train those who sell the equipment to the public. Porto has to make sure that each salesperson in each store knows the features of the various cameras. In other words, he helps them sell Olympus products.

Carmen also helps the camera store dealers with advertising and promotion. He designs ads and is involved in the utilization of the yellow pages, newspapers, radio and TV.

He works with store owners and managers to determine the best product mix and which Olympus products are appropriate for each store. He analyses the kinds of customers each store has. Products that just sit on a dealer's shelf don't benefit the dealer or his customers. The trick is to bring products to each store that will sell as rapidly as possible.

When you consider the number of companies involved in the manufacture and distribution of photographic equipment, there are a large number of marketing and sales representatives. In the Photo Data Research book, *Camera Price Data*, there are 70 companies represented. Of course, not

Carmen Porto of Olympus is caught while visiting one of his camera store accounts.

tion called technical representative. The tech reps support the marketing reps. There are one or two tech reps in each region. Usually, each tech rep will spend a week or so with a marketing rep and then go on to help another one. They train the marketing reps regarding new products and help train store sales personnel. A tech rep may also be involved in specialized professional applications. There are many fewer tech reps than marketing reps. Olympus has only five.

When Porto was a tech rep for Olympus, he had to cover the entire Western Region which includes Washington, Oregon and California. Tech reps are on a straight salary. Most tech reps probably make somewhat less than marketing reps. It was a promotion for Porto to go from tech rep to marketing.

Tech reps are usually recruited from the ranks of professional photographers or from well-trained and educated store personnel. As Porto travels around, he is often asked how store employees can get a job with Olympus. He always recommends that they get a resume together and send it around to the various companies. If you wait until a territory opens up, by the time you get your resume in, the job may already have been filled. He also recommends they up-date the resume from time to time.

Besides marketing reps and tech reps, there are regional managers. As a marketing rep, Porto reports to a regional manager. All of the regional managers Porto knows of, not only with Olympus, but also with other companies, have been marketing or sales reps in the past.

The Olympus main office in the U.S. is in Woodbury, N.Y. The main warehouse and a service center are there also. Additionally, there are service centers at Cypress, California and Rolling Meadows, Illinois. The Olympus world-wide employment is in excess of 7000 people. There are many different jobs at the centers. Some of these are photographic in nature, but not all. Most of the employees are interested in photography even though they may be working in data entry or something of that sort. Many of the people at Olympus come from a photographic background or are interested in photography as a hobby.

every company has a sales crew, but many of them do. While there doesn't appear to be a great deal of turnover among representatives, there are always job opportunities.

In Carmen's opinion, those who pursue this specialty need to be very self-motivated. It's not like being in an office every day. It is up to each rep to get up and go out and make calls. There is no one standing over your shoulder. So they look for someone who is not necessarily over-aggressive, but rather is self-confident. It is preferable for a candidate to have a photographic background, but it is not absolutely necessary. Porto does feel, however, with his photographic background, it makes it much easier to do the job.

Olympus prefers to hire marketing reps with a business or marketing background. A degree in marketing is a plus. In the U.S., there are 37 Olympus marketing reps.

Porto would not divulge any specific salary information about positions in the Olympus Corporation. He has, however, general knowledge about the industry. At Olympus, reps receive a salary plus a commission and funds for expenses. Porto has a company car with a cellular telephone. He believes it would be rare for a sales or marketing representative to take home less than $35,000 a year and he has never heard of anyone making more than $90,000.

Olympus, and most other companies, have another posi-

CAMERA REPAIR

By Harry M. Fleenor

I first became interested in cameras as a hobby when I was seven years old. That's when I received my grandma's Kodak folding camera as a gift. When I was in my early twenties, I developed an interest in camera repair as a result of reading an article about the career in a magazine.

I took some vocational tests and found I had good finger dexterity and mechanical ability. These are two attributes essential to be in camera repair. I took a one-year course in camera repair from the Emily Griffith Opportunity School. After I graduated, I was hired by the Honeywell Corporation

The latest Nikon F4S is shown with a 100 foot back. Photograph courtesy Nikon Inc.

in their repair department. At the time, Honeywell distributed Pentax and Rollei in the U.S. This position was an entry-level one and I received further training on the job. Later, I took a course in electronics in order to keep up with developments in the field.

There are many jobs available in camera repair. In fact, as long as I have been in the field, there have always been more jobs than people to fill them. In order to succeed, you must have good mechanical ability and finger dexterity. These days, you must be trained in electronics as well as camera repair. You must be able to solder excellently, have a steady hand and lots of patience.

It helps if you take a course in repairing a specific camera brand, but this is not absolutely necessary if you are strong in the required abilities and have had vocational school or college training in electronics. The best place to start is in the repair department of a brand-name camera manufacturer. This way, you will receive specific training in that brand and can become a specialist. As new models are introduced, further training is required. If you work for a manufacturer, you will receive the latest information about that brand.

As a trainee, you can expect to find a job which pays about $1000 a month. After you have developed some skill and experience, you will command a higher salary. Generally the pay is based on the number of cameras serviced or repaired and the quality of your work. The highest paid technicians in this field make $30,000 a year. It usually takes a few years to work up to this level.

Manufacturers have repair departments with a number of technicians. Additionally, there are many independent repair companies with employees. Each department or company has a supervisor or head technician. This individual will be paid more than the highest level paid to technicians, somewhere in the range of $30,000 to $50,000.

You can make more by going into business for yourself. Starting a business is risky, but you are less limited. If your business is successful and you are a one-person operation, you will probably take home about the same as you would working for someone else. Of course, you are not limited in the number of hours you can work, so you can easily exceed what you would make in a salaried position.

If you grow to the point where you can hire additional technicians, you can increase your net income. The increase is probably in the nature of 25 percent per person added. But before you start your own shop, I strongly recommend that you take some courses in small business management. You should also read everything you can on starting and running a small business. The success of your shop will depend not only on your repair skills, but also your business management ability.

If you work at a factory service center, you will be trained on new cameras as they are introduced. If you work for yourself or for an independent repair shop, you can keep up to date through factory training programs or through camera training provided by some independent companies. You can count on constant re-training as long as you are in this field.

Today's cameras are electronic high-tech auto everything. Probably there will always be ample opportunities and a shortage of workers. Camera repair people have a particular set of characteristics. They love cameras and many are accomplished photographers. They have a fascination for gadgets and the way things work. They like their work and consider being able to take cameras apart and put them together again a reward in itself. Each camera repaired gives an immediate sense of accomplishment. Everyone I know in the field has a history of taking mechanisms apart just to see how they work.

Harry Fleenor at his work bench in his Oceanside Camera repair shop.

CAREERS IN PHOTOGRAPHY

Chapter 15

PHOTO FINISHING

Photo finishing is a huge business. There are thousands of new jobs available in the field every year. Labs are divided into three categories: custom, wholesale and one-hour. Custom labs charge high prices and perform quality work, mostly for professional photographers. Wholesale labs are generally large plants which take in work from retail outlets such as drug and camera stores. One-hour labs are small operations, although there are large chains involved.

According to data available, there are about 500 custom labs in the U.S., 1600 wholesale labs and 24,000 retail outlets. There are about 2000 one-hour labs among the chains. Since there are many custom labs operated by one or just a few people, the 500 figure is probably too low.

A photo lab is an excellent place for a beginning photographer to get initial experience. Some experts believe it is an ideal place. Since there are so many jobs available, it is easy to get work. Entry-level jobs, however, often pay little more than the minimum wage. Those who are setting out on a career in photography should think of a beginning lab job as an apprenticeship.

ONE-HOUR LABS

By Denine Gentilella

I was ten when I took my first picture. It was of a baby buffalo in the zoo and I used my dad's 110 camera. I remember it as if it were yesterday. I was certain that I had centered the buffalo in the viewfinder. But when the pictures came back from being processed, not only was the buffalo not centered, but also only half of the animal was in the print. I wanted to learn what I did wrong and my interest in photography began.

A year later, I received my first camera for Christmas. I took pictures of such things as my dog dressed up in outfits

One-hour photo labs are found almost everywhere. They offer entry-level jobs for aspiring photographers which provides excellent experience.

like blue jeans and bathing suits. Then, when I was 16, my mother bought me a 35mm Yashica automatic camera. That's when I fell in love with landscape photography, especially sunsets. I took a lot of sunsets.

In my senior year at Commack High School South (on Long Island, New York), I took a course in photography. I borrowed my father's Canon AE-1 and worked with black and white. At first, I was discouraged because I didn't think I could capture beauty without color. Eventually, I found out there is a special kind of beauty you can capture with black and white that you can't get with color. I learned about light and shadows. Silhouettes became an interest and the subject of a class project.

But my biggest interest became sports photography. My first pictures were of my high school's football games. One picture I took was of the offensive line after the quarterback had received the ball from the center and was looking for an open man to receive a pass. I enlarged the quarterback alone to a 5x7. Even though the print was extremely grainy, I was very proud of it. I got hooked on being a sports photographer and went on to an advanced photography class.

When I graduated from high school in 1988, I attended the State University of New York at Farmingdale on Long Island. In my first semester, I took a photography course, but I didn't get a lot out of it. I continued to shoot football though, and got a part-time job in a one-hour lab. I thought that if I wanted to become a photographer, I needed to learn more. If I couldn't learn it in school, maybe I could learn on the job.

To get the job, I just walked in off the street. I was given an application to fill out. Two days later, I was called in for an interview. The manager asked me if I was interested in photography and what my background was in the field. I was hired starting at $5 an hour. During the first year, I was reviewed and given a small raise every three months. During the time I was there, I started as a "counter helper." Then I became a "sorter," and finally a "printer." Eventually I worked up to making enlargements. I was steadily promoted because I had a good attitude and adapted well to different positions.

I worked in that lab for almost two years. In that time, I began to understand color processing. I learned about enlarging, reducing, copy negatives and what custom labs do. I also learned what the machines in one-hour labs can and cannot do.

But most of all, I came to understand coloring. I think color is one of the most important things to understand in any lab. Distinguishing a print with too much green and one with too much magenta and knowing how to correct it is essential to photographic processing.

What is it that is so great about one-hour labs that keeps customers coming back to them? After all, they are much more expensive that taking the film to a drugstore, market or camera store. For many, it is worth extra money to get prints in an hour. But, I think, it is more than that. When you take your pictures to a drugstore, you can't talk with the person who worked on them. Customers at one-hour labs can get professional advise from the employees who actually do the processing. The one-hour lab I worked at on Long Island had equipment to do enlargements. Because of this, and since there were no other one-hour labs nearby, we had a lot of work.

Problems in one-hour labs can cause inconveniences for the customers. In Long Island, most of the counter help were young part-time workers who were not trained well enough to provide a high level of service. And these were the counter workers who were supposed to give advice too. But, someone with an interest in photography has to start somewhere.

Because the Long Island lab didn't have any competition, it got plenty of business. But there was so much work, we couldn't get it done on time or, when we did meet deadlines, the prints were often poor quality. It was hard to do quality work with more and more orders pouring in and not enough time to inspect or redo orders. Looking through prints to make sure they are of good quality is very important. Some one-hour labs make prints, bag them and give them to customers without anyone checking to see what they look like. Even some overnight labs have this problem.

Another problem we had in New York was machines breaking down. If a bulb needed replacing or there were paper jams, the customers had to wait beyond the promised time. This happened at least twice a week because our manager was unfamiliar with the equipment. Since there was no one at the lab who could fix anything, we would have to wait until a repairman could get there.

Due to machine problems, prints would often come out discolored. This was either due to poor color balance or contamination of the chemicals. One drop of a foreign chemical can contaminate an entire tank. And if the tank is developer, it will contaminate all the rest as the film or paper passes through. When there is contamination, all of the tanks have to be drained, cleaned and refilled. This costs a lot of money and time. The owners of one-hour labs don't want to lose money, so sometimes they give the customers bad prints and blame it on their picture taking.

When I was twenty, I moved to California and got a job in another one-hour lab. Some of the problems were the same. But in California, the manager knew almost everything about the machines and we rarely had to call a repairman. There was a lot of competition nearby, so our customers came

Denine Gentilella's first jobs were at one-hour labs where she learned a lot about color negative printing.

to us because they liked the service.

But six months after I started this new job, the lab was sold. The new owners didn't know anything about photography or the laboratory business. They didn't know about chemicals, machines or the products we sold. Then they spent hundreds of thousands on new equipment that they didn't even know how to operate. After another five months, I knew I wasn't going to learn any more at a one-hour lab, so I decided to continue my on-the-job training at a camera shop. When I left the California lab, and after three years experience, I was making $6.75 an hour.

Even though many one-hour labs do not deliver the best quality, I think there is a lot to say for them. But I do believe that if a customer is going to pay high prices—as they do in one-hour labs—they should get good quality.

I am glad for my experiences in one-hour labs. I learned a lot about film, developing, chemicals and color balance. I even learned that with some cameras, such as my dad's 110, when you look through the viewfinder, you don't see exactly what the film does. And then I knew why my buffalo picture didn't come out. I was so close that even though I had it centered in the viewfinder, the image on the film was different.

ONE-HOUR OPPORTUNITIES

The one-hour lab business is divided into three groups: chains, franchises and individual operations. Until recently, there were two large organizations: Fotomat with over 600 stores, Fox Photo with over 300 and One Hour Photo with about the same as Fox. The CPI Corporation, which owned One Hour has purchased Fox making the merged operation the largest in the U.S. with more than 700 locations. The Fox name has been retained for the merged group.

There are a total of more than 24,000 retail photo finishing outlets in the U.S. Almost anyone can get entry-level work in a one-hour. People with little or no experience in photography or photo finishing are trained on the job. Entry-level salaries usually vary between $5 and $6 an hour. There are both full and part-time personnel in these positions. Many employers favor hiring photography students on a part-time basis. Those who work at this level are trained in operating the machines and in serving customers.

After an employee has learned how to operate the processing machinery and has some period of experience in which the skill that goes into making good color prints is acquired, he or she probably will go on to a second level. Or, an employee could be hired into the experienced technician level. Most stores would favor a community college photography graduate or someone with considerable color lab experience. These technicians are paid between $6 and $7 an hour.

A third level is an assistant manager. This person is skilled on all the machines and is good at working with the public. The assistant manager is in charge when the manager or owner is absent. Because of the hours that most one-hours are open, it is almost impossible for the manager or owner to be present all the time. Assistant managers earn from about $7 and hour to as high as $12 and a few at even $15.

The manager or the owner has the overall responsibility for all of the operations and all of the employees in the lab. Managers make in the range from $20,000 to $35,000 a year. Owners, of course, take home the profit.

Some of the larger chains have insurance and retirement plans; few of the individually owned labs do. The employees of a chain may have to wait a period of time before being eligible for benefits. Part-time employees may never be eligible.

A person experienced in the one-hour lab business can go on to higher levels of management in large operations or become an owner of an independent lab. For someone with the training and experience, becoming a lab owner may not be too difficult. The manufacturers of the equipment often will offer very favorable terms and may lend considerable support to a new business. Of course the problem is the considerable competition, not only among other one-hour labs, but also from drug stores and camera stores who offer the same service in about a day.

The one-hour lab business is very large and growing. New products and services are continually being added. Working in a one-hour is a good way to earn some extra money while in school and, at the same time, get some valuable experience. It is not difficult to get a job. Just make the rounds of nearby labs.

WORKING at a COMMERCIAL PHOTO LAB

by Gerry Kopelow

Neither the advent of the one-hour photo processor nor the fancy manipulations offered by custom printers have eclipsed the role of big commercial processing labs within the photo industry. Tens of thousands of ordinary folks (and a surprising number of professionals) do not need instant or super-sophisticated service, so large regional plants that offer high-quality machine processing still thrive. These facilities have some walk-in customers, but the bulk of their trade comes through the mail or via private couriers serving a huge variety of retail outlets. Turn-around time

A commercial lab is a good place for those just starting out to get valuable experience.

The lab supervisor inspects prints to insure quality.

troller, buyer, planning), customer service, general plant maintenance (electrical, plumbing, heating/cooling, structural), chemist and more.

It is not unheard of for employees without much formal education to rise through the ranks to highly paid (middle five-figure) supervisory or management positions. But advancement via this route happens slowly and is dependent on continuous high-performance during years of service at low wages. Quicker progress is guaranteed by studying some combination of commercial photography, photographic technology, photographic chemistry or electronics at a technical college or at a university. Business school or business experience is valuable for those with an interest in management. Labs like to hire skilled people with previous experience in some other related field, as well. For example, those who know the photo-retail trade or have been a photo-manufacturer's representative are favored for customer service or marketing positions. It is interesting to note that marketing and customer service at this level includes dealing with individual as well as corporate customers. The labs take care of some people off the street, but they also handle the photo-finishing needs of big retail outfits like Safeway, Savon, Thrify and Kmart. Following this logic, it is clear that some years of service in various positions at a reputable lab will serve as qualification for employment in other sophisticated industries should such a career shift be desired.

varies from one to ten days. Extensive automation and very high volume keep prices competitively low, although some operations offer pricier custom services as well.

Many photography-related businesses consist of ten people or less, but busy commercial labs are often a lot bigger. Many prospective employees will find a business with fifty, a hundred or two hundred workers appealing because of the variety of occupations and the potential for advancement under one roof. The size of these facilities and the competitive nature of the trade usually translates into a reliance on modern technology and a lot of in-house training. Since large-scale commercial labs consume huge quantities of chemicals, paper and equipment, their employees benefit from up-to-the minute technical support from photo-industry manufacturers. For those who both love photography and are concerned about the impact of photographic procedures on the environment, it is comforting to know that some large labs are very ecology-minded. High volumes make the recycling of silver, chemicals and water an economically attractive proposition.

Occupational possibilities within a commercial lab include film processing technician, printer (both machine operator and custom printer), electronic technician and programmer (repair, maintenance, and modification of sophisticated machinery), shipper/receiver, custodial and security, sales and marketing, management (corporate strategist, hiring and firing), financial management (comp-

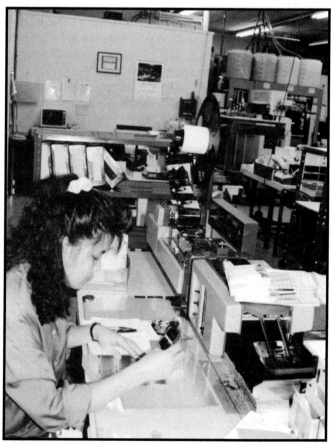

There are many different specialties in a large commercial lab.

CAREERS IN PHOTOGRAPHY

This technician is spotting prints in a large commercial lab.

The attractions of many interesting jobs in photography are somewhat diminished by the mercurial nature of the industry. Photographers fortunes wax and wane with fashion and industrial activity. Retailers suffer from fierce competition from mail-order discounters and puzzling economic cycles. Custom labs depend on the well-being of a few professional shooters or very well-heeled advanced amateurs. The big commercial labs, however, get their business from an incredibly wide cross-section of society. Many of them have been in business for twenty-five or more years. This is comforting to know for those who wish to combine an interest in photography with the security of a long-term career.

Winnipeg Photo Limited, with over 250 employees, is one of the largest processing labs in North America. Established by an amateur photographer in 1934, the operation has grown to the point where its modern 40,000 square-foot plant now services literally hundreds of thousands of individuals through thousands of retailers all across Canada.

Don Berthman started as a printer five years ago and is now Manager of Custom Print Services. Peter Jansen, currently Public Relations Director for Professional Services,

started thirty-six years ago when he was a seventeen year old immigrant tool and die maker from Holland. Peter told me that Winnipeg Photo runs continuous in-house training programs and trade trials of new materials and processes in co-operation with photo industry manufacturers and suppliers. Also, employees are regularly flown, at company expense, to Rochester for technical instruction with Kodak.

Anyone considering a career with a big commercial lab should keep in mind that the ability to work co-operatively with a variety of people is critically important in this industry. Eccentric personalities are welcome in many photographic fields such as advertising or fashion photography. Creative loners thrive on editorial or travel photography. Large scale commercial processors, however, depend on enthusiastic teamwork and cheerful precision.

COMMERCIAL LAB OPPORTUNITIES

Asahi Photo and Video is a large commercial photo lab in Southern California. It is similar to the Canadian lab described in the preceding essay. According to Mr. Kiyoshi Suzuki, there are many career opportunities at this lab as well as others he knows of.

An entry-level job can be obtained without any photographic experience. There is training on-the-job. The starting rate for someone with no experience is $5 an hour. Someone with some experience might start at $6. There are yearly pay raises which are based on the cost-of-living index published by the U.S. government.

The next level is a section supervisor. Supervisors can come from the ranks of lab technicians or from someone who applies with the requisite experience. Beginning supervisors earn between $7 and $8 an hour. Supervisors who have some longevity with the company earn between $20,000 and $24,000 a year. Supervisors not only supervise the lab technicians in their section, but also check the condition of the machinery and are responsible for quality control

The next step above supervisor is assistant manager. Assistant managers made between $25,000 and $28,000 a year. They assist department managers. The highest technical position is department manager. They make in excess of $28,000 a year. Managers are expected to have both industry and photographic knowledge and know the mechanics of the machines in their department.

The company offers health insurance, vacations and sick leave. Personnel are promoted from within as well as hired from outside.

Chapter 16

PHOTOGRAPHY of ART and ARTIFACTS

The photographing of works of art, museum artifacts and museum exhibits is an important activity. Photographers are employed, either on staff or as contractors, by virtually every museum and art gallery. In addition, artists themselves need photographs of their work.

Works of art are photographed for many reasons. Every serious artist has photographs of his or her work. The goal of an artist is to have a "show." This means that the work is displayed in a gallery. When the work is shown in a gallery, sales can be made. The problem for an artist is to arrange for a show. The gallery management decides on whose work will be displayed based, in part, on an examination of a sample of the artist's work. The sample is presented to the gallery in the form of 35mm color slides. Obviously the quality of the slides is of vital importance to artists. Taking pictures of works of art is an activity requiring specialized techniques and equipment.

Valuable works of art also need to be photographed for insurance reasons. Many companies require photographic records of the items insured. These photographs are also important for identification purposes should the work be stolen. So photographs are needed by private collectors, galleries and museums.

Photography is also used to identify and authenticate older works of art and artifacts. As an example, a Leonardo da Vinci masterpiece, "Portrait of a Lady with an Ermine," was sent to the United States for study. The Czartoryski Museum in Cracow asked the U.S. National Gallery to perform certain tests. These included X-radiography and infrared reflectography plus a series of 50X microscopic photographs.

Photographs provide a permanent record of the holdings of museums and galleries. They are used for a number of purposes. They are included in brochures, books and magazine articles about the subjects. They are kept on file in order to authenticate an inventory. They are circulated among scholars for study. And they are often made available for purchase by the public in museum shops.

There are a variety of other organizations that need photographs of art, artifacts and antiquities including auction houses, publishers, government archives, historical societies and universities.

MUSEUM PHOTOGRAPHY

By Robert Schlosser

My initial interest in photography was the result of being in a play so full of dropped lines and missed cues that those of us in the cast all wished we had pictures to remember it by. I realized then that if I had taken pictures of a dress rehearsal, I would have been able to sell them to the players. So I bought myself a second-hand 35mm camera with a couple of lenses and within a few months, I was the "official" photographer for most of the local theater groups. I provided the company with publicity shots and sold prints to the cast.

This resulted in a meager income indeed. But it enabled me to meet people, many of whom asked for portraits, composites, architecturals and other types of photographic work.

One of these amateur actors was an art dealer in need of someone to photograph paintings for his upcoming catalog. Another trip to the local camera store netted me some used lighting equipment and a book on art copying. After two or three of these small catalogs, I began to meet other art dealers as well as collectors.

Through one of my clients, I learned of a job-opening at a major museum. An art copy and sculpture portfolio was assembled with little effort because of all my previous work. The museum liked my portfolio and apprenticed me to a man whose techniques and equipment were old fashioned. But, oddly, his results were always better than mine. I began to pay closer attention and my photographic education really began. Even now, after 20 years in this field, I marvel at his quality.

"The Bacchanal" by Roubiliac is in the collection of the Huntington Library in San Marino, California. This is an example of the type and quality of work required in this specialty. Photograph by Robert Schlosser, courtesy the Huntington Library.

One of the exhibition rooms at the Huntington Library. The photographers at this institution are often required to produce architectural shots like this. Photograph by Robert Schlosser, courtesy the Huntington Library.

Entry-level jobs in the museum photography field usually consist of an apprenticeship to the department head. You will be called an assistant, but what you really are is an apprentice. Your new boss will expect you to do it his way. In spite of what you may think, humor him and do it. In this way, an inexperienced beginner with no habits has an edge over an experienced person with bad habits.

The work at this level will involve carrying equipment, loading holders, adjusting lights, moving objects, taking light meter readings, processing, printing and running to various labs and other suppliers . . . and taking all the blame, of course.

Robert Schlosser (left) works on Dead Sea Scroll negatives with Librarian William Moffett. Photograph by John Sullivan, courtesy the Huntington Library.

There is work in this specialty in an art museum, art gallery, library, auction house, fine art publisher, university collection, state archive, historical society or any place with holdings large or important enough to warrant reproduction for books, catalogs, journals, prints or research.

What is needed is a portfolio specifically designed for these institutions. I have seen one only once in 15 years of hiring in this field. I am usually shown an assortment of images designed to cover a wide variety of photographic fields. I am not impressed. Make some black & white prints and 4x5 chromes of oil paintings, drawings and statuary. Include a few infrared or ultraviolet examples of text retrieval from stained or faded documents. You can create your own originals by experimenting with different types of inks and oils to illustrate these effects. Buy a book or two on the subject.

What do institutions pay after you have gone to the trouble of getting some specific training beyond your general photographic education and designing a custom portfolio? Probably $20,000 to $30,000 a year to start. Invariably, you will start as an assistant. If you are still a student, you should try to get on in a part-time work-study position.

There are a number of mid-level positions. On my staff, for example, there are two microfilmers, two library assistants and one photographic assistant. The microfilmers (micrographic technicians) copy rare books and manuscripts onto microfilm. The library assistants do the billing, ordering and estimates. The assistant should be able to cover for the chief photographer when necessary. Mine can, at least. It may well be that you will have to settle for microfilming or library assistant until a photo assistant job opens up. At least you will be in the department and ready to go.

A top-level position would be the department head or chief photographer. The salary at this level will range between $35,000 and $55,000. The responsibilities include managing personnel, distributing the work load, keeping an equipment and repair budget, supervising jobs and taking care of problems. The Huntington is not only a library, but also an art gallery and botanical garden. So naturally, the work varies from shooting 8x10 color transparencies of "Blue Boy" to making 35mm slides of the night blooming cereus. The orders for these photographs originate not only from the curators on the Huntington staff, but also from publishers and researchers from all over the world. Easily ninety percent of what we shoot is destined for publication.

There are many opportunities to make money outside of the job. People frequently call on me to shoot their personal art work or documents. This often involves travel and much better money. In fact, a friend of mine makes more money doing outside work than on his salaried job!

If you are interested in art, art history or antiquities, this is an interesting and exciting field. My staff and I have been involved in the photographic aspects of the research which is being conducted on the Dead Sea Scrolls. The scrolls themselves must be handled as little as possible in order to preserve them. Part of the work involves photographic reproduction so that scholars everywhere can study the documents. Another function is to photograph them using special techniques which make them more legible.

Gainsborough's "Blue Boy" is one of the famous paintings at the Huntington. This sort of copy work requires accuracy and precision. Photograph by Robert Schlosser, courtesy the Huntington Library.

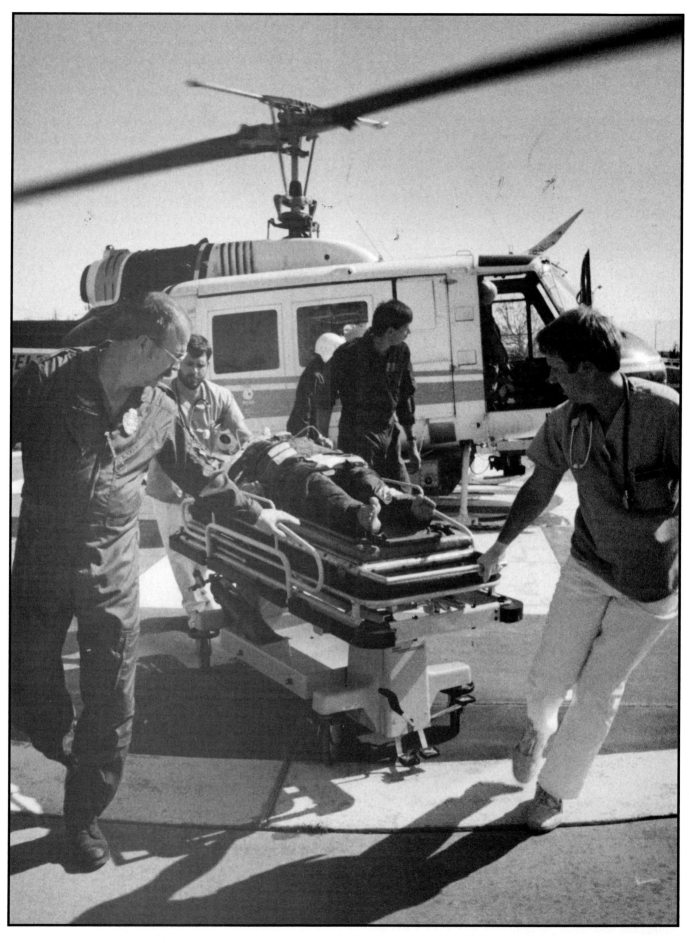

CAREERS IN PHOTOGRAPHY

Chapter 17

PHOTOJOURNALISM

Photojournalism is a very important field in photography. The press plays a vital role in our democratic society. Photojournalists, as the name implies, are a combination of photographers and journalists.

There are a number of specialties within the field of photojournalism. And there are specializations within specialties. You might think that a newspaper photographer is a newspaper photographer. He or she photographs whatever is assigned. This may be true on smaller papers, but on some of the larger dailies, different photographers are often assigned only to certain to kinds of jobs that they specialize in.

All the specialties of photojournalism have one thing in common, however. The photographs end up on the editorial—as opposed to advertising—pages of newspapers and magazines. Some photojournalists work directly for a publication. Others work for an agency which sells news to publications. And some work for themselves.

But regardless of their employer, journalists have a serious obligation. It is to convey the truth to the best of their abilities. At times, this can be a difficult moral problem. Anyone familiar with photographic technology knows that images can be manipulated. This moral obligation is compounded because the public tends to believe pictures more than they do the written word.

The press is specifically mentioned in the United States Constitution. The First Amendment states that, "Congress shall make no law . . . abridging the freedom of speech, or of the press . . ." Thus the press enjoys a unique position in our society. Professional journalists should take their obligations as seriously as they do their rights and freedoms.

One of the photographs on the cover of this book illustrates the probable future of some aspects of photojournalism. Newspaper photography, for the most part, demands immediacy. The picture of the Chinese student standing in front of a tank was taken with an electronic still camera and the image was transmitted over the telephone to CNN headquarters in Atlanta. The normal intermediate steps of developing the film and making a print were eliminated. At the present time, electronic still imaging cannot compete with silver-based photography in terms of either quality or price. But this situation will, in all likelihood, change in the future.

Modern photojournalism demands not only photographic excellence but also physical stamina. This photo was taken while the photographer was running backwards. Photograph by Randy Leffingwell, courtesy the *Los Angeles Times*.

NEWSPAPER PHOTOGRAPHY

By Randy Leffingwell

Newspaper photography may be changing faster than any other career in photography. As recently as 25 years ago, some newspaper photographers still shot assignments with 4x5 Graphic cameras or "compact" Rolleiflex twin-lens reflexes. Flash-on-camera, indoors or out, was standard-operating-procedure. But they also stopped for an "eye-opener" or two on their way in from the first assignment, and could be found back in the local pub for lunch.

Our cameras now are Nikons and Canons with 1/250th second strobe sync, our strobes offer "matrix fill" modes and fire on the "second" curtain, as the shutter closes. We have returned to fill-flash, to open up shadowed faces and make the color engraver's jobs a bit easier. The best work now rarely looks lit and the daily "eye-opener" is a protein powder breakfast at the health club after an early morning workout.

Major metropolitan area newspapers require job applicants to have a college degree. Your major is less important. In most cases too, you will need a minimum of five years experience working for smaller papers. The major metros pay well, $1,000 per week and more. For that money, they do not expect to be training academies. They are looking for journeyman photographers comfortable and competent in any situation.

And that is the key difference between newspaper photography and any other specialization: competency in any situation.

Staff photographers for the *Los Angeles Times* can shoot a court room trial, a black-tie society event, a classical or rock concert, a brush fire, food in the studio, fashion on location, a baseball game, and a celebrity portrait where the subject graciously allows you two minutes to shoot.

Not even the largest newspapers allow the luxury of specialists, photographers proficient in only one or two areas. You should certainly develop special skills, abilities and interests. But often, when an assignment comes along which you think you would be perfect for, you may already be assigned to cover the city council.

The skills you need are varied. You need to know lighting; natural, available and artificial. Also, you need to know manners and social graces. But you also need to know how to use your elbows to fight for a shooting position. You need to know human nature, to understand what your subject may do next or what kind of picture your photo assignment editor is really asking for.

You need to be resourceful, persistent, independent, quick thinking, visually alert, extremely flexible, strong of back and stronger of mind. When a police officer refuses to allow you access at one entry point to a disaster scene, you need to figure another way in. And you need to keep trying. You need to be able to work alone and to trust your own judgment. You need to keep your eyes open as a story unfolds in front of you and be ready to react if it takes a quick, unexpected turn. The equipment is still heavy and newspaper photographers virtually never use assistants or schleppers.

Sound discouraging? What are the rewards? Almost instant gratification. You shoot it in the morning. It is published that afternoon. In Los Angeles, 1.3 million readers daily buy it. It gets passed on from there. Perhaps 5 million people actually see it.

If newspaper photography is changing rapidly, in which direction is it headed? In many ways we may be entering a new golden age of newspaper photography. On one front, new film from Kodak and Fuji and new cameras from Nikon and Canon make getting and reproducing the photos easier. But the photographer's eye, the photographer's sensibilities, are also being used more, published more.

Through the past decade, as daily color arrived at most newspapers, the quality of the image deteriorated. Color was most important and many photographers can tell stories of great images unpublished because they "didn't have color." The novelty has worn off. But also, our visual acuity and sophistication has gotten polished.

Where we used to look for color for color's sake, because we were used to "seeing in black-and-white," now we look in color. We know how to make it work and how to keep it under control when it detracts from the image. Good photographs in color are being published now, not just good color photographs.

And this golden age is about to jump into hyper-space. The heading: electronics and computers. Those who are unwilling to learn are being shuffled off to the side as the field passes them by.

Electronic darkrooms are replacing wet chemistry. Many feel some sense of impending loss, but others will shed no tears. The prospect of no longer working in a dark, aromatic room, hands wet and chapped from brutally strong hypo, is not so terrible. And the capabilities and speed the electronics bring is liberating.

At the present state of the art, electronic still cameras are heavy and cumbersome. Image quality is not nearly so high as even old Tri-X, let alone a modern film like Kodak's Ektar or Fuji's Velvia. But remember what has happened to home computers, portable cellular telephones and home video cameras. In size and price, the drop has been startling.

And the ability to put 25 to 50 images on a 3 1/4 inch floppy disc and "download" it to the office into the photo department's computer by public telephone is only the beginning. Editors and photographers edit their film on video monitors. Cropping and scaling are done in the computer, with captions attached. It is sent by the computer to engraving where it is laser scanned. High quality presses reproduce the image on newsprint less than one hour after it is shot.

And that shoot could have taken place 700 miles from the office. Or seven thousand miles.

As newspaper photography goes high-tech, it is most satisfying to hear editors—word-people, mind you—talking ever more about good images. At the *Los Angeles Times* and at other papers around the country, editors born and raised in the era of television are attuned to the visual representation of life. They understand what we have known forever: good photographs are worth a thousand words.

If your goal is a career in newspaper photography, you can follow two avenues. Both take you through college. But once in, you can chose.

If you major in journalism, you will learn not only the craft of photography but you will also learn the myriad skills of the reporter and editor. These are important. Accuracy of your information in the photograph and the caption is essential and it is your responsibility. (Corrections embarrass a newspaper and at the *Los Angeles Times*, can cost you a day's pay.) In that course of study you will learn the history of our profession and you will also learn journalistic ethics. Do you take a picture or do you "make" a picture? In practice you must do both, but you will learn why and how . . . and when.

Western Kentucky University still has the one of the best photojournalism sequences in the U.S. Others are available at San Francisco State, the University of Ohio and California State University at Long Beach. The best monitor of education quality it to pay attention to which school's students win the Hearst Contest Sweepstakes.

The benefit of these schools is that you get hands-on experience practicing and refining your skills while in school. Further, these schools maintain ties with local and regional newspapers and can steer you to summer jobs (called internships) and full-time positions after graduation.

The other route you can follow once in college is to major in any area of interest to you: English, history, psychology, art history or whatever. You can sign up for photography courses on the approval of the professor. However, this can lead to delays of a semester or more to get in.

The liberal arts education perhaps rounds you out more than straight journalism. It exposes you to the world outside journalism as a participant rather than as an observer, which you are in journalism. Of the college graduates on staff at the *Los Angeles Times*, the census is about mixed between journalism and non-journalism school graduates.

Of course, you can do the same at any of the journalism schools. All require course study leading to a minor degree outside their schools.

What to consider as your major or minor? As a newspaper photographer, you are primarily going to be photographing people. Any course of study that helps you understand people better would not be a bad idea: anthropology, psychology, sociology. Of course, you are also setting out to be a visual communicator. So studying design or art history won't be far off the mark either.

Your first job, with luck, will be a summer job at a newspaper. An internship is really a summer vacation replacement. Few newspapers are set up to offer a real training program. If you are lucky, you will land somewhere which will enable you to go out with staff photographers for several days or weeks and observe and shoot along with them.

By all means observe. You may be "College Photographer of the Year," but the working techniques of a staffer who is expected to produce a picture on deadline that will tell the story AND reproduce on that paper's presses will be well worth paying attention to. Yes, of course, shoot along side. Or around the other side if you see a better picture. But if you are smart, you'll remember you are there to learn, not show off.

Learn as much as you can. Because at some point during that summer, you will be treated as a staffer. You will get the same kind of assignments and—if you've proven the ability—you get some of the best assignments. If you're a

hot talent and have a good eye, a smart photo assignment editor will give you room to do good work. Summer internships are usually paid at a salary level somewhat lower than starting salaries on those newspapers. You'll be able to live—you won't have to sleep in your car—but mostly you're there to work.

It is important to realize that the competition is fierce for internships; fiercer for full-time jobs. In 1989, the *Los Angeles Times* had two summer photo interns. We had nearly 500 applications.

To get any job, you'll need to show a portfolio. Quality is essential: image and print. An intern the *Times* hired several years ago sent us good images poorly printed. We reckoned we could teach the photographer how to print. But the muddy gray prints were emblematic of several other deeper flaws in working skills and even in thinking. It was not a successful internship, for the photographer or for us.

When you select images to show a perspective employer, try to pattern your assortment after what you see published in that paper. This means in most cases a general mix of subjects. The photographers who select summer interns recognize that spectacular spot news is not always available on your campus. But include something, because it shows us your ability to think under stress and react quickly in a different way from sports action.

We are mostly interested in seeing good, telling images. Good composition is essential because it grabs our eyes. Edit your work tightly and ruthlessly. Never send more than 40 transparencies (or prints if you can afford them). We tend to remember the one or two applicants who sent us several hundred images. And we don't remember them too kindly.

We treat portfolios as if they were our own work. We are careful with them. You will get your portfolio back, usually quickly unless we need to show it to more editors . . . and we

Photojournalism is almost as old as photography itself. This Civil War shot shows how slow lenses and film were in the mid-nineteenth century. Movement could not be captured because exposures were so long. Photograph courtesy the Library of Congress.

want to interview you.

The last full-time job was not advertised in any of the trade papers, *Editor & Publisher* or *NewsPhotographer*, and we still had dozens of applications, alerted by word of mouth. Newspapers virtually never go recruiting. They simply don't need to. There is much more talent available out there than positions.

Opportunities for advancement? Frankly, limited. As you become a better photographer, you can move up to better newspapers for a better salary. Some papers have "Senior Photographer" positions. These usually involve shooting better assignments and long-term project work. Some newspapers with their own Sunday magazine assign or rotate staffers through a position there. Magazine photography is a vastly different discipline from newspaper photojournalism.

But frequently magazine art directors are reluctant to trust newspaper photographers' skills and abilities on big stories. The art directors have a certain "style" in mind for the visual look of the story, and most of them think of newspaper shooters as fires, wrecks and handshakes.

Ironically, it is the versatility which is required of us that undermines us in circumstances like these. The average *LA Times* staffer's day may be modified slightly. One editor will want a courtroom trial shot "like Weegee;" another will want the fashion shot "like Helmut Newton," yet another will ask for a celebrity portrait shot "like George Hurell" or Greg Gorman. You must be able to ape all of those.

What results is that you never have an opportunity to develop your own style. You are too busy perfecting everybody else's. If the art director said, shoot this "like Bruce Davidson, or Guy Bourdin or Gregory Heisler," you could easily do it. Asked how you would do it yourself, you might draw a blank. But, because of your generalist skills, you might also bring many more ideas to the shoot that the art director had at first.

Beyond the magazine and senior photographer position sits management: photo assignment editor, photo editor, chief photographer, director of photography. Depending on the paper, these jobs are often combinations of nurse-maid, cheer leader, bureaucrat, diplomat, scold, big brother and occupier-of-the-desk-at-which-the-buck-stops.

For a newspaper receptive to photography, the Director of Photography can enjoy a challenging, exhausting career. Working with various editors (the *Los Angeles Times* has more than a dozen section editors who all need photography) to bring better images to their sections, can make you prematurely gray.

It can also make you an absolute hero in the eyes of your staff. As you work for better assignments, better display, travel, your staff benefits. Morale improves. You caused it. Fewer bucks stop at your desk.

Photo directors are generally well paid, as they should be for the grief and hard work they endure. Major metros will pay bosses much more than slaves to keep the slaves in line and content.

The future of newspaper photography? Ultimately it is uncertain. The economy since the late 1980s has left all business on shaky ground. If businesses can't afford to advertise, then newspapers can't afford to stay in business. Few newspapers in the country are thinking of expanding their staffs. Many are letting attrition, retirements and resignations of staffers trim their budgets for them. But some have had to take more drastic steps. Like closing. The *Los Angeles Herald-Examiner* left a dozen photographers out on the streets. Some have still not found full-time jobs.

As an official in the *Los Angeles Times* parent company, Times-Mirror recently put it, speaking about the entire newspaper, "Electronics and computers are the future. If you're uncomfortable with that, your future is limited . . . "

So if you want your future unlimited, you have another list of courses to add to your already full curriculum.

PUBLIC RELATIONS

True or false: All the pictures you see and articles you read in newspapers and magazines are shot and written by staff photographers and writers. Answer: false.

To one extent or another, virtually all publications as well as radio and TV rely on what is called a "handout;" the ubiquitous press release. These handouts are produced by or for organizations in order to further their own aims. Think of it as disguised advertising. Research shows that when these releases or handouts are used, the effect is at least as good and often superior to paid advertising. Consequently, many organizations spend significant amounts of money on press and media relationships. This process usually comes under the heading of "public relations."

Some larger organizations have departments with employees to perform public relations functions. Others hire an independent public relations agency on a fee basis. But however the functions are accomplished, there are many career opportunities in public relations for both still and motion picture or video photographers and for those with related or associated skills.

Some in-house public relations departments employ staff photographers. Others hire independent photographers for a fee on a need basis. The same is true of PR agencies. Some will hire out; others have photographers and other technicians on staff. Some organizations with personnel on staff still look towards outside organizations for particularly difficult or specialized assignments. For example an organization with a staff photographer may hire an outside motion picture production company to produce a PR film.

A lot of photography for PR purposes is basically photojournalism with a twist. The photographs are slanted to favor a specific purpose. The purpose is defined by the employing organization.

So a good PR photographer must first be a photojournalist. Most news media will not accept handout photos unless they at least meet minimum professional standards. In other words, the photographs must be at least as good as those produced by staff photographers.

But if a photographer is a skilled photojournalist, why would he or she want to work making PR photographs? The answer is money and opportunity. Often PR photographers make more than staff photojournalists with equal skills. Actually, PR photography sometimes takes more skill than just recording news. PR photographers must be able to not only shoot news, but also slant it. Or as they say in PR circles, "Put a spin on it."

The most innocuous PR photo is a shot of Joe Blow who has just been selected as the president of the XYZ Corporation. If the company is important enough or an advertiser, the local paper may send a staffer who will shoot a quick head shot or two-some handshaker with the chairman of the board or the retiring ex-president.

But a PR photographer had better do more. A photograph of the new president supplied by the PR staff should emphasize characteristics the company wants to get across to the general public, i.e. honesty for the bank president, reliability for the car company, intelligence for the computer company.

Where are the employment possibilities in PR photography? 1) Companies and other organizations with a PR staff and/or a photography staff. 2) Public relations and advertising agencies with photographic staffs. 3) Photography companies who provide services to organizations and agencies. 4) Individual photographers in business for themselves (freelance) who provide PR services.

If someone is interested in entering the field of PR photography, how should he or she train? The route to a career in PR photography is similar to one for photojournalism. A high school student should take photography courses and work on the school newspaper and yearbook. He or she should also try to take newsworthy photographs on campus and provide these to local news media.

While not a requirement, a college degree is important to a successful career in PR. Those who are most successful can write too. A major in journalism and/or photojournalism is a plus. And again, participation in school media should definitely be included in a college career.

College (and sometimes high school) students can often make arrangements to work as an intern in a business or other organization outside the school. Sometimes these internships are arranged by the school; occasionally students make their own individual arrangements. Additional academic credit is usually earned by interns (also called work-study programs). Internships are very important for future PR photographers and should be a part of an individual curriculum if at all possible. Some interns are paid, usually the minimum wage, and some work for free.

If your school or college cannot or will not arrange a suitable internship or work-study assignment, you should try to secure one yourself. If you cannot succeed in selling yourself for free labor or minimum wage, you probably will not succeed in PR.

How can a student make arrangements for an internship? First, make a resume and portfolio. Second, pick out a number of target organizations. Your goal should be to secure an internship with an in-house organization rather than trying to freelance. In this way, you will not only learn by doing, but also learn from others.

Your targets should be organizations with PR departments and a photo staff. You may not have to look farther than your own school. Almost all colleges and universities have a PR function or employ an agency. And while few high schools do, the school district usually does.

Then look to nearby organizations such as medium to large companies, government departments and PR and advertising agencies. After you have made a list of targets, start calling and asking for the PR department or director. If there is none, cross the target off your list. When you connect, explain your business in as few words as possible and make appointments. Dress well, be neat, clean, polite and show up on time. Present a copy of your resume and show your portfolio. You may be turned down a few times, but don't give up. You will be successful if you call on enough organizations. (Obviously there are more PR opportunities in New York or Los Angeles than in Deluth or Bangor.)

When you graduate and apply for your first real position, on-the-job experience and a good recommendation from your work-study supervisor will carry a lot more weight than any other course you may have taken.

Jobs and wages in PR photography vary depending on the specific job and the part of the country you are working in. Entry-level staff positions are often in the lab. Hourly wages for lab workers range from $10 to $50 an hour. Those who go out and take pictures make more. In smaller departments, photographers often do their own lab work. Sometimes the lab work is farmed out to a custom or commercial lab. At the high end, some talents make hundreds of dollars a day. Some well-known photographers take PR assignments and make many thousands. Ansel Adams, for instance, shot for the University of California and the Yosemite Park and Curry Company among others.

Many of those in PR work come to it from journalism. PR photography can be satisfying as well as lucrative. There is a real thrill in creating a photograph and then seeing it used in a publication. When you work directly for a newspaper or magazine, you expect your work to be printed. After all, that's what they are paying you for. But in PR, it's a contest to see if you can do such a superior job that the media will print your work. At the same time, of course, your photographs must promote the goals of your employers. Those whose work is consistently used in the media will always be in great demand.

There are PR employment opportunities, not only for still photographers, but also in video and motion pictures. PR organizations often produce news clips for distribution to TV stations. Some even produce full-length shows. And others produce motion pictures and slide presentations to further the interests of their employers.

A photographer who can do lab work, shoot stills, videos and movies will surely have a competitive edge over others limited to a single skill. And those who can do some writing too are miles ahead.

Chapter 18

PORTRAITURE

Portraiture is almost as old as man himself. Some of the earliest evidence of our ancestors is in the form of drawings on the walls of caves. The most common pictures are those of our forefathers. Portraits are among the world's greatest works of art.

The development of photography provides us a more accurate image than does painting, drawing or sculpture. We have a much better idea of what Lincoln looked like than we do Washington. Most of the first photographs were portraits. It is rare today to unearth a daguerreotype of another subject.

From a historic and sociological standpoint, photographic portraiture is among the most important types of images we record. From the beginning of photography, portraiture was a profession. But today, it comes in all types and forms.

A large company which sells mailing lists has the names and addresses of more than 26,000 portrait photographers in the U.S. There are probably more. Some of these are large corporations employing thousands while others are one-person operations. Portrait photography is everywhere. In a large shopping mall, one is likely to find a portrait studio operated by an individual, chain studios in the department stores, passport photography in a one-hour and a machine in a booth where, for two dollars fed into a slot, a portrait can be taken by the subject.

DEPARTMENT STORE PORTRAITURE

Some of the largest operations are found in department stores such as Sears. The stores usually contract with a separate company and merely lease the space. The arrangement may involve cooperative advertising and possibly a percentage of the gross or net.

Almost every Sears store, for example, has a portrait studio. And there are more than 1200 Sears stores! Smaller stores may have only a few photographers while larger ones may have twelve or fifteen. Each studio has a manager and larger ones have assistant managers.

All shooting is done with long-roll cameras in a fixed position. Each setup has a variety of backgrounds, but the strobe lights are in fixed positions as is the posing location. All the photographer has to do is raise or lower the camera on its track and shoot. Of course, the important thing is expressions.

Department store studios are open long hours. They are often open until 9 or 9:30 every night and during the Christmas holiday season until 11PM. Many of the employees are part-time and the manager has to arrange a schedule so that there will always be sufficient personnel present.

New employees are located through ads in newspapers or from those who come in looking for a job. Often, photographers will also be required to work at selling portraiture too. New hires are trained on the job. Because of very rigid controls and highly automated equipment, it is possible for someone with very little photographic experience to learn rapidly. Probably personality is as important as technical expertise.

An entry-level job as a trainee pays at the minimum wage or possibly whatever starting salary other starting workers in the store receive. If a prospective employee applies with some training or experience, the starting pay could very well be more than the minimum. One large organization gives raises every six months, depending on performance. The raise is between one and ten percent.

Most department store studios are happy to employ students on a work-study or internship basis. These students—who are always part-time—are usually paid the minimum

This portrait of President Abraham Lincoln was taken by the famous Civil War photographer, Matthew Brady. The advent of the photographic portrait allows us to have a much better idea of how someone looked than does painting, drawing or sculpture. Photograph by Matthew Brady, courtesy the Library of Congress.

wage and the studio manager will cooperate with the college or trade school with regard to assigning a grade.

The majority of clients in department store studios are families with children and the pictures are often of the children alone. The work is demanding and somewhat high-pressure. There are probably more women than men working in this situation.

For the most part, promotions come from within. If a studio is large enough, there will be an assistant manager who probably makes in the $7 to $12 an hour range. Managers make from $7 to as much as possibly $20 an hour.

Department store photography is a high-volume business. A larger store may have around 200 sittings a week and this may increase during special times such as Christmas or Valentines Day to 400. All of the processing is sent out to labs which specialize in this sort of work. Orders are returned in "packages" which may consist of an 11x14, two 8x10's, two 5x7's and a number of wallets-size prints. The packages are printed before the client returns so that the customer can walk out with prints. Every pose is printed. Those not purchased are tossed. It is less expensive to throw away prints than it is to take orders from proofs and have the client come back a third time.

Department store portraiture is an excellent training ground for anyone interested in photography. Jobs are plentiful and not difficult to get. This is a very good stop to be recorded on your resume because it indicates an ability to work under pressure as well as being able to get along with all sorts of people.

SCHOOL PHOTOGRAPHY

School photography is a HUGE business. That's the good news for photographers. The bad news is that photographers employed by school photography companies don't make a lot of money.

Virtually every student, kindergarten through college, is photographed every year. Schools need portraits for a number of reasons. Some schools use as many as five. A small photo is needed for student ID cards, for the student files, for the Rollodex in the office, for the counseling office and for the yearbook.

Additionally, students are photographed as members of student activities, clubs and teams. Dances and other social events are covered too. Some of these photos are purchased by the schools while others are bought by the students or their families.

Few schools employ individual photographers. Companies organized specifically to shoot schools bid for school contracts. These companies are the employers. And, for the most part, the processing and printing is sent to labs that specialize in schools. The business is highly organized and rather rigid.

There are thousands of school photography companies large and small. And there are many labs as well as equip-

Karen Carter has been shooting department store portraits for over six years. Now she is a studio manager. Note the automated long-roll camera.

ment and supply firms involved. The industry, taken as a whole, employs large numbers.

Some school companies specialize within the specialty. There are those who shoot only sports teams, or dances, or senior portraits. Others offer a complete service including the faculty. Except for some very small schools, individual portraits are shot with specialized long-roll cameras, either 35mm or 70mm. The nightmare in school photography is to lose a shoot due to a technical glitch, either an equipment or operator malfunction. Sometimes a situation can be saved, sometimes not. Portraits can be re-shot, but dances cannot be rescheduled or games replayed.

From a photographic standpoint, everything is rigid. Cameras are tripod or stand-mounted and fixed in place. The lens is pre-focused and locked in place with a set screw. The posing spot and the lights are located by exact measurement. Technical expertise comes in the set-up and making double sure everything works. The creativity is in getting expressions.

School photographers are often young people just starting out in their careers. Others may be wedding photographers who shoot weddings only on weekends working at schools which are open only during the week. While rates vary from place to place, generally speaking, photographers make between $6 and $12 an hour. Those who shoot at dances often make more since the events are in the evenings. Time and one-half or a flat rate between $50 and $100 is usual.

Some of the work is sporadic; some is part-time. Individual portrait shooting usually starts in late August—or whenever the fall term begins—and ends by October. All of the yearbook work is usually done by February or March so there is time to print the books.

In spite of the modest pay, working for a school company has a lot of advantages. For someone just starting out, it is excellent experience. There is just a short time to take each individual portrait or couple at a dance. If the expressions are not just right, sales will suffer. And school children are not necessarily the easiest to handle.

Jobs are not difficult to get. To locate companies, just call school administrative offices and ask for the name and telephone number of the company with the contract. Shoots are often performed by crews of three: a photographer, an assistant and a clerk or cashier to keep track of the money and orders.

Unfortunately, because the working hours will probably conflict with classes, school portraiture is not very convenient for students. But shoots such as dances and other events can be done by photography students. For the most part, school photography companies prefer to hire those with some photographic experience.

INDEPENDENT PORTRAIT STUDIOS

There are many types of portrait studios. Many are one-person or mom and pop operations. This kind of studio will often have very few or no employees in addition to the owner. And if a studio has one employee, that person is often a receptionist. Many studios send out all their processing work to commercial or custom labs while others do everything in-house. If a small studio has an additional photographic employee, he or she usually works the lab.

Other studios are a little larger and may have more than one location and a number of employees. Because of the large variety of portrait studios, it is difficult to make generalizations. Beginning salaries depend on training and experience, but a full-time starting wage will probably be in the $19,000 to $20,000 range. Starting work consists of such chores as cutting negatives, putting together orders, sending out for prints, working in the lab, generally assisting and cleaning up.

Many independent studios will cooperate with colleges or trade schools and accept interns on work-study programs. Individual students can often approach studio owners or managers and make their own arrangements. Those in this category will probably be paid the minimum wage.

This portrait by Jim Britt reveals a great deal of the style and flare which have made the photographer famous. Photograph by Jim Britt.

After an employee has some experience and starts shooting, he or she can probably expect to make between $20,000 to $25,000 a year. There will probably still be such additional work as cutting negatives and so forth. A top level-employee in an independent studio can probably expect to make from $35,000 to $50,000 a year. This person may also be an assistant manager or a manager and be expected to take care of all aspects of running the studio. Some of the pay may be in the form of commissions, so how much is made will depend on sales and managerial abilities as well as photographic ones.

Some portrait studios do weddings as well. Since weddings are always held on weekends and studios are usually open during normal business hours, this makes for a full week. Also, some studios send photographers out to do portraits on location.

There are few photographers who will not benefit from at least a period of shooting portraits. At the very least, it is an option someone just starting out should consider.

Chapter 19

THE RETAIL TRADE

There are many thousands of retail establishments dealing with photographic equipment and supplies. There are millions of customers whose needs have to be served. Large numbers of people make their livings through photography. And photography is, in terms of money spent, the most popular hobby in the world.

Many thousands of workers are employed in the photographic retail trade. They work behind counters or on the telephone, advising, explaining and selling. Unlike other photographic jobs, retail sales personnel are sometimes hired without training or experience. So this is an area of photography where it may be relatively easy for a beginner to get a job and start earning money right away. Working behind a retail camera counter is also good experience, regardless of one's ultimate career goal.

There are a number of different types of retail establishments which deal with photographic products. 1) Camera stores. 2) Department stores, drug stores and discount outlets. 3) Mail-order dealers. 4) Show dealers.

Some of these are combinations. There are those who have a mail-order business and also a camera store. There are those who have a camera store and deal at shows. Sometimes a camera department within a larger operation such as a department store or discount house is larger than a stand-alone camera store down the street.

Except for the very smallest camera store whose sole worker is its owner plus possibly the spouse, a photographic retail operation is an employer. For the most part, camera store sales people are not highly paid. So there may be considerable turn-over and consequently there are continual job opportunities. On the other hand, some employees in the retail trade are well paid and in these cases, there may be very little turn-over.

A retail establishment can provide an excellent part-time job for someone going to school to become a photographic professional. It will probably pay more than working in fast-food restaurants. And it will surely provide a better learning experience. An added plus for some students is extra credit for working in a field related to the major course of study.

Paul's Photo in Torrance, California.

Retail offers a number of opportunities for individuals to go into business for themselves. Many are part-time and may involve very little capital. These include being a show dealer or mail order dealer. These careers are discussed in the second volume of this series, *Photo Business Careers*.

WORKING IN A CAMERA STORE

By Anne Sharp

Many photographers have started their careers working in a camera store. Whether as a student or aspiring professional working up through the ranks, retail work has provided them with income, knowledge of equipment and helpful discounts.

There are many retail camera stores scattered throughout cities and communities. So if you want to work, you can probably find a job fairly close to your home or school. Of course in smaller communities there may be fewer opportunities, especially in university towns where there are invariably more applicants for such jobs.

The usual starting salary for a retail camera store employee is around $5 an hour (this could vary depending on the area of the country and local economy). In any case, it is close to the minimum wage.

As an entry level employee, you are not expected to know a lot, but rather to learn a great deal fairly quickly. An employer looking to hire someone at the entry level will seek a person who has some photographic knowledge and a definite interest in the medium.

Retail camera store work entails not only selling new camera equipment but also used systems, dealing with photofinishing, repairs and film sales. An entry-level employee will be expected to work mainly in the latter areas. There are many details to learn, particularly if the store deals with several photofinishing companies. Film sales also require much attention and knowledge, because clients will

Herb Agid's Riviera Camera, where Anne Sharp worked, is an example of a small retail operation.

often ask for suggestions on which film to use in differing situations.

Inexperienced employees are usually not assigned to camera sales because it requires a good deal of knowledge of camera systems and photography in general. Clients feel more secure when an experienced salesperson is helping them and may even get annoyed with an employee who can't explain why one lens is better than another. Rather than risk losing a sale, a camera store owner will entrust experienced salespeople with the camera sales.

It may take awhile before an entry-level employee is allowed to make some camera sales, but there is often more opportunity to make some extra income. So it is desirable to move ahead into this area as rapidly as possible. Employers often offer perks for camera sales. This can be in the form of a small percentage of the sale or passing on to the employee the sales spiff offered by the camera manufacturer. A sales spiff is an amount of money, usually $3, $5 or $10 and sometimes $20, which is given by a camera manufacturer to a retail salesperson for selling a camera. It is logical that the higher the value of the camera sold, the greater the spiff.

Jobs in entry-level retail are not that hard to get. There is usually a big turn over because students customarily fill these positions and eventually move ahead to bigger and better things. Mid-level positions may not be as available since this group is paid more and is a little more stable. Whereas entry level jobs can start at minimum wage and go to maybe $6 an hour, a mid-level position can start at $6.50 an hour at the low-end up to $8.50 at the high-end plus commissions for sales.

At this level you would not only be expected to handle photofinishing and film sales, but you would probably be selling cameras and lenses too. Your duties may include taking inventory, pricing and stocking. There are many items to keep track of in this business and many details with which you need to become familiar. The mid-level employee should know about films and photofinishing and should be self-reliant in deciding what needs to be done, taking the initiative to go about these tasks.

The top-level position in a retail camera store, if not the owner, is the manager. This person is in charge of all aspects of running the business and is controlled only by the owner. The manager does most of the purchasing, sets the prices, hires and fires personnel and, depending on the involvement of the owner, will handle most of the camera sales. Some owners are very involved with running the business and others rely on a competent manager. The low-end managerial position pays about $9 an hour and the high-end is around $13 plus commissions. These positions are not as easy to get because they pay more and require more stable personnel.

When you apply for a job in retail sales, ask a lot of questions such as starting salary, spiffs, possibilities of profit sharing, health care and employee discounts. The latter can be very helpful for students and people starting a career in photography, since employee discounts range from 25 percent to buying at cost. You may have to look for your own health insurance, since sometimes only large corporations can afford to offer these benefits.

Large retail corporations are able to offer their employees more in many aspects. As an example, one large retail chain I researched offers a starting salary of $6 to $7 an hour plus spiffs and a five percent incentive when they sell proprietary company products. There is also a two percent sales commission.

In addition, the company provides full benefits including medical, dental, optical, life insurance, sick leave and retirement.

Entry-level employees in this corporation are not expected to know about camera retail when they start, but are trained on the job by the company. They look for energetic, polite, dynamic personalities. A good knowledgeable employee can advance quickly to a middle-management position with a salary range of between $24,000 and $26,000. These are store managers and floating managers. Higher level employees are district managers and earn between $30,000 and $40,000. The next level is regional manager with a salary of $50,000 to $60,000. For the most part, higher-level personnel are promoted from within.

Some successful individually-owned retail stores are able to provide some kind of health care coverage and still stay in business. For example, one local store owner offers his employees an HMO besides paying them between $5 and $12 an hour (depending on experience) and offering a shared commission on serial numbered items which is divided at the end of the month.

There is not much of a future in retail work beyond the salary unless you decide to go into business for yourself or you work to the top of a large retail chain. An interesting fact to note is that manufacturers often hire their product representatives from retail stores. This is because they have trained the retail personnel in the use of their equipment and get to know the good employees over time.

One thing to remember when considering a career in retail is that anyone involved in a retail business should enjoy dealing with people on a day-to-day basis. Sometimes it takes a lot of patience, but you still need to present a smiling, courteous and helpful attitude to your clients or the business will suffer.

The retail camera store business is in continual flux since it has to keep up with changes in the industry. New developments occur every year. Competition among the major manufacturers has become even more pronounced during the last few years. One-hour labs have taken a lot of work away from retail camera stores along with much of the profitability. The response of some stores has been to buy processing machines and go into the one-hour business themselves (if you can't beat'em then join'em). But now retail camera stores are faced with the fusion of still photography and video which further complicates an already complicated business. It's hard to stay in business, especially since, to remain competitive, the mark-up on camera equipment has to be rather low.

Successful retail stores are those that offer a knowledgeable staff and are well stocked, not only with a quantity of products but also variety. As I see it, the future success of retail camera stores will depend on the competency and technical knowledge of the staff.

To start out in this career, I would advise finding out as much as you can about new trends in the camera business as well as acquiring a knowledge of older camera systems. Read any information you can on films and cameras. There are many photography magazines that have articles every month on these subjects. Read price lists on cameras and become familiar with the equipment produced.

As for your future in retail camera sales, this can be a pit stop on the way to a career as a professional photographer or it may lead you into some other aspect of the business. Some camera store owners offer profit sharing and you may end up eventually owning your own business.

Above all, if you don't enjoy retail work or don't like dealing with the public, look at something else. Life is too short to hang around doing something you don't enjoy. Finally, develop a plan; here is where you are, this is where you want to be and determine a way to get there.

Anne Sharp selling film at Riviera Camera in Redondo Beach.

Chapter 20

SCIENTIFIC PHOTOGRAPHY

Photography is used extensively in almost every field of science. There are opportunities for photographers, not only in staff positions, but also as independent contractors.

The fact is, however, that many scientists take their own pictures. Virtually all scientists who use microscopes are fully capable of doing their own photography. And astronomers invariably are also their own photographers. There are, however, opportunities to work in photo labs which support various scientific endeavors.

Photography is used in hospitals, but usually medical photographers are only found in teaching hospitals. Most of the photography is performed in conjunction with the teaching function. Many doctors are fully capable of taking their own pictures as are many X-ray technicians. Those photographers interested in and looking for work should go to teaching institutions.

So, even though photography is a essential ingredient for most sciences, there are not as many career opportunities for photographers as one might think. Some specialized fields, however, do employ significant numbers. Usually a photographer specializing in a particular science has to have education and training in the science as well as in photography.

INSTRUMENTATION PHOTOGRAPHY

By Wesley Lambert

What in the world is instrumentation photography? Even many professional photographers have never heard of it. Instrumentation photography uses the photographic medium in the engineering process. There are many jobs in this field; some in private industry, many in the government including the services.

The best-known uses of instrumentation photography are in connection with rockets, missiles and space. It is important for scientists and engineers to be able to study what happens to a space vehicle from the time the engines start until it reaches orbit. High-speed motion picture cameras are used for this purpose.

Designing, building, testing and using very specialized photographic equipment for the analyzation of motion is a field somewhat apart from the rest of the photographic industry. Many of those in this field work for the U.S. government. This was the path my career took and I more or less grew up with the instrumentation specialty.

While I was in high school, I got a job working for a small motion picture company in San Francisco. I was just a flunky, of course, but I learned a lot. The company processed and printed movie film, made film sound recorders and still enlargers. I helped on industrial movies and worked on the service and repair of projectors.

After my service in the U.S. Navy, I decided I wanted to have a career in photography. I worked for a time in San Francisco and then I went to a photo school to further my skill in portraiture. While I was in school, I worked in a camera store and took pictures of construction projects.

After graduation, I got a job with the Army as a civilian employee. Civilians who work for the U.S. government are graded into steps. These steps are called, "GS" ratings. The ratings have to do with the yearly amount of money you earn. Currently, the lowest amount paid to a GS-1 is $11,015. The highest at GS-18 is $97,317. There are certain senior executives who make more than this.

These are civil service jobs, of course. This means that you are hired on the basis of a competitive exam. First, the government advertises that a job is open. Then all of those who apply are judged on their education, experience and exam performance. The exams can consist of a written, oral or performance test, or a combination. Each job is given a GS rating. As an example, a photographer in a Range Instrumentation Systems Department of the Photo Instrumentation Branch is rated at GS-11. The salary at this level is $31,116 to start. There are step increases for each year of service to ten years when the salary is $40,449.

Wes Lambert (right) explains on of the camera systems he developed to Dr. William Eggerton at the Point Mugu Naval Missile Center in California. Official U.S. Navy photograph.

I started with the Army at GS-5; the title was General Photographer. In those days, of course, the pay was less; but today, the first-year salary for a GS-5 is $16,973. I was assigned to the Dugway Proving Grounds which is in the desert about 80 miles west of Salt Lake City.

One of my first jobs had to do with photographing the trajectory of a small rocket. The engineers were having trouble stabilizing the flight path of these rockets. I used my Sept motion picture camera and a sequential camera to help solve the problem. I altered the shutter so that the effective speed was approximately 1/1000 of a second at 16 frames per second.

Another job was to photograph the detonation of the weapon when the rocket struck. For this, I positioned a number of 4x5 still cameras around the impact area. The purpose of the photographs was to measure the size and positioning of the poison gas clouds. The problem with this sort of photography is the moment of exposure. How do you trip the shutters? Without going into detail, the answer is, with electronics. An instrumentation photographer must not only be familiar with both still and motion picture photography, but also electronics.

Some years later, I moved to the Naval Ordnance Test Station at China Lake, California and was promoted to Photo Technologist. To achieve this job title, you must have a college degree. My first assignment was in the Tracking Mount Section. High speed motion picture cameras with very long lenses were mounted on heavily modified machine gun mounts. They recorded the ground launch or air launch, flight and intercept of missiles with their targets. Next, I moved to the Cine Theodolite Section where we photographically tracked and determined the acceleration of ground-launched missiles. We used a very large, high-speed still camera mounted within a huge mechanical assembly which provided a means of traversing the camera in azimuth, elevation and roll. This system was so large it was mounted on a trailer made of two front ends of a pickup truck.

During my work with the Navy, I was involved in instrumentation photography of the Polaris missile. This is a nuclear missile which is launched underwater from a submarine. It is one of the most important elements in the defense of our country because anyone who attacks the U.S. can be assured of retaliation.

As my career progressed, I went on from taking photographs and writing reports to the actual design of instrumentation photographic systems. I participated in the design, development and testing of new camera mounts to track the flights of missiles, aerial camera pods for use on jet fighter aircraft and a wet-hull fiberglass submarine for Navy photo divers.

Instrumentation photography is challenging, interesting, exciting and, occasionally even dangerous. It is used for all sorts of other engineering and scientific projects in addition to the military applications I worked on. I retired from government service at a GS-13 level which today pays a salary of approximately $60,000 a year.

Those interested in government service in this specialty should also be aware that there are a number of important benefits in addition to the salary. In some cases, my family and I were provided with housing. The medical benefits and retirement plan are outstanding in comparison with many in the private industry.

X-RAY TECHNOLOGY

When most people think about photography and related careers, they don't include X-rays. But X-ray photography is very important. X-ray photographs are vital diagnostic tools. Without them, our health would suffer. X-ray photography is also employed in product design and in safety applications in order to visualize such things as cracks and fatigue in metals.

According to the U.S. Bureau of Labor Statistics, radiologic technologists and technicians will achieve the third highest percentage of growth between 1988 and 2000. (The first is paralegals, the second, medical assistants.) Most people call radiologic technologists, X-ray technicians. In a medical setting, an X-ray technician takes X-ray photographs of parts of the body.

X-ray photographs are exposed by radiation from a different part of the spectrum than is visible to us. The pictures, however, are on film. X-ray technicians who work in a medical setting are required to be licensed. Generally, a license can be obtained only by completing an approved course of study in an accredited institution. It is possible to complete an X-ray technology course at a community college.

There are two types of training programs one can go through in order to become a radiologic technologist. One is hospital based; the other is college or university based. It takes four years to complete a program.

One advantage to taking a college or university program is that a degree can also be achieved. In a community college, the degree is an Associate in Science; in a 4-year institution, it is a Bachelor of Science. A bachelors degree carries more prestige and offers better chances for advancement. Attending a community college is less expensive and may be more convenient. Generally, a bachelors degree is required for management or teaching positions.

A number of academic science courses are required including anatomy, physiology, algebra, physics and chemistry. In a community college, two years of academic work must be completed before starting radiologic training which is another two years. Completion of the same or similar academic work is required before starting a hospital-based program.

Whether hospital or college based, the two years of radiologic training is full time. The program includes classroom work as well as on-the-job training. The clinical rotation part—which involves working in a hospital—is 25 hours a week.

Many states require a state-issued license before a

graduate is allowed to practice. Most employers and states without a licensing procedure require a certificate issued by the American Registry of Radiolocic Technology. To get a state license or a certificate requires taking a test. A prerequisite to taking a test is graduation from an accredited program, whether hospital or college based. It is best to achieve the certificate in addition to a license since the certificate is recognized in all states.

There are many jobs available for radiologic technologists. All hospitals have positions plus many clinics and doctors' offices. In addition, some technologists work for a "registry." A registry contracts with institutions to supply technologists.

Those who start in a hospital make between $14 and $16 an hour. Most hospitals also give generous benefits including full medical and dental. Policies vary, but raises are given on at least a yearly basis. Some technologists may chose to work without benefits, in which case the hourly rate may be as high as $20. Those who work for a registry make considerably more; up to $30 an hour.

There is also a demand for radiologic technologists who take additional training in a specialty such as radiologic therapy. Those who specialize in oncology (cancer), which takes an additional year of training, start at around $30 an hour in a hospital. Those who work on contract make about $1500 a week.

There are all sorts of other specializations, some of which require additional education; others can be learned on the job. Those who acquire specialties are paid more. In addition, there are supervisory and teaching jobs.

Radiologic technology is an expanding field. New devices and techniques are continually being developed. But it is also hard work. Technologists spend most of their day on their feet lifting patients and carrying cassettes of film around. Anyone who is good at science and math and who enjoys helping people should at least consider the field.

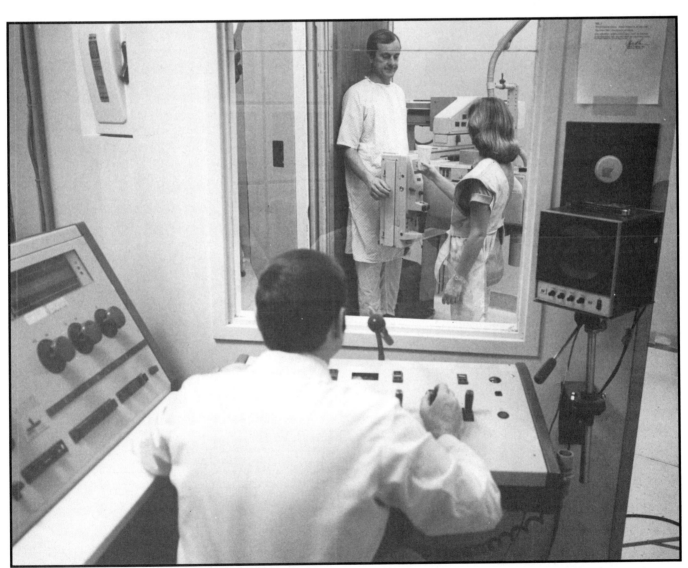

Radiologic technologists work in hospital settings with patients. Photograph courtesy The Saul Heiser School of Radiologic Technology at Daniel Freeman Memorial Hospital.

SURFER

OCTOBER 1983 VOL. 24 No. 10 $2.95 14246

The Surf-Skate Synthesis
Everything You Didn't Want to Hear About Verticals and Air!

First Thrusters, Now Clusters
Multi-Fins Take Off!

Focus on Flashdances
State of the Art Surf Photos

Combat Surf!
The Last Expedition to El Salvador?

Sydney
Great New Surf Cities Series

ON THE COVER
Jason Majors pulls off a very skate-orientated lip bash at Pupukea on Oahu's North Shore. Many modern surf moves seem to have been inspired by high-performance skating, and in this issue we re-examine the links between the two sports. Photo: Jim Russi.

Chapter 21

SPORTS PHOTOGRAPHY

There are as many types of sports photography as there are sports. Often, different sports require different techniques. There are many different jobs too. When thinking about sports photography, probably being a staffer for *Sports Illustrated* is the first thing that comes to mind. But this is the top of the heap and there are not that many photographers on the staff. Of course, there are many other sports magazines, most of them specializing in a particular sport, but for the most part, they do not employ staff photographers. Most of their pictures are produced by freelancers, from pros on assignment or from stock.

Sports magazines are just the tip of the iceberg in this specialty. Many photojournalists shoot sports. Virtually every newspaper carries sports pictures every issue. And many of the advertisements in magazines and newspapers are centered around sports. There are many sports-related products such as wearing apparel and cosmetics as well as sporting equipment. And advertisements for products and services unrelated to sports often use a sports setting.

There are thousands of organized sporting activities. Whenever there is a team, there is almost always a team picture and pictures of individual members. The team picture business is as well-organized as the wedding and yearbook businesses are. Every Little League, Pop Warner and ASYO Soccer team everywhere represents a rich resource of photo buyers. The list goes on: adult bowling leagues, adult slow-pitch softball, the mixed-doubles tennis tournament at the municipal park. A significant percentage of the population is engaged in an organized sporting activity. Everyone wants pictures to commemorate their participation.

Sports trading cards are another specialty. Cards of the members of the professional teams are sold everywhere. Shooting, publishing, distributing and selling these cards is an important business.

EDITORIAL SPORTS

By Jim Russi

My area of photography is editorial sports for magazines. The sports I shoot are surfing, professional beach volleyball, snow skiing, water skiing, wind surfing and motorcycle racing. For the most part, I shoot for the many different specialty magazines.

For almost every sport, there is at least one, and often more magazines devoted to it. There are literally hundreds of these publications. Think of a sport and you will find a magazine. Every one is filled with photographs. And every issue of every magazine needs more new and different pictures.

This is an example of the spectacular sports cover shots which have made the photographer well-known. Photograph by Jim Russi, courtesy *Surfer* magazine.

There are a number of sources. Some are taken by staff photographers. A staffer works on salary for the publication. Others are taken by independent contractors on assignment. Quite a number are taken by freelancers who shoot on spec and then try to sell their images. And a few are purchased from stock.

In the specialization of sports photography, it is unrealistic to plan on being a staff photographer for a magazine. There are very, very few such positions and seldom is there a vacancy.

On daily newspapers, most of the pictures in the sports sections are shot by staff photographers. On some of the larger papers, some photographers specialize in sports. But for the most part, photojournalists who work for newspapers must be generalists.

If you are interested in a career in sports photography, you will in all probability have to work for yourself. In order to get started, of course, you will have to first learn photography. The path I took was to earn a 4-year degree in photography from the Brooks Institute in Santa Barbara. My opinion is that this was a very worthwhile avenue to take since by the time I graduated, I was a fairly accomplished photographer. I also took quite a few other courses in addition to photography. I feel that these have stood me in good stead in running a business. There are many other good schools besides Brooks. Some of the community colleges are excellent; almost all of them offer some photography. I believe that a minimum education to get started would be an AA degree in photography from a community college.

Assuming you have your initial training behind you, how do you get started in editorial sports photography? The first thing you have to learn is how to cover sports. If you are in school and there is a school newspaper or yearbook, try to get on the staff to shoot sports. This will provide valuable practice.

Even with some school experience, you will have to go out and spend your own time and film and shoot and shoot until you learn. One way to do this is to pick out a sport you are already familiar with or interested in. Then buy copies of the magazines which are devoted to this sport. This will give you a good idea of the kinds of pictures the editors pay money for.

Go out and make contacts with the people involved with this sport in your neighborhood. Consistence and persistence is the key.

Then, when you become good enough to produce professional-level images, begin submitting to the magazines of your choice. To shoot for these magazines, you have to shoot transparencies, Kodachrome or Fujichrome in 35mm. I would suggest looking in the masthead of the magazine for the name of the photo editor and call and try to make an appointment to show your work. If you don't get to the editor the first time, keep calling. The key is pleasant persistence.

If someone is interested in sports photography just to make money, I think it is possible to find many other easier ways to make money. But if you love photography, and feel you must pursue it as a profession, you have to follow your heart. There will be many hard times, many frustrations, many aggravations. And they continue. I have been in this business for some years now and I still have frustrations and aggravations. But I am doing what I enjoy. I'm thankful that I am able to make enough money to make a living at this. But it is difficult. And you have to love it. If you don't love it, do something else. Basically the way to break into editorial sports photography is to shoot and shoot and keep submitting your work. While you are doing this, you won't be able to make a living at it. So you must have a way to support yourself. What you will need is a trust fund or a good night job so you can shoot in the daytime.

You will have come along in editorial sports when you start to get some stuff printed. When this happens, you can start to pursue magazines in order to get assignments. At this point, you can try to get the publications to give you advances for expenses. But even at this level, you will very probably need some sort of outside income.

Once you are recognized because of having a lot of pictures published, you can try for one of the few staff positions with one of the magazines. Also, some photographers are kept on retainers by magazines. Getting a retainer means that the magazine pays you some money in advance to cover certain events. But those on a retainer are still freelancers; they are working for themselves rather than on salary.

If you are in business for yourself, marketing is one of the most important aspects. You should not depend on one magazine, but have contacts with as many magazines as possible. I also place work with stock photo agencies and some work is placed with foreign magazines. I continually look for as many areas as I can spread out into insofar as marketing my work is concerned.

Anyone starting out in the field of editorial sports has to be very persistent. You have to have a thick skin because you will be rejected. If you want to get your ego beaten, this is a great field to get into. You may experience many rejections before you have even one success. And this continues throughout a career in editorial sports photography, as far as I can see. This is something you have to learn to live with. It is very difficult for an artist, but it is important.

SPORTS ADVERTISING

By Jim Russi

The other part of my business is fashion shooting. It is challenging, but also rewarding. There are very difficult situations and very difficult people you have to work with. Fashion was my major at Brooks. But I got involved in fashion work through my editorial sports shooting. This got my name known and I got tear sheets for my portfolio.

Making the switch from editorial sports to sports fashion is not easy. The money is much better, but the jobs are harder to get. For editorial sports, I get around $125 for a page from the lowest paying magazine. This goes up to $500 in *Sports Illustrated*.

In advertising, I get $500 at the low end for a regional ad. On an international level, I get up to $1500. So there is quite a bit more money in advertising than in editorial. But this is why the competition is fierce and the work harder to get.

In fashion, you can learn by being an assistant. This is not true in editorial sports. First, I strongly suggest going to school and learning the trade. If you can afford it, I would recommend Brooks or the Art Center or some comparable institution. I think a minimum should be a degree from a community college.

I would recommend that anyone interested in professional photography work as an assistant for someone who is really good. You can learn a lot. This is worthwhile even if you have to work for free.

I don't pay my assistants until they start to prove themselves. When they become helpful enough and valuable enough, I start paying them. I start them very low, around the minimum wage level. When an assistant gets really good, they get $100 a day. After that, they have usually learned enough and they go out on their own. That's okay with me, I love to train and I'm not afraid of the competition.

In sports fashion, I have to be able to offer my clients as much service as possible. In the future, I think, everyone who is successful in this specialty will need to be not only very competent, but also provide a complete service. Small clothing companies are looking to photographers to have an entourage of stylists, make-up artists, models and even printers and graphic artists. I think it is important to be able to make a complete package for some of these small companies who don't want to spend the money to go to a large advertising agency. So in this sense, the photographer becomes his own mini ad agency. There are a lot of headaches involved in this. So it is important to learn about printing and all of the processes rather than just leaving it to someone else.

Go to school and get an education if you are interested in sport fashion and sports advertising. If this is impossible, get an assistant job. Don't worry about getting paid at first. Just feel lucky if you can get on with someone who is very good.

In spite of the problems, I love to produce images. My biggest reward is when my work is published.

Photograph by Jim Russi.

Chapter 22

STAFF PHOTOGRAPHERS

Some photographers work on salary for organizations whose purpose is other than photography. These individuals are usually referred to as staff photographers. Photographers who are employed on the staffs of newspapers, magazines and other publications are called photojournalists.

All sorts of organizations large and small employ photographers in various capacities. Some just shoot, some just work in a lab and others must be very versatile. Governmental agencies from the White House on down employ photographers. And most companies of any size have a photo department.

CORPORATE PHOTOGRAPHY

By Pat Willits

I am presently the corporate photographer for Occidental Petroleum Corporation. This is a staff position and I work on salary. The job is demanding, exciting and interesting. How did I get where I am and what do I do?

I originally came to Occidental with a background in graphics. My first position with the company was as an artist and typesetter. I liked photography, so I began to take some evening courses at a nearby adult institute. I was lucky to have inspirational and talented instructors. Eventually, I took all of the photo courses offered at the institute. So I started taking classes at the University of California at Los Angeles Extension (night school).

I practiced around the company on everything and everyone. After a while, I started offering my services for

Some corporate photographers have opportunities to travel and meet famous personages. This shot was taken in Highgrove, England. Dr. Armand Hammer is on the right with the Prince and Princess. Photograph by Pat Willits, courtesy the Occidental Petroleum Corp.

company events and parties. People started asking me to cover things. At this time, Occidental did not have an in-house photography department as it does now.

For important events, the company would hire an outside professional. One year I photographed our annual stockholders' meeting along with the pro. This made it easier for me since all of my shots were just an extra bonus for the company. Nevertheless, it was exciting and very hard work.

The then Occidental Chairman of the Board, Dr. Armand Hammer was a famous art collector. With my background, I am interested in art too, so I wrote some memos to Dr. Hammer asking him if I could cover some of his art openings. After he saw some of my other work, he eventually gave his approval. My real goal was to become the Occidental company photographer. All of this time, I continued to take evening classes and practiced, practiced, practiced.

Finally, my goal came in sight. But the company wanted me to become more proficient. So I was sent to Brooks Institute of Photography in Santa Barbara as a full-time student for a four-month course. Occidental paid for all expenses and continued my salary. I studied a lot about the technical aspects and took courses in industrial photography. It was a rewarding experience and fun to attend a school where everyone had the same interests. I worked hard and learned a lot.

When I returned to Occidental, I was appointed to the newly created position of Staff Photographer, a full-time job. Eventually, the photography department grew and I was appointed to the position of Corporate Photographer.

In this job, I perform specialized photographic work for various company officers, board members, the executive staff and company departments. Among other things, I do some of the annual report photography and shoot executive portraits, photographs used for training, public relations, public information and for legal purposes. I even do aerial photography when it is needed. I work closely with various photography labs and help in the library where all of our negatives, transparencies and prints are cataloged.

I use a wide variety of professional equipment. I have had the opportunity to travel a lot of the world and in the course of my work, I have met quite a number of famous personalities.

In doing research for this essay, I surveyed six other large companies with photography departments (in addition to Occidental) to find out the range of salaries which are paid to corporate photographers. The companies were First Interstate Bank, Mattel Corporation, Arco, Hughes Aircraft, Lockheed Aircraft and the American Automobile Association. The low average annual salary was (rounded-off) $26,000 and the high average was $39,000. The lowest salary paid was $22,000 and the highest, $47,000. All of these companies offer liberal benefits including health insurance and retirement plans. I have an expense account and I believe most of the others do too.

As a woman in photography, I have always felt somewhat like a pioneer because, at least in the area I am in, it was a male dominated career. I have always enjoyed art, and photography helps fill this interest. When everything comes together just right and you know you have a good photograph, it is a very satisfying feeling. I believe it is important to get a solid technical education if you want a career in photography. And I know my background in art has been very helpful too.

GOVERNMENT PHOTOGRAPHY

By Dan Madden

When I was about 12 years old, I had the opportunity to visit with the official photographer for the Chicago Police Department's Bureau of Investigation. He told me about the time he was in Washington and went to shoot the Lincoln Memorial. The shot he wanted was blocked by a small child standing there gazing at the massive statue of the seated Abraham Lincoln. When the child finally left, he took his picture. But then he realized he had just missed the picture of a lifetime; the shot of the child and the president. This story made a lasting impression on me.

As a teenager, I found myself in the U.S. Navy. I was serving as a Communications Technician when someone "up there" decided I should be re-assigned to the base newspaper. The Navy messed up because I really enjoyed the work. I had the opportunity to get to know and work with the base photographer. He taught me the basics of shooting and processing. I often helped him in the lab and on assignments. It was a lark for me, but it turned out to be a three-month training period.

The photographer was transferred to another base and I was assigned to take his place. To do so, I had to take and pass the Navy journalist exam. Six months later, the Navy realized that there was no job category for a journalist at that base, so I was transferred to a destroyer and did two tours in Vietnam and Southeast Asia. On my last Navy job, I was assigned to an admiral in Long Beach. So when I got out, I

Los Angeles County photographer Dan Madden on assignment at the annual Los Angeles County Sheriff's Posse Ride. Photograph by Jim Camp, courtesy Los Angeles County.

settled in Southern California.

After my Navy experience, I knew I wanted to be a photographer, so I enrolled at Los Angeles Trade Technical College where I studied not only photography, but also printing. Since most professional photographs end up being printed, I thought it important to learn what goes on in that process. I also took courses at Long Beach Community College and the Art Center.

I am presently employed as a photographer for Los Angeles County. There is a great variety to this job; some of it is even exciting such as when I was sent to San Francisco to record the effects of the Loma Prieta earthquake. A lot of the work is shooting the seemingly endless number of "grip and grin" photo opportunities, judicial enrobing ceremonies and portraits. The challenge is to put as much life in these routine assignments as the more sensational work.

Getting an entry-level job (called Photographer I) with Los Angeles County is not easy. There are not too many spots and you will be competing against several hundred other applicants in an open examination situation. A Photographer I makes a starting annual salary of $25,704. There are step increases which can boost this pay to $31,944 over a two-year span.

The Photographer II level at Los Angeles County pays a top salary of $35,400. Jobs at this level are harder to find. But then this is true of almost all better paying jobs, isn't it? At this level, a photographer will have to have some specialized training and experience.

The top-level positions are rarely open and require years of experience in the particular field. They also require management skills including the ability to supervise other working photographers and to deal with budgetary demands. The pay is about $50,000 a year.

Governments at all levels will always need staff photographers. But these photographers, if they are going to advance and prosper, will have to be thinkers and not simply button pushers. Part of the thinking process is knowing what those giving out assignments really want. One time I was told to get a picture of a "train crossing." After some questioning, I discovered what they really wanted was a "train blowing smoke," a major difference!

It is important for a government photographer, or any photographer, to continually expand his or her technological horizons. We have to push ourselves and our creativity and be willing to take the extra step. And when you work for the government, perhaps the best advice of all is, "Don't let the bureaucrats get you down."

Here, I think is a great quote for photographers: "I have always felt that the highest human expression comes in our creative endeavors, those which draw upon all our posers of imagination, intelligence and understanding." — Dr. Armand Hammer.

Los Angeles County sent staff photographer Dan Madden to document the effects of the Loma Prieta earthquake for use by the emergency preparedness services in Los Angeles. Photograph by Dan Madden, courtesy Los Angeles County.

STAFF PHOTOGRAPHERS

CRUISE SHIP PHOTOGRAPHY

By James Weintraub

Being a staff photographer on a cruise ship is a little-known specialty. Every cruise ship has at least one photographer and most have a number. Cruising is a very popular vacation and it is becoming more so. Additional ships are constantly being built. Cruising used to be confined to the rich. But no longer. Some don't charge much more than a good hotel. There is even a one-day cruise out of San Diego, California which costs less than $100 including one night in a San Diego hotel. So there are many photographer jobs.

Photographers don't necessarily work directly for a cruise ship line. Photographic services can be a concession. There are two large companies which provide photographers and photographic services to cruise lines. They are Cruise Ship Pictures of London and Miami and John Davis of London.

For the most part, those who work on cruise ships are young and single. Most come to the work directly from a college major in photography. Some others have experience as studio assistants, in a lab or doing wedding photography. For most, this is not a career for a lifetime. Some work at it for two or three years; others stay with it longer. But there seem to be very few who are in their thirties and almost none in their forties.

The largest company is Cruise Ship Pictures with almost 40 ships. Those who work for this firm do not receive a salary; all the work is on commission. So the amount of money each photographer makes depends on how many passengers there are, how good the ship is and how good the photographer is.

Shooting on a cruise ship is really hard work. Because of the cost of a ship, they only stay in port long enough to take on passengers and provisions. So the photographers have to work all the time with no days off.

Every cruise ship has a staff of photographers on board and a full-service laboratory. Photograph courtesy Princess Cruises.

CAREERS IN PHOTOGRAPHY

I am a professional photographer. To see what ship photography is like, I took a three-day cruise on The Viking Princess. The first day the ship went to Catalina Island off the coast of Southern California, the second evening to Ensenada, Mexico, about 70 miles south of the U.S./Mexican border and the third day returned to its home port of Los Angeles.

The photo crew consisted of six people; in this case, five men and one woman. One of the men was designated by the company as the Chief Photographer. All of the processing, printing and selling was done on board. Each photographer shared in the work. Each must be able to shoot, process, print and sell.

Early in the morning of the second day, passengers started to get off the ship to visit Catalina. Each passenger or pair was photographed as they got off the ship. There was a set-up with the name of the ship on a life ring and a "Catalina Island" sign. Between seventy and eighty percent of the passengers will usually get off. This means 1000 to 1100 people.

There is a complete lab on the ship with the same or similar equipment found in one-hour photo labs. The Catalina departure pictures were processed and printed by 1PM. Then the prints were displayed in a gallery where two of the photographers worked on a rotating basis taking orders and selling. The gallery was open until midnight every day.

The next evening as the ship cruised to Mexico, there was a formal dance. The photographers had a set-up with a backdrop similar to those used at high school or college dances. Everyone was photographed while entering. At each of these occasions, they shoot 80 or 90 rolls of 12-exposure 120 color negative. All of the pictures were processed and printed that same night and displayed in the gallery the next day.

The crew also shot a number of other occasions: the departure from Los Angeles, cocktail parties and in the lounges. They usually shoot another 60 or 70 rolls each day. Again, everything is developed and printed immediately. Nothing is ever left over until the next day. This is really high-pressure work.

Even though the photographers have to work every day without any days off, there are a number of benefits. They don't work continuously all day and night. They usually get a few hours off every afternoon and maybe an hour or so in the evening. And all of their expenses are paid for. They don't even have to own any of the equipment. They get all of their meals—and this is some of the best cuisine in the world. They also have accommodations and even medical care since there is a doctor, nurse and clinic on every ship.

Some of the ship photographers really make a lot of money. The top-level photographers working for Cruise Ship Pictures make between $50,000 and $60,000 a year. Entry-level people make around $15,000 to start. And there are no living expenses other than clothes. Depending on the circumstances, it is possible that there is no income tax. This was the case with one English photographer I talked with. There is, however, a six-week vacation each year. The photographers are not paid during this period.

The Viking Princess never stops. It goes on alternating three and four-day cruises every week. You really have to be a single person to do this. You can't bring a family on board. A few of the people are married, but the wife or husband works at another position on the ship such as in the casino.

This ship can take almost 1800 passengers. But the ship is not always filled to capacity. At slower times of the year, there may be as few as 1200. There is a crew of 600.

The photographers with Cruise Ship Pictures get to see a lot of the world. The company doesn't keep them on the same ship forever. Most have been in the Mediterranean, the Caribbean, the American West Coast and the South China Sea out of Hong Kong.

Working as a cruise ship photographer is a real adventure for a young person. And, in comparison with other photographers in the same age bracket, the money is very good. Someone who has completed a photographic education could very well work for a number of years on a ship and save a significant amount . . . maybe enough to open a studio.

Those interested in exploring this specialty have to make contact with whoever does the hiring for each line. Cruise Ship Pictures can be contacted in Miami or London. The most direct way of finding out where to apply for a job is to contact the headquarters office of each cruise line and ask who takes care of photography. Cruise lines are listed in the yellow pages and travel agents always have brochures.

CAREERS IN PHOTOGRAPHY

Chapter 23

TEACHING PHOTOGRAPHY

Many thousands of instructors are employed teaching about photography. Most high schools, colleges and universities have one or more photography teachers. And there are a number of other settings for photographic educators: photography schools, night schools, workshops, seminars and correspondence schools. For some, teaching is a career; for others it is a part-time pursuit.

There are many teaching opportunities outside public school districts and institutions of higher education. For example, Bob Shell, *Shutterbug* editor and a contributor to this book, teaches workshops on glamour. Anne Sharp, Marketing Director of Photo Data Research (publisher of this book), teaches a night course at a community art center. Most photographic periodicals list a large number of workshops and seminars. For the most part, these endeavors are part-time and rarely lead to a full-time career. Salaries paid vary widely. Anne receives a small stipend while Bob, who organizes his own workshops, makes a handsome profit.

COLLEGES and UNIVERSITIES

College and university teachers are almost always paid more than high school teachers and they invariably teach fewer hours. A high school teacher who teaches five periods (a period may not be a full hour to allow going from classroom to classroom) a day works with students twenty-five hours a week. Community college teachers usually teach fifteen hours a week while university teachers appear in front of their students only twelve hours and some a few as nine. Of course a college or university teacher may spend considerable extra time counseling students or doing research. Full-time community college teachers are generally required to be on campus five days a week while this requirement in a university may be only four. College and university teachers are almost always required to be in their offices a

certain number of scheduled hours a week to counsel students.

Teaching in a public community (or junior) college requires a state issued credential in most states. But the requirements for a community college credential may be very different from one which will allow you to teach in a high school. You cannot assume you are qualified for a community college position unless you have a specialized credential. Many states require that their community college teachers have a masters degree. If you are interested in the specific requirement where you live, call the Department of Education in your State capitol or the dean of instruction at a community college.

Salaries for college and university teachers vary widely from state to state and between private and public institutions. Probably the very lowest full-time position pays at least $20,000 and wages for a tenured full professor with a doctorate can approach $100,000. Few photography teachers, however, will be offered a full professorship in a university. First of all, there are very few photographers or photography teachers with a Ph.D. And even then, photography is not considered to be an academic discipline on the same level as philosophy, political science and physics.

Universities and four-year (as opposed to community or two-year) colleges do not require teachers to have a credential or state certification. Generally speaking, a university teacher is hired by the department or school within the university in which he or she is going to teach. The dean of instruction and sometimes the college president have input towards a decision too. But it would be unheard of for a college to hire a teacher without the approval of the department chairperson. While the department chair usually is the most important decision maker, sometimes other senior teaching staff are consulted too. Universities and four-year colleges generally do not hire people without a Ph.D. There are sometimes exceptions in cases such as photography where not too many have achieved such a degree. But when a teacher is hired without a Ph.D., he or she is sometimes asked to agree to pursue the degree and it is understood that tenure will not be offered without it.

Many colleges and universities offer night school (sometimes called extended day or extension) courses. These may

---

Photograph by Glen A. Derbyshire, courtesy Brooks Institute of Photography.

be taught by the full-time staff; but often part-time teachers are employed. Additionally, some colleges and universities employ part-time teachers for day-time classes, particularly in such areas as photography. Many full-time teachers have first been hired as part-time instructors or adjunct professors.

HIGH SCHOOL TEACHING

There are many photography teachers working in public schools. Most are in high schools. Some teach photography full-time while others teach a mixture of photography classes and another discipline. Most public high school districts offer night school courses and many include one or more courses in photography. High school classes in journalism and yearbook may include photography.

Public schools in the U.S. are creatures of each state and teachers must be licensed or certified by the state in which they are employed. In most states, the license is called a credential. Virtually the only way a full-time public school teacher can receive a credential is through a university degree which includes education courses mandated by the state. Most states require at least a bachelor degree and some require graduate courses or degrees. Some states issue credentials based in part on experience.

The requirements for night school teachers are much less stringent. Night school credentials are often based on experience in the field, in this case, photography. Most experienced professional photographers will have little problem in receiving a night school credential.

How can you find out about credentials? Each state has a department of education which is involved, among other things, in the certification of teachers. Write to the state department of education in the capital city of your state. Ask about teacher requirements for the position in which you are interested, whether it be night school, high school or public community college.

Another way is to visit a school of education at a university. Since the state requires a college education for teachers, virtually all universities include teacher training in their course offerings. If you have been talking with someone in a public school about teaching, there will be an administrator in the school district who can advise you about the requirements for state certification.

A teacher in a private school is not required by the state to have a credential. Because private high schools may be smaller or, in some cases, specialized in some way, probably fewer offer courses in photography in comparison with public high schools. Additionally, many fewer private schools offer night school classes than do their public counterparts. So while the good news is that it is probably easier for a photographer to get a job in a private school, the bad news is that there are fewer positions to fill. While the state does not require private school teachers to be credentialed, some private schools demand that their teachers have one anyway.

Being a teacher in a high school is a career in itself, regardless of the subject taught. Very few high school English teachers are published authors. By the same token, a high school photography teacher need not necessarily be an experienced professional photographer. Many high school photography teachers have achieved their career goal by taking the courses in a university required by the state for a credential and photography courses too. Most states issue what is called a "general" credential which allows the recipient to teach any subject at all in high school. So while it might be difficult to get a job, it may be legal for someone to teach photography in a public high school without any photographic education or experience.

What are the working conditions and salary for a public high school teacher? Full-time teachers usually start at between $18,000 and $24,000 a year. But this is for a ten-month school year. Teachers who work in summer school are paid extra. Salaries for experienced teachers are higher, with a high end in the neighborhood of $40,000 to $75,000.

Salaries paid in public school districts are a matter of public record. If you are interested, you can go to a public school district head office and ask to examine the teacher salary schedule. Some teachers augment their regular salary by teaching in night school and/or summer school.

In 1989 (the last year figures are available from the U.S. Department of Education), the average annual teacher salary was $31,304. This number is misleading though, because a lot depends on where you live. In South Dakota, the average was $21,300 while in Connecticut, it was $40,496.

There are many advantages in being a public school teacher. First of all, as everyone who has attended high school knows, there are many more holidays than are recognized elsewhere. The two-month summer vacation allows teachers to further their university educations, for leisurely travel and other pursuits.

The work day usually begins at either 8AM or 9AM and most are through by 3PM at the latest. While other teachers may be burdened by grading students' written assignments, photography teachers don't have this problem. Most high school teachers teach 5 one-hour classes each day with an hour off for lunch and another hour off for office work.

The salaries of public school teachers are increased in one of three ways: time-in-service, education and overall increases. As a teacher completes more and more years in a school district, the salary is increased. This is one way districts encourage loyalty since little if any time-in-service is transferable to another school district. Teachers are generally rewarded when they take additional university courses. Many districts pay significantly higher salaries to those with advanced degrees. Most districts require a doctorate in order to achieve the highest possible salary. Sometimes, all teachers in a district are given salary raises, often because of union action.

In comparison to positions elsewhere, job security for public school (and college and university) teachers is extraordinary. This is due to a concept called tenure. After a certain number of years of service and upon satisfaction of certain requirements, teachers can achieve tenure. A tenured teacher cannot be fired without cause. The causes may not include doing a lousy job; they are often criminal in nature such as sexually or physically abusing a student.

Those who work in public night school are usually paid by the hour. Night school classes are often two or three-hour sessions, generally between 7PM and 10PM. Some night schools have Saturday classes too. Wages for night school teachers fall between $10 and $45 an hour with most in the $15 to $30 range. Those who teach night school at public schools generally do not get the fringe benefits received by full-time teachers.

One way some people start teaching is by substituting. Some states allow prospective teachers to substitute teach while they are working on their credentials. When a photography teacher is absent, the school must employ a substitute. Most principals would prefer to have someone experienced in photography rather than just a baby sitter.

NIGHT SCHOOL TEACHING

By Anne Sharp

The opportunity to teach a night school class in photography presented itself to me in an unusual way. I was asked by the community art center if I knew someone who could teach a photography class, or if I myself would be interested.

Of course this request was not made out of the blue. I had performed the duties of night manager at the Palos Verdes Art Center for a period and had, during that time, made a few friends there. In addition, I was (and am) a paying member of the art center and had volunteered my photographic services on occasion. So, when they suddenly needed to replace their beginning photography teacher, I was a natural point of reference. This is not the normal procedure these institutions take when hiring teachers. They usually request that an applicant submit a portfolio and educational history. Records of awards received and shows entered should be listed. Also any prospective teacher will be expected to have a curriculum proposal ready for approval.

In night school, there is enormous freedom in the approach and area of photography you can cover. However you need to remember that the course should have a broad enough appeal so it will attract a certain number of students or it will not be economically feasible for the school to carry the course.

People who take photography classes in community centers fit into several categories. Occasionally there are high school students who want to pursue a subject of interest not available at their school. Mothers and housewives sign up with the intention of improving their personal photographic skills. This group enjoys photography and usually just wants to learn how to take better pictures. Often, however, some become so involved and fascinated with the medium that they keep taking classes and may end up going professional.

The retiree is another student that often will become a dedicated photography student and might eventually become a professional or an advanced amateur. Just as involved can be the career or working person taking the photography class as a creative outlet. Because these people have other occupations and do not have a lot of time (remember they are taking the class for personal enrichment and enjoyment), they do not want to be saddled with tons of information and assignments. Most appreciate getting very clear and concise information. In my beginning photography class, I reduced the information needed for one three-hour lesson to one page. I call it the cooking recipe technique; all the necessary information is there, simple to read, with no frills.

The lessons are usually three hours long once a week for ten weeks. Pay is usually between eighteen and twenty-three dollars an hour, so you wouldn't want to count on this as a sole means of support, but rather a supplement to your income while starting your own business or extra money while attending school. This experience could be very valuable if you ever wanted to apply for a teaching position in a university or community college.

To teach you need a solid foundation in photography either through school or from experience. A knowledge of the chemical, technical and artistic elements are necessary. This can be acquired in any university or community college with a good photography department.

I was working on my B.A. in fine arts at the University of California at Davis when I discovered a love for photography. The emphasis at Davis was on the artistic, esthetic and compositional elements of photography. However my teacher had a background in chemistry and was an avid photo historian besides being an excellent photographer, so I was fortunate to get a well-rounded photographic education.

Where do you go once you have decided that teaching is for you? Well, a good place to start would be your local community art center. Most public high schools offer evening adult education classes. Community and junior colleges also provide a selection of night courses. Many universities have extension courses which are generally evening classes and may or may not offer the students university credit. Additionally, some cities offer evening classes through various community activity programs.

In any case, you have to be a little creative both in finding the teaching position and in structuring your own course materials. Teaching can be personally rewarding and you may find that you make many friends among your students. It also cements, so to speak, your photographic education by forcing you to research and expand your own knowledge of the medium.

Before you apply for a night school teaching job, you should prepare yourself. You should have a resume and a portfolio. Your resume should be slanted towards a teaching position rather than a photography job. Remember that most of those responsible for hiring teachers will be as impressed with your educational achievements as your photographic ones.

CAREERS IN PHOTOGRAPHY

Chapter 24

WEDDING PHOTOGRAPHY

By James and Laura Weintraub

Wedding photography is unique. First of all, most weddings take place on weekends. So generally, you have to work all day and often evenings every Saturday and Sunday. The wedding only happens once. You can't go back and shoot it again. There is a lot of pressure because of this and because it is a very emotional event for everyone involved. And you are a wedding guest too. So you have to have a friendly personality and be able to fit in.

We (Jim and Laura are a husband and wife team. Jim is in charge of photography and Laura handles the business end.) have three levels of employees: trainees, assistants and associates. Actually, all of these are part-time since this is weekend work. Trainees are usually community college students. Assistants are trainees with at least one year's experience. And associates are the top guns; the main photographer at a wedding.

Most of our associates have a job during the week and most of the jobs are in photography. For instance, one associate is a full-time fashion and portrait photographer. Another is at the sheriffs department as a photographer, and a third freelances in fashion.

We pay by the hour. The trainees get the minimum wage, the assistants start at $15 an hour and can go to $30. An associate gets from $35 to $50. The associates have to own their own equipment and a backup system and assistants have to own some of their own equipment.

Our trainees are students. Mostly they are majoring in photography at a community college. They have to work as a trainee for a minimum of one year. During that time, they have to go out on jobs at least two weekends every month. This is a minimum. Usually it is more than two.

If a trainee is successful and has been with us at least a year, he or she can go on to becoming an assistant. An assistant goes along to help the associate at the wedding. And they are a back-up photographer. After the wedding, the assistant may go on to cover the reception alone while the associate goes to another wedding. An assistant who catches

Photograph by James Weintraub.

on quickly and produces well could go to $20 very rapidly. At this level, an assistant starts to own some of his equipment and maybe also uses some of ours. A significant part of how much an assistant gets is how much equipment he owns and how well he has learned the art of wedding photography.

The highest level is associate or main photographer. At that point you must own all your own equipment. The format we require is 2 1/4 or 6x6. We shoot everything in medium format. For the most part, this is Hasselblad. The company owned equipment is all Hasselblad. Of course, an associate could have another brand such as Rollei or Bronica, but few do. He has to have a backup body, back-up flash units, a selection of lenses—wide-angle, normal and telephoto (150mm)—and two professional strobe units. We double-light everything.

An associate must be able to handle the entire wedding, from start to finish, on his own. Usually this is a six hour stretch. So there are usually three people for a wedding: a trainee, an assistant and an associate. The trainee stays with the associate and his function is to haul the equipment around, help getting set up and act generally as a gofer. Trainees don't do any shooting.

Being a trainee is an excellent learning experience. Only about one-third of our trainees go on to become assistants. Trainees not only learn a lot about shooting, but they also find out whether or not this is the field they want to specialize in. Some like it, some find out they don't want to do weddings and a few find out they don't want to spend their life in photography.

When we have an opening for a trainee, we put an ad on a 3X5 card on the nearby community college photography department bulletin board. We want people just starting out. Students in 4-year colleges either want too much money, are too set in their ways or won't give us enough time. They don't seem to have the patience; they don't want to pay their dues.

When we sell a wedding plan, it often includes video. But we don't do video ourselves. We sub-contract it out to other companies. The clients pay us and we pay the video company. When the tape is delivered, it says, "A Weintraub Production" on it. We have input on the editing of all of the tapes.

We do an average of twelve weddings each month. We

James and Laura Weintraub.

think of ourselves as photographic wedding artists, not just wedding photographers. We don't just document an event; we try to create romance and love in our pictures. According to industry statistics, $16,000 is spent on each wedding in the U.S. (Of course, these are formal weddings. Left out are those who just fly to Vegas for a weekend or go to a Justice of the Peace.) Almost ten percent of that is spent on photography and video. In the major population centers, the figure may be closer to $25,000.

The things we look for in employees are dedication, a desire to learn and, most of all, loyalty. There is no substitute for practice and development. The only way to do it is to go out and find studios that will take on people as trainees, or assistants. Then one day you can become an associate photographer.

In our specialty, it is hard to find a course in a college or trade school that will teach you wedding photography. There are some weekend seminars and workshops, but the only way we see to learn is to apprentice in one way or another.

One thing we require is for our people to become members of the Professional Photographers of America. This gives them lots of information about the industry in general. I urge anyone interested in this specialty to join the Professional Photographers of America. Within that organization, there are two lower levels. Each state has a Professional Photographers of California, New York, Illinois, etc. And the larger cities have a Professional Photographers of Los Angeles, Chicago, Miami, etc. There are meetings where experienced specialists give presentations. There are also publications and the organization operates the Winona School of Professional Photography. Members can even achieve a masters degree in photography. There are also print competitions and I would urge anyone to become involved and test themselves against what others are doing.

What we want in employees is personality, perseverance and pride. Personality is very important in this field. You are a wedding guest, after all. You have to be able to stand up under pressure; every wedding has pressure. A wedding only happens once. You cannot fail. You have to have perseverance. If your primary system fails and something happens to your backup, you have to be able to pick up your 35mm and go right on like nothing happened. You can't quit. And you have to do the very best you can. This is one of the most important occasions in peoples' lives. You cannot let them down.

We have some other requirements in addition to basic photographic knowledge. Our employees have to be well-groomed. They must have a very good appearance. We don't want any long hair and earrings on men. They also have to have an out-going personality. They have to be able to mingle comfortably with the wedding party and guests.

We require basic photographic knowledge before we will hire someone as a trainee. They have to own a 35mm camera—not a point and shoot—and they have to have completed at least one basic course in black and white photography at a community college or trade school and be enrolled as a photo major. They also have to pass a written test given at the studio.

We do not usually hire anyone directly as an assistant. The only way someone can become an assistant is to come up from being a trainee. Our studio has a very particular style. This takes some time to achieve. Even for someone with experience, to achieve this style takes at least six months.

Photograph by James Weintraub.

CAREERS IN PHOTOGRAPHY

Photograph by James Weintraub.

CAREERS IN PHOTOGRAPHY

Chapter 25

LOOKING FOR A JOB

Looking for a job is a job in itself. Those who study about and organize this task are almost always more successful than those who approach it in a hit or miss manner.

Naturally, you want to be successful in your job hunt or you wouldn't be taking the time and trouble to read this. Obviously, because you are reading this, you want to get a job in some sort of field related to photography. Good. There are many jobs available; the work can be interesting and sometimes even exciting. And you will presumably be doing something you like to do.

Almost every professional photographer was an amateur before becoming a professional. This is not necessarily true of other pursuits. Who among us would want to be operated on by an amateur surgeon or consult an amateur lawyer? But photography is different. It is not just a profession, it is also a hobby. As a matter of fact, it is one of the most popular hobbies in the world. And the hobby aspect of photography provides countless jobs.

If you want to find a job in photography and you are not already an amateur photographer, ask yourself, why not? Those who are really and truly interested in photography are avid amateurs. If you don't fall into the avid category, maybe now is a good time to take a good look at yourself. Is this something you really want? In many areas of photography, there is a lot of competition for available jobs. This is because most people would like to be able to make their living doing their hobby. So when you embark on your search for a job, you will undoubtedly be in competition with others who are truly dedicated to their craft. Without a similar dedication, you are not likely to be successful.

Now we have passed the first hurdle. You are an avid amateur photographer, dedicated to the craft. Next, take the time to finish this chapter before you do anything else. Then read through the rest of the book. Next, go back and study the parts which are of particular interest to you.

Before you start to look, prepare a resume and, if appropriate, a portfolio. Make a resume even if you have never had a job before and you may not think there is enough data to put down.

Next, select a target. What kind of a job do you want? Obviously, the target has to be reasonable. You may say to yourself that you want to be a fashion photographer in New York, shooting for top designers and magazines. Is this a reasonable target for you? If you just graduated from high school, it is not. This may be an eventual goal, but it is not a reasonable target for an immediate job hunt.

Do you already have a target in mind? Decide whether what you have in mind is a target or a goal. A target is something that you are immediately qualified for. If you don't have a specific target in mind, study the parts of this book which tell about different fields. Try to find something that appeals to you. The chapters about each field should also help you decide if you are qualified. It is seldom a very good idea to try to get a job for which you are not fully qualified. Sometimes you can get away with it by faking and get hired. But most fields of photography are technical in nature. Maybe you can get a job working in a lab, but if you don't know how to make a good, professional quality print, this failing will become obvious very soon. So take a good look at your qualifications.

If you already have considerable education and training, you know the technical tasks you are qualified to perform. If you are starting out and just want to get work, the entry-level jobs are somewhat limited. But there are a number of assistant-type jobs. The two most numerous entry-level positions are in camera stores and one-hour labs.

Now that you have picked a target and you have a good resume and portfolio, you are ready to organize your search. Make a list of the organizations where there is work. If you are at entry level, most camera stores and one-hour labs are continually hiring. This is because they don't pay a lot. But if you are just starting out, no one is going to pay you a great deal anyway. First you need experience, and a camera store or one-hour lab is a good place to get some.

Traveling to and from a job is always a problem. Look at your target organizations and list them according to the distance from your home. If everything else is equal, many employers will hire a candidate who lives the nearest. This way late and absentee problems due to car trouble or the bus

Canadian commercial photographer Gerry Kopelow's assistant, Mike Holder (left), takes an incident light meter reading on location. Photograph by Gerry Kopelow.

not coming are minimized. It's also more pleasant for you not to have to travel too far.

Your next step is to contact your targets by telephone. The first thing you need to accomplish on the telephone is to find out who the individual is you have to contact. This depends on the type of organization you have targeted and its size. If you are applying for a civil service position, there will be a rigid routine you will have to adhere to. If you are applying to a small or medium-size camera store, you will probably have to talk to the owner.

When you have found the person to talk with, explain what your interest is. You should be able to do this clearly and rapidly. If this is your first time, maybe it would be a good idea to write out a script beforehand and practice with a friend. In some fields, telephone manners are important. So your prospective employer may be judging you even as you speak on the phone.

If your target organization needs someone right away, you will probably be able to arrange an interview with your first phone call. Or you may be asked to send your resume and a letter. If this is the case, be sure to send a good letter. It should be typed and free of any grammar or spelling errors. Some employers ask for a letter and resume because these materials will indicate your written communicative abilities.

But at any rate, you won't be hired without an interview. The first and most important thing about a job interview is to BE ON TIME. Plan on arriving at least five minutes early. No one wants an employee who is late to work.

Prepare yourself for the interview. Find out exactly where the interview is to take place and how to get there. If you are taking public transportation, be sure of the bus or subway connections. If you are driving, know the route and where to park. Plan for a problem. The bus or your car may break down. Leave with plenty of time to solve an unexpected occurrence. Most employers have already heard about car or bus trouble a million times. You are unlikely to land a job if you are late, regardless of the reason.

Be neat and clean. Brush your teeth. Have a friend check your breath. You clothes should be clean and appropriate for the job you are seeking. Many employers are put off by certain styles. Some will not hire men with long hair or earrings. Others will not hire women who wear too short skirts, excessive makeup or jewelry. And so on. You should know if you are within the norm for your community. If you don't, ask for advice.

Before you are interviewed, you may be asked to fill out an employment application form. Take your resume file with you or some notes so that you are able to fill out an application rapidly and accurately. Never lie on an application. You will be asked to sign the application. An untruth is cause for dismissal. Write carefully and neatly. If you cannot write good cursive script, print.

The interview is your one chance for the job. So be prepared to do your best. Don't sit until asked to. Sit up straight and look the interviewer in the eye. Speak when spoken to. When you are asked a question, answer clearly and briefly. Don't ramble on and on. Each answer shouldn't take more than a minute. Bring copies of your resume and offer to leave one. Bring your portfolio and offer it for inspection, but don't hand it over until asked.

If you are not hired immediately, this does not necessarily mean you won't get a job. Many employers have a number of applicants and will want to interview all the candidates before deciding. If you are not given a definite "yes" or "no" during the interview, before you leave, ask when a decision will be made.

Many employers want to hire someone who is persistent. So call back in a week or after the time you were told a decision would be made.

RESUMES

A resume is like a calling card for someone looking for a job. If you don't have one, you are like a salesman without a business card. Without a resume, you immediately fall into the category of beginner, amateur or lowest-level employee.

It is never too soon to start working on your resume. Your resume should be a summary of information which you believe will let you receive the most favorable consideration from an employer. To begin, keep a file and collect every bit of data about yourself and the training, education and experiences you have.

Some people prepare a single resume. But this is like having the same sales pitch regardless of the prospect. A better idea is to make a resume depending on the organization or class of organizations you are going after. For example, if you took a summer workshop with Bret Weston and you are trying to get a job in a gallery, this would be something to emphasize. But if you are calling on a one-hour lab, it would be less important.

There are two types of resumes, one which is more or less a summary and another which is very complete. The summary or short resume should fit on one single sheet of typing paper the same size as a page in this book. The resume must be typed and free from errors. If you have changes to make, don't write them in; type a new one. Make sure the paper is clean and without erasures. If you cannot prepare an excellent resume, the better part of valor is to have one done for you by a service. Resume experts are listed in the yellow pages of the phone book. The short resume is what an interviewer or employer will use to remember you.

Some employers may request more complete and detailed information. When this happens, you need to have ready a complete resume. A complete resume should list every single detail. As an example, a short resume might list that you are a graduate of Brooks Institute of Photography in Santa Barbara. A detailed one would list the major courses of study you accomplished. A short resume would include that you were employed for two years as a photographer at the XYZ Corporation while the complete one would detail the type of photography you did and perhaps some of your major projects.

The categories of information you should include in a resume are personal data, education, training, military service, previous employment, references and other pertinent activities. As you progress, you should make an effort to collect letters of recommendation. You should have letters from your major instructors, the head of your instructional department and your employment supervisors.

These letters form the basis of your references. Most employers are not interested in references from your pastor, attorney or tennis buddy. But letters from people and institutions they may have heard about are significant.

Before starting to type your resume, you need to make a list which accounts for your activities from the time you graduated (or left) high school. Employers or interviewers can be suspicious of time gaps. What were you doing for those eight months? In jail? Is this the kind of person who would just goof off for eight months? Is this person so inept that he or she couldn't land a job for eight months? Do I really want to hire him or her? You can see the kinds of speculation significant gaps can create.

PORTFOLIOS

By Bob Shell

Photographers who hope to sell their services or be hired in a staff position need a portfolio. If you are selling yourself to someone in a creative field, you need a drop-dead portfolio.

If you have a sloppy and unorganized portfolio, this is a good indication that you yourself are sloppy and unorganized ... hardly the sort of person who will make a good employee. Another indication that a photographer is not very professional is a portfolio that includes one of everything: portraits, food, hi-tech, products, industrial, architectural, wedding, etc.

Before you look for a job, either as an employee or as an independent contractor, you should research your target. Tailor your portfolio to the market. In a small city or town, photographers often take on any sort of assignment. In larger communities, virtually everyone specializes. But even in a town situation, you should become known for your technique. Without a discernible technique, it may be assumed that you are unable to concentrate on a project.

If you are just starting out or are still a student, you need to take time to develop a portfolio. A portfolio should, at the very least, represent a decent body of work. The biggest problem most beginners have in assembling a portfolio is a lack of editing. Each picture should be the very best you can produce. Throw out everything that isn't first class.

If you have had some experiences at being paid for your work, it is important to include examples. If your work has been published, include "tear sheets." A tear sheet is the page on which the work was printed. It is often a good idea to include the original prints or transparencies too, so that the portfolio displays how well your work reproduces. Publication is important. Even if it is only your school newspaper or yearbook, put it in. As you accumulate more experience, continue editing and weed out less than excellent examples.

The next question is, how many examples represent a decent body of work? If you have only shot a limited amount of work, you should not be ashamed to have only five or six images. But they should be different. Five or six shots of the same model with the same background are not sufficient. Probably the largest number of images would be no more than thirty. And this would be a very large portfolio. You should be able to demonstrate your talents in a short span of time.

What kind of work should be in your portfolio? Today, most photographers are expected to be able to shoot in both black and white and color. Your portfolio should reflect this ability. The only exception might be if you are applying to a newspaper which doesn't print color.

Black and white prints should be made very carefully. It may take you two or three hours in the darkroom to produce one print suitable for your portfolio. And you may have to burn countless pieces of paper. Your portfolio represents what you can do. Don't even think about saving paper. Your prints should be free of scratches or dust. If you cannot spot prints so imperfections are not visible, re-wash your negatives. If that doesn't work, use another image or get it retouched by an expert.

Your choice in color is whether to use transparencies or prints. 35mm transparencies are not particularly impressive; 8x10's are. And, in some cases, transparencies are more impressive than prints. Even if you shoot in 35mm, you can have a custom lab make larger transparencies. But, of course, you will pick up some contrast and lose a little quality. A good compromise might be to include both transparencies and prints. But remember, these are general suggestions; you have to tailor your own portfolio to the market you have targeted.

Color prints should be made with the same care as black and whites. Recently, some very fine color negative emulsions have been introduced. The Kodak Ektar series is an example of a color negative material which can produce prints of reproduction quality. Make sure the film you are using fits the situation. You cannot be expected to shoot night football with an ISO 25 film. But you should not take product pictures with high speed materials just because it might be easier in terms of depth-of-field.

Whether or not your color prints should be made from transparencies or negatives is an open question. Until very recently, only transparencies were acceptable for professional reproduction. Lately, however, more and more printing plants are making separations from prints. A color print allows you a greater degree of control since you can crop and dodge.

If your prints are from transparencies, probably your best bet is Cibachrome. Without getting into the extreme expense of dye transfer, Cibachrome can probably produce the best quality. Use the glossy surface rather than the matte. The latest Cibachrome emulsions have gone a long way towards curing the problem of print contrast from contrasty transparencies. But still, be careful of high contrast in transparencies. The best color prints are often made from lower contrast originals.

If you are unable to make your own color prints, take some considerable care in selecting a really good custom lab. The high-volume mail-order labs won't even come close to what is required. Hand-made prints start at about $20 for an 8x10, so plan on spending some money. If your budget is limited, include only a few dynamite color prints. This is preferable to a lot of lack-luster ones.

Another decision is size. How large should the prints be? 8x10, of course, is a standard size. Anything smaller is really not acceptable. 16x20 is impressive, but cumbersome. In my opinion, 11x14 is a good compromise. There are a number of carry cases and binders on the market in that size. But again, your portfolio has to be tailored for your market. There is nothing wrong with 8x10. If you are including transparencies, an 8x10 can be mounted on black 11x14 art board with a window cut out. Transparencies should be covered with a clear vinyl jacket so that they can be viewed over a light table without damaging the transparency or getting it dirty.

The final question is, how should your work be presented? There are a great variety of products on the market. Take some time and shop around. Look in art supply stores as well as camera shops. The two most common products are binders and cases with a binder built in.

The sort of product commonly found in retail stores will probably suffice for many purposes. But if you are targeting advertising agencies and magazines, you should investigate some of the more recent trends in portfolio presentation. Some photographers even employ a professional designer to assemble their portfolios.

Remember, your portfolio is evolutionary. Keep working on it all the time. When you shoot a job, think about taking a few more frames for yourself. Improve your collection. Give yourself assignments. And expose yourself to the work of others. Study the best magazines and books; visit galleries and museums. Don't just look at photographs. Include other works of art.

GETTING A JOB AS A PHOTO ASSISTANT

By Dennis Miller

Okay, so you want to be a professional photographer. Most likely though, you are going to have to assist for a while just to keep body and soul together. That's not even considering you will need to learn a thousand things about the business not taught in any curriculum.

Many of us, myself included, graduate from school with the idea and promise that we are prepared to be photographers. This is a mistaken idea. It's not necessarily bad, just slightly misleading.

Unless you have a huge source of daddy's money or perhaps a rich spouse, the step from student to professional photographer will be large, scary and expensive. This is one of the reasons it is a good idea to consider the interim step of assisting. It allows you to fine focus your goals while making money and gaining experience rather than taking the plunge abruptly and blindly.

A photo assistant is an educated day laborer who helps professional photographers during shoots. He or she is a beast of burden who is as patient and strong as a pack mule, quick as a rabbit when the pressure is on, discreet as a head of state when something hits the fan and loyal and trustworthy as an Eagle Scout.

Most students, after they graduate from a trade school or college with a photo major, assist for three to six years. This is an excellent way to prepare to start their career as a professional. During this time, contacts are made, the business end of photography is learned as well as local expectations and practices.

Assisting provides a 24-hour a day graduate school. As an assistant, you will never really leave work; it will always be with you. You will always be looking and appraising visuals strewn everywhere such as magazines, television, billboards and so forth. To survive, you had better love photography and be the very best assistant you can be for the duration. The better you are, the more you will learn. And the more you learn, the better prepared you will be for the day when you go out on your own.

Without one or more assistants, most advertising and commercial photographs would not be possible. For the photographer, assistants are friends, confidants and students. For assistants, it is on-the-job training.

It is difficult to predict exactly what your start-up costs will be when you strike out on your own. But whatever you think it might be now, it will probably be more. Paying for advertising, equipment, insurance, studio space and overhead takes cash. And do you still owe on that old student loan? Assisting is the best way to earn and save that cash. And, if you are astute, you'll learn more about the business of photography than you dreamed possible.

No matter how much formal training and education you have and no matter how good it was, there is simply no substitute for experience. I'm sure you have heard the expression, "Only the experienced need apply." Well, how do you get experience in professional photography? You're not born with it! Assisting doesn't give you direct experience, but it does confer the next best thing. By keeping your eyes, ears and mind open, you can learn how a professional solves problems. And sometimes, a job will come along that is just too small for the boss. If you have established a good rapport, he just might refer it to you. Now you will get some experience.

Assisting allows you to make contacts, establish yourself

in your community and find out what your market really needs and wants. Technical knowledge is not enough, but it is an essential ingredient. Assisting helps you to look for the clues as to how you should position yourself for success.

As a beginning assistant, you will probably spend the first few years doing everything but taking pictures. The closest you will get will probably be on weekends, shooting for your own portfolio. During the week, you'll be painting, cleaning, running errands and maybe even picking up the dry cleaning.

One of the things students are often not told in school is that they will seldom be able to actually shoot when they start out. As a result, young photographers frequently become discouraged and some even quit the business. My experience is that after three years, about half of the assistants will be working at something unrelated to photography.

Others don't quit, but they become impatient. They decide to strike out on their own too soon and are doomed by their own inexperience. An assistant must be patient and understand that the boss (the professional photographer) doesn't need help taking pictures. Rather someone is needed

Dennis Miller worked as an assistant for a number of years before starting his own photography business. The photograph illustrates one of the assistant jobs: packing and shipping. Photograph by Steve Smith.

to do all the other things that must be accomplished so film can be exposed. So what if you spend all week painting, cleaning and calling caterers. At least you will know what paint works for what, what cleaning solutions to use and where to find good caterers. Scoff if you like, but this knowledge and much more will prove invaluable later.

If you are mentally prepared for the unusual things that sometimes happen, you will be able to handle situations better. Forewarned is forearmed. If you know what to look for, you may learn more as an assistant than you will when you are on your own. This helps explain why some of the unusual requests really have a basis in logic. And you will learn what you might realistically expect from assistants when you are the employer.

When I first started as an assistant, the only demands were to lift stuff, move stuff and not do anything really stupid. Today, things have changed. With larger but tighter budgets, a great deal of responsibility falls on assistants. Even though it is an entry-level position, assistants are commonly called on to perform more and more complex and important tasks.

We have all been told that lighting is three-quarters of most photographs. By the same token, preparation is three-quarters of most assisting. Whether it is hiring the right caterer, renting cars, buying film or just getting enough sleep so you can be sharp the day of the shoot, preparation is everything. Failure in any detail can endanger the entire job. If you are successful, you are a hero. You will gain the trust and learn insights from your boss who is your teacher as well as your employer. Assisting is your springboard to the business of photography.

How do you find work as an assistant? Where should you look in order to find pros from whom you can really learn? I started out in a medium-size city in the Eastern U.S. There were no freelance assistants there at the time. I began working for a local professional photographer full-time. If we had a full week, I worked 40 hours or more. If we had a slow week, I worked less; sometimes a lot less. When we were busy, the job was great. But when it was slow, it was hard to pay the bills. Eventually, I moved to Los Angeles in search of fame and fortune.

In Los Angeles, as in most cities now, there are lots of freelance assistants, and in my experience, at least a decent amount of work available. If you really want to learn, I recommend going to some big city. Only a big city has the caliber of talent, the diversity of experience and the overall opportunity. Then, if you wish to go back to your hometown, no problem. Once you've paid your dues, you'll be able to go almost anywhere and work.

But for now, how do you find work? First, I suggest going to your local large bookstore and buying copies of some reference books. Buy one each of *American Showcase* or *Corporate Showcase*, the *Workbook* and perhaps *NY Gold*, for the New York City area. There are several regional books similar to these books, but geared to a specific area. I have also gone to a local large library and found a surprising array of these books in the reference section.

Sit down and study what you see. The photographs may be designed to attract art directors and titillate designers, but they also serve to illuminate assistants. By carefully looking through these books, you can spot photographers whose work excites you. These are the people from whom you are likely to learn the most. You can help them and be paid at the same time, while they are helping prepare you for going out on your own.

After studying the aforementioned books, you have an idea of who to call, write, fax and badger. In order to sell yourself as an assistant to these potential clients, you need only the desire, the love of photography and a skin thicker than an elephant's hide. Along more practical lines, I would suggest a car, a phone, an answering machine, a digital watch, a diary/appointment book and a prep kit.

Although each individual photographer may have different requirements you may have to fill, you are ready. Make a list of the photographers whose work excites you or makes you wonder, "How the heck did he do that?" Go after the photographers whose images you would like to have in your own portfolio. These are the people who will form the core of your call list.

Make a phone log of these people and their numbers. Then start to call, announce who you are and why you are calling. Most likely they won't surprise you with an immediate request to come to work right away. But put each name in your diary for a return call and keep calling back at regular intervals. Whenever you happen to be in the neighborhood, stop by and visit. But be sure to call first. You are much more likely to be hired if you are not unknown. At least they will know you won't embarrass them with your looks or your smell.

Let's face it. It's a pain to go and meet with photographers and tie up part of the day in traffic, use up gas and all for no money. But look at it from the employer's point of view. Let's say he has a shoot coming up for a tough client and his usual assistant isn't available. This is your chance, so don't blow it. Even though it may be inconvenient for you, you can hardly blame the photographer for wanting to meet you beforehand. And you don't expect him to drive over to your place, do you?

The bottom line is, try to meet new people every free day you have. Keep doing this until you don't have any more free time because you have so much work. I can't stress too much the importance of staying in touch. The tactic that has worked well for me was to be very tenacious, but still not make a pest of myself. I always asked potential clients to tell me if I should cross over the line.

My favorite story about finding work is about the "Denver Mafia." This was a group of assistants who graduated from various schools in the Denver area and then moved to Los Angeles temporarily, to pay their dues. The remarkable thing about them was their modus operandi. Moving to a new city can be difficult. You can frequently go a long time before accumulating enough clients to pay the bills and start to get comfortable in your new home. The Denver Mafia became highly proficient at networking. If one member was busy when a call came with work, there was always another in the group available. They referred within their group so assiduously that when new members rolled into town from Denver, they almost always had work waiting for them.

Even though I have now gone pro myself, I often talk with assistants. I try to get a feel for what they are doing in order to find work. Some send out resumes, usually full of all kinds of information, but also sometimes dull. Some make a lot of phone calls. These things are good, but there is a way to make your efforts even more effective. Design a piece of promotional literature, develop a mailing list and send it to photographers you have targeted.

Here is what I did, and it was simple and effective. I got a pair of destroyed gloves, a pair of tattered sneakers covered with paint and dirt, a roll of black masking tape, a strobe meter and a sync cord, all placed on a shipping carton that said, "Hong Kong," "LAX," and "Fragile." Then I took a black and white photograph of this still life of the tools of an assistant's trade. I had a bunch of 5x7's made at a local lab and added a mini-resume extolling my many virtues on the back of each print. The total cost was about $1 each.

I mailed out 40 to people I wanted to work for and learn from. From this one mailing, I got five regular customers plus two or three occasional ones. This is a great return for direct mail.

The promotional piece allowed me to stand out from the crowd of assistants seeking work. Whether the recipients hired me or not, they remembered. It kept me busy for months. For a $40 or $50 investment, you can't afford not to do something like this now and then.

So get busy and make a promo. Good luck and successful assisting.

(This essay was adapted, in part, from an article which appeared in the Winter 1990 issue of *PhotoPro*.)

Here is the shot Dennis Miller used for his promotional mailing piece. Photography by Dennis Miller.

CAREERS IN PHOTOGRAPHY

Chapter 26

WORKING FOR OTHERS

Now you have a job related, in one way or another, to photography. Great! You are on your way in the pursuit of a career. While you are on this job, remember your career goal. Is this job an interim step, or is it your final destination?

If you answered, the final destination, you need to develop a new goal. A career is like a battle. If you are not winning, you are losing. And the best defense is a good offense. Career-wise, you always need to be on the offensive. Set a new goal and start working towards it. Your final goal should be a secure and happy retirement where you can go back to where you began: an avid amateur photographer.

Your present job may be just a step along the way. What are your objectives insofar as this job is concerned? In other words, what do you hope to achieve while on this job? One answer should be, to learn. A second should be, to set a record. And a third might be, to develop your technique. You may have others. The time to define them is now. For many, it helps to write these objectives in a private diary.

Write down the specific things you hope to learn. Setting a record is important to the achievement of your goal. The record of your achievements at this job and how your employer evaluates your performance will very probably affect the rest of your career. Try to write very specific technique objectives in your diary. And develop any other objectives you may have. Set time limits for the achievement of all these objectives. You should recognize that your employer's interests may not be the same as yours. Your job may be such that your employer wants to get the most possible production out of you. He or she may be uninterested if you learn anything new or different.

In order to leave a good record, you need to become aware of your employer's objectives. If you are employed in a private enterprise, your employer has to make a profit. Without a profit, the company will, sooner or later, go out of business. If you are employed in a governmental, not-for-profit or non-profit activity, your superiors' interest is in protecting their organization.

A large shoot may require a number of assistants. This is an excellent way to get started. Photograph by Glen A. Derbyshire, courtesy Brooks Institute of Photography.

MY IDEA OF A GOOD EMPLOYEE

The following very short essays were written by contributors to this book (or to the second volume, *Photo Business Careers*) who have been in positions to employ or supervise workers. Their viewpoints come from individual experience.

PAUL R. COMON (*Owns and operates a large camera store*). What do I expect from a new employee? Enthusiasm! If he or she is sincerely enthusiastic and likes people, the rest can be easily learned. The ideal employee is a terrific salesperson, gets along with everyone, is intelligent, honest, knowledgeable, neat, clean, punctual and dependable. Some of these traits are mandatory, but an employer cannot expect most employees to exhibit all of them.

GERRY KOPELOW (*Owns and operates a commercial studio*). For a long time I resisted hiring any help. After a while I recognized this resistance to be a little irrational. It was puzzling that even when I became quite overworked I was still reluctant to become an employer. Finally I realized that what I disliked about the employer-employee relationship was having to tell someone else what to do.

I have never had a job working for someone else. My natural inclination is to structure my own time and do what I think best at any given moment. As a child of the egalitarian sixties. I believed that this sort of life was best for everyone. The idea of ordering people around was offensive. Nevertheless, the harsh realities of business and my own physical and emotional limitations soon put an end to this idealistic state of affairs. For several years now, I have employed a variety of part-time and full-time assistants and lab technicians.

I now understand that there are people who flourish in an environment that is organized by others. I think this characteristic is valuable in an employee insofar as it is an indicator of potential harmony. The ability to function within a preexisting structure does not eliminate intelligence, honesty, or imagination as critical characteristics; rather it guarantees a sort of inter-personal bottom line.

I am a commercial photographer and I am hired by my clients to perform a service. Anyone who works for me is automatically enrolled in that same enterprise. Consequently, they must perform various tasks in ways that suit me. In my business, these tasks are often technically complicated and esthetically sophisticated; dull people don't cut it. I hire people after a personal meeting and a quick review of their formal qualifications and references. I trust my intuition when hiring, but I rely on performance to weed out unsatisfactory people after a trial period.

Because my work is complex, I can use a simple criterion for evaluating those who work with me. I assign a job, describe how I have done the job myself in the past, and I very carefully list the results I want to see. I do not insist that my methods be followed. I simply insist that the results I want are achieved by civilized, sensible means. I am willing to go through the process three times, in depth, for every task, however small. I look for someone else to hire if three times is not enough.

ALICE AND PETER GOWLAND (*World-famous glamour photography team*). Speaking specifically of assistants with our photographic work, we look for men and women who know as much or more about photography as we do. We want someone who can anticipate our needs, who is physically strong and is not lazy. An assistant with a station wagon or van is a real find because we frequently need assistance in picking up props or hauling gear and people to locations. One these requirements are filled, we look for a sense of humor. We do not want to work with people who are moody or irritable. And no smokers!

TOM COUNTRYMAN (*Industrial motion picture producer*). In commercial and industrial photography, everyone for whom you do a job becomes your employer. If you cannot show up on time, you won't be working for that person in the future.

Every day of our lives, we learn something new and everyone we work with has different and possibly better ways of doing things. Most of my employees started out as just plain helpers and went on to become cameramen, directors or heads of their own companies.

Our cameras are the tools of our trade, and if an employee doesn't know the equipment and how to take care of it, then he or she won't be able to fulfill an assignment.

DAN MADDEN (*Photographer, Los Angeles County*). What I look for in an employee is the ability to show up to work on time. If the person is conscientious enough to be on time, they are usually self-starters who care about what they are doing. In the government photography field, you need to be present, but not noticed, unless you are assigned to take charge of a shoot. Then you have to be polite, yet in charge. And after the shoot you quietly fade into the background.

You need to be sensitive to the needs of your client and the other photographers around you. If you are in the political

arena, you will probably be working around news media photographers. You need to be aware of their job and its needs, since their photographs will probably put your client into thousands or millions of homes. Perhaps your stepping out of the way is a better service to your client than holding your claimed ground.

You must be a self-starter, able to function without direction and be pleasant. No matter how rottten a mood you are in, you must never display that to a client. No one likes to look at a sourpuss. Vent you steam at the water filter in the darkroom, if you must, but hit the light with a smile.

DENNIS MILLER (*Owns and operates an independent industrial photography company*). When I am asked what I look for in an assistant, I find that it can be a difficult question to answer. Often, it is suggested to me, that a good assistant is one who will follow directions. When someone says that to me, I know right away that they have either had a very bad time finding someone with whom to work or, more likely, they are afraid to delegate.

Finding someone you can trust and then immediately delegating as much as you can logically expect the assistant to do is of paramount importance. The assistants I like to work with most are self-starters. They are willing and able to make decisions on their own, are good detail people and, of course, are hard workers.

Most importantly, they are people I can trust. I'm not just talking about trusting them not to steal. I also want to be able to trust their judgment, sensibilities and skills. I want them to be me when I can't be there. These are people to whom I can delegate responsibilities. All other attributes are poor seconds to trust.

BOB SHELL (*Editor of Shutterbug magazine*). In today's world, the biggest stumbling block in finding a good employee is education. I need someone who can read, spell and put together a grammatically correct sentence. Punctuation is another shortcoming. They simply don't seem to teach this stuff in today's schools. I expect punctuality and precision when I assign tasks. Like most professional photographers, I am a perfectionist and cannot tolerate sloppy work. I expect an employee to be clean and neat, but I do not think an employer should dictate hair style, makeup or dress so long as they are not beyond a reasonable range of current taste. I also want an employee who is not intimidated by me, who will ask questions if he or she doesn't understand something. If I ask something which doesn't seem to make sense, I expect to be told so.

The only things I will not tolerate in an employee are an arrogant or hostile attitude and a lack of common sense.

RANDY LEFFINGWELL (*Photojournalist at the Los Angeles Times*). My sole experience is in hiring assistants, never a full-time permanent employee. At first I didn't pay much attention to it, but the primary consideration I now have looking for an assistant is physical conditioning. I work very long, hard days. And frequently at the end of the longest hardest day, as the light gets critical, I start running. I need someone who can keep up.

An assistant must be a quick study. I am willing to repeat myself, but not too often. I want someone who is a self-starter and is willing to assume responsibility. I would cherish someone with a sixth sense. The very best "assistants" I have ever "hired" have been other photographers who, interested in the shoot or the challenges of the shoot, offered their services. They have the ideal "sixth sense" about what is needed: equipment, correction gels, another light.

I always pay them as much as I possibly can. An assistant must know or learn quickly how cameras load, strobes connect and work, how Polaroid film works and how it is handled, and—in my case—should know where the nearest fast-food outlet is that sells iced tea, preferably extra large, preferably two of them.

ART EVANS (*Chief Executive Officer at Photo Data Research, a publisher of photography books*). For me, the first and most important thing I expect in an employee is reliability. I want to work with someone who is always on time and never misses a day of work except on occasions of genuine emergency. Naturally then, good health is important. One time I had a young assistant who took a work day off to go to a rock concert. She truly believed that this was more important than going to her job . . . which she no longer had.

I don't enjoy telling people what to do, so I like a quick study. This attribute has to be tempered with a little common sense, however. I once had an associate who charged ahead and did three days of work without really understanding what the job requirements were. It turned out that these were three lost days; the work had to be done over again.

I really can't work with someone who doesn't speak the language. The language of photography, I mean. It is much too difficult to communicate if one side of the conversation doesn't understand the terms and definitions.

Loyalty, I think is an important attribute. Invariably, someone with whom you work will discover many things about the business and even your affairs. But these should remain private and not become the subject of gossip. For me, gossiping on the job is verboten. Part of loyalty is truthfulness. Working with others requires communication. If a co-worker does not tell the truth, communication is flawed and the work will suffer.

I like an associate who is willing to try just about anything (legal). Photography has to do with imagination and innovation. An open mind is a valuable asset.

JIM RUSSI (*Sports and advertising photographer*). A good assistant has a creative imagination, a good eye and is not afraid to express different ideas. A ton of technical knowledge is not required, but a fairly good understanding of photography is necessary. An assistant should know the different lenses and some lighting techniques.

Someone who can anticipate my needs is appreciated and knows automatically which lens to hand me and when. He or she will notice when I'm at the end of a roll and will be ready to hand over either a loaded camera or a fresh roll. A good assistant will recognize when a reflector or flash may be needed and won't be offended if I say, "No, not now."

An assistant should be physically fit, strong, agile and quick, since he or she will be required to climb ladders, run around and move things. Since there is often the need to humor a model or client, I like an assistant who is personable and works well with people.

Many photographers jealously guard their trade secrets. However, I like to teach and enjoy an employee who is eager to learn. The only exception to this is in the heat of a shoot when I only have a few minutes to capture the golden glow of the sunset.

I expect the assistant to become familiar and handy with my equipment. An assistant is more valuable if they are a good photographer, especially when I'm shooting a water action photograph. In this case, I will be in the water and my assistant, if he or she is a good photographer, will be shooting from the beach with my 800mm lens.

Photographers just starting out can learn a lot working as an assistant on important shoots. Photograph by Dennis Miller.

WORKING FOR OTHERS

139

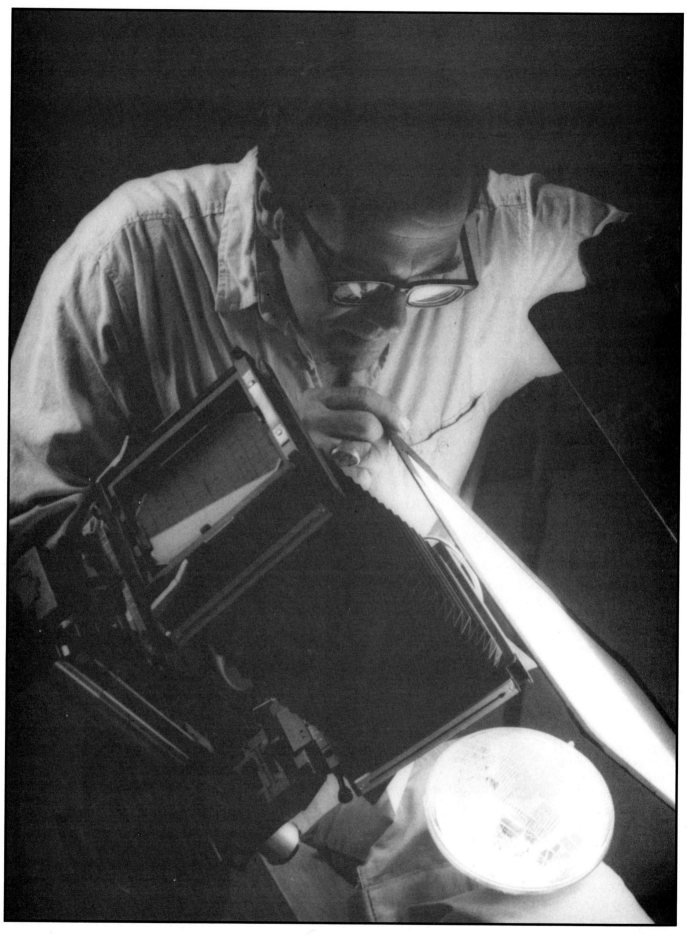

Chapter 27

PHOTOGRAPHY and MORALITY

This book is about photographic careers; how to get started and how to get ahead. But it would be incomplete if nothing is said about how photographers should act once they have a job. Some very successful and excellent photographers feel very strongly about the matter of morals and the profession. Some of the contributors to this book also wanted to contribute towards the thinking of those who will come after.

PAUL COMON

Honesty in photography can be a very fine line.

In decades past, misdeeds committed by world leaders were hushed up. In the nineties, the pendulum is swinging in the other direction. Have we gone too far? We see the private lives of politicians, entertainers, judges and religious leaders scrutinized under quartz lights and video lenses.

Any celebrity is fair game. But when the decade ends, will there be any heroes left? Even before Columbus-bashing, the "experts" were exposing the famous nineteenth century photographer, Edward S. Curtis, calling him, among other things, a huckster. They claim he didn't portray American Indians in a realistic way because he did not photograph them in blue jeans. He always eliminated any hint of the encroaching Anglo culture adopted by his subjects.

It is a cruel photographer who intentionally distorts an image with malice in mind. But is a photograph that glamorizes also offensive?

Any day now, a gossip monger may reveal to the public some rodent-like traits of Mickey Mouse. Perhaps the pendulum will swing far enough and the world will discover how many critics and "foremost authorities" live in glass houses. In the interim, photographic masterpieces like "The Vanishing Race" will continue to captivate viewers who see them for what they are: works of art, nothing more, nothing less.

Photograph by Glen A Derbyshire, courtesy Brooks Institute of Photography.

ART EVANS

During the 1960 election campaign, I was studying towards a masters degree in political science. In a seminar on American politics, each student was assigned a research project. Since I was already a photographer, I chose the topic of photojournalism and the presidential campaign.

Richard Nixon and John F. Kennedy were the two candidates. During the course of my research, I collected hundreds of pictures of Nixon and Kennedy from newspapers and news magazines. When it was possible, I identified the photographers. I then analyzed the pictures and, when possible, the politics of the photographers. I do not claim to have been the only student to have undertaken such a project. But in mine, some interesting indications came to light. Kennedy almost always appeared more attractive than did Nixon. Nixon, of course, had the problem of a heavy beard. But many of the Nixon shots were taken from low angles while just as many Kennedy shots were taken from high ones. As any photographer knows, pictures of people taken from low angels make their jaws appear large and their foreheads small, stubborn and stupid, as it were. A photograph taken from a high angle makes the forehead larger than the lower part of the face thus emphasizing the intelligence of the subject.

This was not all. The expressions of Kennedy were usually benign while those of Nixon often were threatening. Of course news photographers don't always pick the shot actually printed, editors do. But nevertheless, the differences were striking.

An investigation of a sample of the photographers revealed that they were, by a very large majority, registered Democrats or at least rather liberal. It would appear that many photographers in that campaign allowed their political sentiments to intrude on their professional work.

What is the morality of this? Should a photographer in these circumstances do as some in 1960 did? The election was very, very close. A change in only a few votes would have put Nixon in the White House instead of Kennedy.

Those few votes could have made a vast difference in subsequent events. Eisenhower was always against having

American troops in Vietnam. Maybe Nixon would have followed Ike's advice instead of what Kennedy and Johnson did. And John F. Kennedy might be alive today. We could keep on with speculation.

But the point is, do photojournalists have the right to skew their images? We could ask, do any journalists? But print journalism is different from photography. We all know that what we read was written by someone. But when we see a news photograph, we tend to think of it as a depiction of reality.

So do photographers have a higher duty than their brethren who work in other media? In this day of electronic imaging, it is possible to create a photograph of the U.S. president chopping off the head of a baby. And it can be done so it looks very real. But what about less blatant manipulations? Where does responsible journalism leave off and propaganda begin?

GERRY KOPELOW

We all want to believe that we know right from wrong. Yet what is perceived to be a moral absolute varies from culture to culture and from one historical period to another. Whatever the circumstances, we depend on accurate information to make the proper choices around ethical issues.

It is difficult to establish ethical standards governing the production and use of photographs, particularly commercial photographs, because photography itself has an ambiguous relationship to the truth. Contrary to what many people would like to believe, photographs do not always accurately record objective reality. In addition, whatever the reality reflected in particular images, those images may serve many purposes, not all of which are wholesome. If we are to depend on accurate information to make moral judgments, can we trust photographers and the users of photography to show us a reliable truth?

In my view, ethical standards for commercial photography are shaped by the reactions of the photographer to the demands of the client and then further shaped by the treatment or modification of the resulting images by the designer/retoucher/production house/editor/advertiser et al. The integrity of the process is hard to gage. It would require knowing how the viewer's response to the final image would compare to the viewer's response to the real-life situation that the image purports to represent. I believe that if an image is produced in an ethical manner, the trusting viewer will benefit. If an image is produced in an unethical manner, the trusting viewer will be harmed.

The entire process is further complicated by the knowledge that the viewer is not necessarily an innocent. The various target audiences for commercial photographs are jaded to some degree. They depend on age, intelligence and life experience. This is why photographers should have a good education. We must understand the social milieu in which we work. Like lawyers, doctors, judges, journalists and politicians, we photographers are charged with serving the public. Even though this obligation is not defined by law, it is no less binding.

Grand sentiments notwithstanding, we have to realize that photography is only a part of a vast advertising machine. Individuals can only be responsible for their own deeds. However, if in the normal course of business, a moral lesson is to be taught, I believe it is best taught by example. On the one hand, we cannot easily be forced to do unsavory things. If cigarettes cause cancer, we do not have to shoot slick ads for the tobacco companies. On the other hand, we cannot be easily forced to do wholesome things. If the United Way needs support from skilled communicators, we must rise to the occasion by an act of will.

Like Pogo said: "I have seen the enemy, and the enemy are us."

RANDY LEFFINGWELL

Ethics. Morality. Weighty concepts. Why should we as photographers worry about them if it seems that many of the people we photograph are significant because of their lack of these same things.

Photographers have a terrific legacy to carry around in two trite cliches: "The camera never lies," and "a picture is worth a thousand words."

Any of us with any experience with very wide angle or very long telephoto lenses knows we can distort reality. We can place someone's head at the edge of the frame shot with a 24mm and make them into a Saturday Night Live Cone Head. If we back off and shoot the same face with a 300mm, we flatten the face so much that we change the subject's appearance.

The same long lens can compress the distance to make one mile of Las Vegas Boulevard look like a neon nightmare. And the same wide angle can stretch distance to make our subject look taller than any of the neon signs on Times Square.

But we know these tricks, and we know when we use them and to what purposes we make our cameras tell little white lies.

A far greater danger is looming on the horizon as newspapers and magazines evolve electronically. With a sweep of a computer mouse, we can change a background color, a subject's hair color or an entire subject. We can make Bruce Willis pregnant, neatly affixing his head onto Demi Moore's full-term body.

But that is editorial illustration; and fun, too, you might suggest. So it is. But the same trickster with a mastery of the Scitex computer might be called on next to change something more substantial.

Hypothetically, a newspaper might receive a photo of any Iraqi military official walking through a rubble-strewn street scene. By careful pixel editing, it is possible to replace the unnamed, insignificant military officer's face with that of Saddam Hussein. The editorial content of the picture changes enormously and its value as page one lead art increases,

CAREERS IN PHOTOGRAPHY

especially if the original officer bore a modest resemblance to the country's leader. If the photo is an "exclusive," meaning their photographer was the only one to shoot it, who's to say it wasn't really Saddam Hussein? The camera never lies.

Another hypothetical: U.S. Secretary of State James Baker goes on an information-seeking walking tour through a particularly war-ravaged section of Jerusalem. In an open world press, many photographers would have nearly identical shots and trickery would be difficult. But in a closed society with a controlled press, a talented electronic retoucher could remove all the street debris. It would take time but the street could go from war-torn to resort-like. Baker is no longer a compassionate official but an American on holiday while the rest of the world agonizes over tragedy. The picture is worth a thousand words.

In the midst of this prophesy of doom and deception, there is a spot of good news. By and large, at most newspapers and magazines, the people entrusted with these electronic picture editing tasks are photographers; former street photographers who have been promoted out of the line of fire and into management.

Thus, the good news is pretty good. The chances of a manipulated image appearing without a disclaimer in any major publication in the United States are slim.

But the bad news is as bad. There are commercial electronic retouching studios and labs in business which offer these same services to any client with sufficient budget. These services are expensive. But face it, advertising and public relations seek to sell or promote their product. A flaw in an otherwise usable shoot will likely be retouched.

Then again, this all goes out the window in a society where the media is controlled and the access to information is limited.

So if all this makes readers nervous, gives viewers cause to worry, keeps audiences up at night, take heart! At least in the U.S., it makes photographers nervous, causes photographers worry, and keeps photographers up at night as well.

BOB SHELL

A number of recent experiences have led me to believe that the shortest book in the world might well be the one entitled, "Photographer's Ethics." Photographers seem to have adopted the selfish, "what's in it for me," attitude and have begun to drift more and more away from the ethical high ground they once occupied. For example, many photographers today espouse trendy causes. But when you see their own lifestyles, you quickly realize that they are only involved for the publicity and PR value.

Consider the case of the photographer who espouses the conservation of natural resources and recycling, but uses bundles of paper towels in the darkroom and studio to save the time and trouble of washing cloth towels. Consider the photographer who speaks grandly of environmental concerns, but shoots a photo of an endangered species chicks in a nest by cutting away tree branches which shield the babies

from predators, and scares the mother away permanently. Consider the press photographer who stages a re-enactment of a newsworthy event and passes the pictures off as authentic. Consider the advertising photographer who "doctors" before and after photos taken for a weight-loss center and who uses different focal length lenses and different lighting to take before and afters for a plastic surgeon. Consider the commercial photographer who uses photographs of a model for all sorts of purposes not covered in the release and neglects to pay the model for the additional use. Consider the photographer, shooting for a lawyer, who uses lighting and various manipulations to make injuries received in an accident appear worse than the are. And finally, consider the photographer who appears on a talk show and claims to be a vegan (one who does not use animal products for any purpose). Does this guy even know what film is made of?

Everyone involved in commercial photography has been asked to improve the appearance of products for photographic purposes. All advertising photography includes an element of puffery; the idealization of the product to make it appear more desirable. This is legitimate and one of the reasons good photographers command high prices. But when the line between puffery and deception is crossed, ethical questions arise.

It is time, it seems to me, to speak out for a code of ethics. Unless we do, the image of professional photographers and the respect earned through suffering and hard work will be diminished. We must come to respect the images we create, understand the power in our hands and the damage we can do. We have the ability to sway masses of people. Our pictures can generate positive social change and social awareness. They can also be used to mislead and for unethical purposes.

Questions regarding ethics will become more and more important as image manipulation becomes increasingly sophisticated through the use of computers. Many of us remember the hew and cry raised when the *National Geographic* used a Scitex system to relocate an Egyptian pyramid in order to create a more pleasing composition. In another example, the same publication took the hat from one Russian and put it on another. No one would have batted an eye if these had been done for an ad where such manipulation has long been accepted. But editorial content is a different kettle of fish. Now we hear stories of network television news teams staging events or even inciting crowds to violence in order to create more exciting footage.

I have always had great respect for David Bailey. He has the ability to create powerfully moving images. Several years ago, after considerable self-searching, Bailey realized he could no longer accept jobs to shoot fur coats. He had seen the brutality and insensitivity of the fur industry and so he decided to refuse jobs depicting furs as fashionable or classy. To atone for his past photographic sins, he produced a very powerful television commercial and a poster for Greenpeace.

How many photographers would accept a job to shoot pictures for ads about poison intended to kill people? If you answered, none, think again. What about all the photographs which depict smoking as a glamourous pursuit indulged in by young and beautiful people? We are all aware that smoking kills more people every year than traffic accidents and illegal drugs combined. Yet many skilled professional photographers accept commissions to produce the slick pictures that sell this poison. I don't know how these guys sleep at night. I suppose that if cocaine was legal, there would be no shortage of photographers taking pictures of gorgeous young people snorting white powder or smoking crack.

We need to realize that with the power of images we create comes responsibility. Too many of us are stuck in the, "anything for a buck," mentality which divorces cause from effect. They pretend that the use of their images in advertising has nothing to do with the effect on society of the ads.

(This essay was adapted from an article by Mr. Shell which appeared in the Summer 1990 issue of *PhotoPro*.)

ANNE SHARP

A dilemma many photographers face at some point in their careers is the question of morality as it relates to the depiction of sexually explicit or violent imagery. Where does art end and pornography begin and how fine is the line dividing the two? I'm afraid that we often don't know until we stumble across it in the form of a lawsuit or lose an account because a photo is too explicit, or, would you believe, not suggestive enough.

One example of the extremely controversial nature of this subject was the cancellation on June 13, 1989 of the photographer Robert Mapplethorpe's retrospective at the Corcoran Gallery in Washington D.C. due to the explicitly homoerotic and violent nature of some of the images. This lead not only to a tremendous conflict between artists and bureaucrats but also to the resignation soon thereafter of the Gallery's curator. In addition, the National Endowment for the Arts (N.E.A.), which had financed the show to the amount of $30,000, underwent attack and risked losing its budget.

The show eventually found a home in Washington at the Washington Project for the Arts where it opened July 20, 1989 with controversial, but great success.

However, that was not the end of the show's woes. Obscenity charges were filed against the Contemporary Arts Center in Cincinnati when Mapplethorpe's retrospective opened there in April 1990. The art gallery was finally found not guilty of obscenity and acquitted in October 1990.

So how can we define this area of photographic morality for the artist and for those who use the camera for commercial purposes? Like a sliver of glass, the answer seems to be embedded somewhere in the heel of socio-cultural and religious values, illusive and annoying. But, you may say, there is an overwhelming variety of socio-cultural and religious values in the world. And so there are.

If you traveled around the world, you would notice that a street corner newsstand in Iran lacks the sexually suggestive magazines and ads you find at a newsstand in Sweden or Italy and for a very good reason; their religion does not allow it.

That would throw some sticks in some advertiser's wheels in this country.

How often do we see advertisements taking advantage of "sex appeal" in our society by depicting scantily clad men and women promoting products? Some have become incredibly savvy at manipulating the medium. One such advertiser gone to the point of using a nude man and woman together, chest to chest, standing on a swing (I'm thinking of a recent black and white perfume ad I saw). It gave a feeling of controlled sensuality. Somehow, positioning the couple on a swing with a side view (not showing anything specific) took away the "sex" from the situation. The use of black and white for the ad served to objectify the couple, giving them more the quality of a marble sculpture than flesh and blood. Now who could object to a marble statue of nude figures lacking in specific detail? Not many in our culture, but try pulling it off in Tehran.

It seems that, when it comes to photography, as in art, context is everything. In the ad, had the context of the nude figures been different, it could have scandalized instead of sensualized. At the same time, in our society and in western Europe, such an ad is acceptable. But change the socio-cultural religious context and a person could be ostracized from society or jailed for such an ad.

Imagine taking the copy of the "David" of Michelangelo and "The Rape of The Sabines" from Piazza Della Signoria, the central plaza in Florence that they grace, and drop them off in the center of a major Muslim city. I think you would get some reactions and they wouldn't be positive.

By the same token, the United States is more puritanical than many countries in Europe. Take as an example the ban on topless sunbathing on our public beaches when in France and Italy it is not unusual to see a number of topless sunbathers on any public beach. Certain areas of the United States are more conservative than others. A lawsuit was filed against Mapplethorpe's show in Cincinnati, a conservative area, whereas in Philadelphia, Chicago, Hartford, Berkeley and Boston, the exhibition was generally accepted and very successful.

Robert Mapplethorpe was an artist and his means of expression was photography, but many commercial photographers today deal with different aspects of the same issue that his retrospective brought to the public's attention so tumultuously. A photographer could lose an account by being too explicit and yet lose another client by not being suggestive enough. A photographer I know lost an account because the images presented to the client were not sexual enough. On the other hand this same photographer has had other clients comment that their images are almost too sensual.

So, what is the answer? There is none, but maybe some guidelines will help. First, determine your own limits as a photographer. Next, study the community in which you work or the audience to which your work is exposed and understand what is socially, culturally and religiously acceptable.

If you are shooting for a magazine or for an ad to be placed in a certain magazine, you need to know what is acceptable and what is expected for each one. An ad or photograph appropriate for *Cosmopolitan* will not necessarily be acceptable for *Time*.

The bottom line is to know what the client expects and what the community accepts. There is a fine line to be aware of which sometimes could just be the difference of using black and white instead of color.

Those who decide to cross the line and not compromise their artistic ideas when in potentially controversial territory should find a good lawyer, just in case.

Photograph by Krisjan Carroll.

PHOTOGRAPHY and MORALITY

CAREERS IN PHOTOGRAPHY

Chapter 28

THE CONTRIBUTORS

The purpose of this chapter is to relate some of the lives of those who have contributed to this book. The concept is to convey career ideas to those who are just starting in photography. The experiences of others is reality, not theory. Every contributor has been successful to one extent or another. At the same time, every path has been different. Before starting on your own path, it might be useful to take a look at the routes others have taken.

BILL ALNES

Bill Alnes was born and raised in Southern California. He attended Long Beach City College where he was awarded an Associate Degree in Aeronautics.

His first job was for the Flying Tiger Line where he worked as an airframe and power plant mechanic on heavy jets. He is presently a Senior Aircraft Maintenance Instructor working for Federal Express.

Bill served for four years in the Navy working on military aircraft at the Point Mugu Naval Air Station. His first flying experience came when he joined the Point Mugu Aero Club. He earned his private pilot license while still in the Navy. After being discharged, he earned his commercial pilot rating. In 1979 he completed rebuilding his 1946 Aeronca 7DC which he still flies.

In 1973, Alnes bought his first camera, a Canon FTB. He attended photography classes at El Camino College in Torrance, California. He has his own darkroom at home. He does most of his work with a 6x7 Pentax and 35mm. He also uses a 4x5 special application aerial camera he made himself.

KRISJAN CARROLL

Krisjan Carroll attended the Art Center in high school where she took live drawing, painting and advertising design. After graduating from high school, she assisted her father in his Los Angeles design studio. Originally, she intended to follow in his footsteps.

When Krisjan was twenty, she was accepted by the California Institute of the Arts where she majored in design illustration. After a year and a half, she changed her major to fine arts so that she would have access to the school's photography equipment and supplies.

Her first work after she left school was shooting portfolios and composites for modeling agencies. She also worked in a custom lab, assisted and worked with *Cameo* magazine. Finally Carroll found stable employment working for boudoir studios. Eventually, she opened her own studio with a partner.

PAUL R. COMON

Paul Comon entered the photographic profession in 1952. He is the president of Paul's Photo Inc. of Torrance and Monteleone Photographic, Inc. of Redondo Beach, California. He has been a board member of the Southern California Photo Dealers' Guild since 1981.

Comon received his early photographic training from Sir Charles Morgan. After earning a degree in photography, he completed his formal education at the Julian Hiatt Institute of Photography. After a stint in commercial photography, Paul settled into his current occupation, owning and operating a retail camera store. Along the way, he taught photography in night school in the Torrance Unified School District.

Paul's hobbies revolve around photography. He is an avid collector of photographica as well as a weekend pictorialist. He has the distinction of having pictures published in two consecutive issues of the *Hasselblad Forum* and has contributed to the *Leica Viewfinder*.

Comon collects things photographic. He has over 2000 cameras as well as numerous peripherals and accessories. His collection of paper, however, is truly extensive. He has many signed, first edition copies of photography books plus cabinets full of information: catalogs, press releases, magazines, articles, brochures, technical manuals, instruction books and bits of data from a 38-year accumulation.

Comon is married and has four grown children, one of whom is making photography a family tradition.

TOM COUNTRYMAN

Tom Countryman became interested in photography during World War II when he recorded on film the events of the African and Italian campaigns for the 34th Infantry Division.

Alice and Peter Gowland at work in their studio in Santa Monica, California. Photograph by Joseph Dickerson

After the war, he studied engineering at South Dakota State College and the University of Oklahoma. He worked on the yearbook and student newspaper while minoring in photojournalism. In his junior year, he decided his real interest lay in photography, so he left the engineering school and took a two-year course in commercial photography at the Fred Archer School of Photography in Los Angeles.

After graduating from Archer, he opened a commercial photo studio, but was shortly called back into the Army for the Korean War as the Photo Officer for the 43rd Infantry Division.

Countryman was released from Army duty after two years and moved to Minneapolis to run the motion picture division of a large commercial photography company.

In 1956, Tom started his own motion picture company and, a few years later, took in a partner. The firm of Countryman-Klang soon became one of the largest in the Twin Cities with its own building and a full-time staff of up to seventeen.

After the death of his partner in 1987, Countryman began to phase out the motion picture production part of his business and turned his interests to the development, construction and operation of motion picture cameras cars and camera cranes. His initial interest in engineering had come full circle.

Tom is an avid sports car enthusiast. He raced a number of different Porsches with the Sports Car Club of America for some twenty years.

ART EVANS

Arthur Evans is the author of a number of books about photography. He has also written books on other subjects as well as a great many magazine articles. Evans is presently the editorial director and chief executive officer of Photo Data Research, the publisher of this book.

Evans was educated at the United States Military Academy at West Point, California State University, the University of California at Los Angeles, California Western University and the University of Southern California. He has bachelor, masters and doctoral degrees plus three California teaching credentials.

Dr. Evans has extensive experience in both still and motion picture photography. He has worked on magazines and in advertising and public relations. He was an Assistant Professor and Chairman of the Photography Department at Orange Coast College in Costa Mesa, California; the Vice President for Production at Paramount-Oxford Films and the Senior Vice President of Pyramid Films.

His still photography has been featured in numerous group and one-man shows including a solo exhibition at Lincoln Center in New York City. His work is in a number of permanent collections including the Oakland Museum, the Santa Barbara Art Museum and galleries at the University of Southern California and Occidental College.

With over 100 credits, his motion picture work has garnered numerous awards including the George Washington Medal from the Freedoms Foundation. He is a member of the Society of Motion Picture and Television Engineers, the Association for Educational Communications and Technology, the Masquers Club and the West Point Society.

Art Evans served in the active Army, the California National Guard, the US Army Reserve and is a retired officer. He is a licensed racing driver active in vintage competition, has a collection of vintage racing cars and a collection of over 80 Rolleiflex cameras.

HARRY FLEENOR

Harry M. Fleenor III is the owner of Oceanside Camera Repair. He specializes in the repair of Rollei twin-lens reflex, SL66, Rollei 35 cameras plus the Pentax Spotmatic, M and K series cameras. His shop also repairs Fuji and Ricoh autofocus cameras.

Fleenor learned camera repair at the Emily Griffith Opportunity School in Denver. He later took courses in electronics from the National Camera Repair School. Harry worked for seven and one-half years as a camera technician at Holleywell when that company distributed Rollei products in the U.S. He has had his own business for the past ten years.

Fleenor is married and has three grown children, one of whom works with him as a camera repair technician.

DENINE GENTILELLA

Denine Gentilella is a student at California State University at Dominguez Hills. She works part-time in a camera store.

Denine first became interested in photography at age nine or ten. When she went to high school, she took two photography classes: beginning and advanced. As a graduation gift, she received her fist interchangeable lens camera.

After high school, Gentilella attended the State University of New York at Farmingdale. She took photography course there and graduated with an Associate in Arts degree in liberal arts. While she was a student in New York, she worked in a one-hour lab.

In 1990, Denine's family moved to California and she moved with them. She is presently studying communications with an emphasis on public relations.

MARY GARAND

Mary Garand owns and operates a retouching business in Torrance, California called "Professional Finish." She also teaches retouching and restoration techniques. Her reputation is such that she draws work from all over the country.

Garand was initially educated and worked in drafting. During her drafting career, she became skilled at doing airbrush renderings. In 1980, she decided to change from drafting to photography, so she attended the Veronica Cass Retouching Academy at Hudson, Florida. After graduation she established her own retouching business.

ALICE AND PETER GOWLAND

Although Peter Gowland's name is one of the best-known in photography, in actuality Peter has a very important partner: his wife Alice. Alice's background is in writing and business while Peter's is in photography. But when pressed, Alice can also take pictures and is an expert darkroom technician.

Peter was schooled in London at the British Military Academy. When his family moved to the U.S., he continued at the Hollywood Professional School. Gowland's father, Gibson, starred in the famous Eric von Stroheim movie, *Greed*, among others and his mother acted and wrote scripts.

After graduating from school, Peter worked as an extra and bit player. One time he doubled for an actor named Ronald Reagan. While working in Hollywood, Gowland took up the hobby of photography. Peter met and married a Lockheed Aircraft secretary named Alice Adams in 1941 and got a job in the North American Aviation Photography Department. Later he was a photographer in the U.S. Air Force in Germany.

After Peter was discharged in 1946, he and Alice bought a home in Southern California with the GI Bill. They decided to start a freelance photography business and used their home as a studio.

The Gowlands have produced two daughters, twenty-one books, nine *Playboy* center folds and twenty documentary motion pictures. The team has sold more than 1000 magazine covers to such publications as *Cosmopolitan, Playboy, Better Homes and Gardens* and *Popular Photography*. They have sold pictures and taken assignments from United Airlines, Continental Airlines, Pan Am, Delta, Pacific Southwest Airlines, Aloha, Hughes Airwest, Smirnoff Vodka, Lancer's Wine, Black Velvet, Kodak, Polaroid, General Electric, NBC and Ridge Tool among others.

Peter has invented and manufactures twenty-eight different specialized cameras and movie equipment. His clients include Kodak, Polaroid, the FBI, the U.S. Army, Navy, Air Force and Postal Department.

The list of famous personages photographed by Gowland starts with Mohammed Ali and ends with Andy Williams with too many in between to list.

GERRY KOPELOW

Gerry Kopelow is a professional photographer and writer. He lives on sixty rural acres near Winnipeg, Manitoba, Canada. Now in his forties, Gerry began his photographic career in high school. By age sixteen he was working on assignment for the National Film Board of Canada. His early photographs appeared in several juried exhibitions and related fine art publications. At nineteen, he received a grant from the Canada Council for the Visual Arts (similar to a Guggenheim grant). By age twenty he was shooting award-winning commercial assignments for a variety of advertising, architectural and corporate clients.

All Gerry's photographic skills are self-taught. His work has appeared in such publications as *The New York Times Magazine, Architectural Record*, and *Popular Photography*. Other clients include The Canadian Broadcasting Corporation, Great West Life Insurance Company, and Canadian Airlines.

He has written several technical articles for *Popular Photography* and has recently completed two books on photography: *How to Photograph Buildings and Interiors*, (Princeton Architectural Press) and *The Professional Photographer's Business Book*, (Images Press). Current projects include a technical guide to modern films for still photography, *Film Data*, to be published by Photo Data Research as well as the creation of technical seminars for working photographers and photography students.

WESLEY LAMBERT

Wes Lambert is retired from a photographic career in the federal government civil service. He is currently involved in researching the history of early motion picture equipment. His hand-cranked movie camera collection is one of the best in the world. He edits a newsletter on the subject.

After serving in the Navy and working at various photographic jobs, Lambert took a civil service job as a "General Photographer" and worked at the U.S. Army Proving Grounds at Dugway, Utah. Almost immediately, he was assigned to instrumentation photography projects. After Dugway, he moved to the Naval Ordnance Test Station at China Lake, California.

Wesley was involved in all types of both motion picture and still picture instrumentation photography. Later in his career, he participated in the design, development and construction of specialized instrumentation camera equipment and tracking mounts.

RANDY LEFFINGWELL

Randy Leffingwell's first experiences with a camera were dodging his father's attempts to record every family holiday event on film. Somewhere along the line, that fear and loathing of photography did an about-face and by his sophomore year at Kansas University, Leffingwell was shooting for the campus daily newspaper. This led to summer internships. In May, 1968, he went to Paris to shoot the student riots for Agence France-Presse. In 1969, he interned at the Lawrence, Kansas Journal-World and in 1970, at the Chicago Daily News.

Randy returned to college each fall and continued to shoot for the student paper and the school yearbook. Occasionally, he went to class and did some homework. Upon graduation, he was hired to work for the Kansas City Star-Times where he stayed for two years. Then he moved to his native Chicago and worked for the Sun-Times for ten years.

Leffingwell had always had a love for cars, so he left the newspaper business to become the Associate Editor for *Auto-Week* magazine. After a year, he resigned and moved to California where he freelanced for eighteen months.

In 1984, he was hired by the *Los Angeles Times* and he has been there ever since. Leffingwell admits he prefers shooting things that don't talk back such as food, automobiles and architecture. But he is, in fact, a general assignment photographer and has served as the night photo editor.

Randy Leffingwell is the author and photographer of two books, *American Muscle* and *The American Farm Tractor* and is completing this third, a history of Porsche cars as told by the participants. "Doing a book," he says, "is like taking on another full-time job, but the creative satisfaction makes all the work worthwhile."

DAN MADDEN

Dan Madden is a photographer in the chief administrative office of the County of Los Angeles.

Madden was born and grew up on the south side of Chicago. His father was a police officer. His initial interest in life was piano which he started at nine years old and continued through the American Conservatory.

After four years in the Navy, Dan was discharged in Long Beach, California where he decided to make his home. He is married with two children.

Madden has worked for Los Angeles County since leaving the Navy in 1970. He is a board member of the Press Photographers Association of Greater Los Angeles and an honorary member of the Long Beach Police Officers Association. He is presently working on a committee which plans to publish a book titled, "Media Guidelines for Press Photographers." The purpose of the book is to help public safety officials in dealing with the news media.

DENNIS MILLER

Dennis Miller is a location photographer, specializing in corporate photography and based in Los Angeles.

He graduated from the State University College of New York at Buffalo with a bachelor of science in art education degree and a New York teaching credential. He majored in art education and minored in photography. After graduation, he moved to Los Angeles and, for a number of years, worked as an assistant.

In addition to working at his photography business, Dennis also guest lectures to advanced photography classes at various colleges and universities on the West Coast. He also writes for photography magazines and for National Public Radio.

BART OLDENBURG

Bart Oldenburg has spent the last twenty-three years in various sides of photography. In 1969, he graduated with a bachelors degree in photojournalism from Kent State University. Since he was an ROTC cadet, he was called to active duty in the U.S. Army. His first assignment was as an assistant motion picture director in New York City. During all of 1971, he was in charge of all combat photography for the U.S. Army in Vietnam.

After being released from active duty in the Army, he achieved a masters degree in instructional design and development from Florida State University. Since then, he has been employed in the aerospace industry in the education and training side of photography. He has published articles on video-disc production techniques and artificial intelligence applications. He is currently in charge of management training at a large Los Angeles based aerospace firm.

JIM RUSSI

Jim Russi owns and operates his own photography business in Southern California. He specializes in sports and sports fashion. His work has appeared in many magazines including *Sports Illustrated, Surfer, Powder, Sports Style* and *Surfing Life*. The sports he shoots are surfing, professional beach volleyball, skiing, wind surfing and motorcycle racing. He also shoots advertising fashion for a large number of clients who manufacture sports wear, sun glasses and accessories.

Russi grew up in the Los Angeles area and attended Palos Verdes High School where he worked on the school yearbook and newspaper as the photo editor. He graduated from Brooks Institute of Photography in Santa Barbara where he earned a bachelor of arts degree with a major in fashion illustration and advertising photography. He also studied underwater photography which he uses not only to shoot surfing but also advertising. Before setting out on his own, he worked as an assistant to Annie Liebovitz and also freelanced shooting sports.

ROBERT SCHLOSSER

Robert Schlosser is head of the Photography Department at the Huntington Library in San Marino, California. The Huntington is a library, art gallery and botanical garden. It is also one of the leading research institutions in the world.

Schlosser was born in 1947 in Detroit, Michigan. In 1962, the Schlosser family moved to Bad Hamburg, West Germany where Bob's father was working for the Sperry Rand Corp. Bob graduated from high school in Frankfurt and then attended Schiller College near Stuttgart.

In 1966, he moved to Los Angeles and joined the Merchant Marine for a two-year stint. In 1968, he moved to Santa Barbara where he worked as a freelance photographer until 1974 when he was hired by the Huntington Library as an Assistant Photographer. In 1977, he was promoted to be head of the department. Schlosser is married with two children.

ANNE SHARP

Anne Sharp is the marketing director for Photo Data Research and a freelance photographer. She also teaches night courses in photography at the Palos Verdes Art Center. In the past she has worked in the photo retail business and photographed real estate on a freelance basis for the *Peninsula News*.

While growing up, her father's work with Dupont took the family to live in Delaware for eight years, Geneva, Switzerland for five years and finally to Los Angeles where they settled in the suburb of Palos Verdes.

Anne attended the International School of Geneva Switzerland and Palos Verdes High School. She received her B.A. in Fine Arts from the University of California at Davis and participated in the Education Abroad Program at the Academy of Fine Arts in Venice, Italy.

Upon completion of her degree, she returned to live and work in Italy where she became involved in photographing the Butteri (cowboys) of the Maremma in Tuscany. During this time she also photographed for hotel brochures.

Anne has two boys ages 5 and 9.

BOB SHELL

Bob Shell is internationally known as a photographer and writer. He is currently the editor of *Shutterbug*, the world's third largest monthly photo magazine and the technical editor of *PhotoPro*, a new magazine for professionals. He writes regularly for a number of foreign magazines including *Color Foto* (German), *Photo Answers* (English) and *Asahi Camera* (Japanese). Bob has done assignment photography for *The New York Times*, *National Geographic*, the National Wildlife Federation and many others. He has also done publicity photography for Rod Stewart, Steve Winwood, Ron Wood, Ozzy Osborne and Johnny Cash. His advertising clients include Lamborghini, Nikon, Bronica, Olympus and Paul Buff, Inc. He has worked on assignment in eight European countries as well as Malaysia and Japan. The projects have ranged from frozen pizza to high fashion.

Shell's glamour and nudes are in demand worldwide. He has agency representation for the sale of prints in Tokyo, Rome, Frankfurt and London. His images have appeared on book covers, magazines, cassette covers, greeting cards and even jigsaw puzzles. In Japan, his photographs illustrate the dust jackets of Danielle Steel's novels.

Bob has written two books, *Pro-Guide: The Canon EOS System* and *Pro-Guide: The Hasselblad System*, both published by Hove Foto Books. Additionally, he has written sections for other books and a large number of magazine articles. He also teaches workshops several times a year.

Mr. Shell is a member of the Board of Directors of Photo Data Research, the publisher of this book.

JOHN UPTON

John Upton is one of the most distinguished photographic educators in the U.S. He is a full professor and chairman of the Photography Department at Orange Coast College in Costa Mesa, California.

Upton started his photographic studies at the California School of Fine Arts where he studied under Edward Weston, Ansel Adams and Minor White. Subsequently, he studied the history of photography with Beaumont Newhall at the University of Rochester. He has a M.F.A. degree from the California State University at Long Beach.

For five years, John owned and operated a commercial photography studio. In 1963, he started working at Orange Coast College as an instructor. In 1966, he took over as head of the department.

Upton co-authored with Barbara London the widely-used college-level text, *Photography*. This book is in its fourth edition and has sold almost a million copies. He has served as a trustee of the Friends of Photography, and on the board of the Society for Photographic Education and also Photo Data Research. He was a visiting curator at the International Museum of Photography at the George Eastman House and was a panelist for the National Endowment of the Arts.

JAMES AND LAURA WEINTRAUB

James and Laura Weintraub are a husband and wife team specializing in wedding photography. They were both born in Los Angeles and both have had extensive experience in both photography and advertising.

James began his photography career in high school were he was the photo editor for the yearbook. This inspired him to pursue a career in photography. After high school, he attended Pierce College and majored in photojournalism and business administration. He then attended California State University at Northridge where he served as the photo editor for the school's monthly magazine.

James' first job out of school was working for a now-defunct Los Angeles newspaper, the *Herald Examiner*. He worked as a photojournalist and as an advertising executive. During this time, he met his future wife, Laura, who was working as an advertising executive on the *Los Angeles Times*.

In 1986, they were married. They both were still working for the newspapers, but James started to freelance in his spare time. He worked at several studios, among which was one operated by Rocky Gunn, a nationally acclaimed wedding photographer.

Inspired by Gunn, the duo decided to start their own business and specialize in wedding photography. They opened their studio in 1988. Today, they handle over 150 weddings a year.

PAT WILLITS

Pat Willits grew up and attended high school in Oklahoma City. After high school, she studied commercial art for two years at Central State University in Edmond, Oklahoma. At her first job, she worked as a typesetter and assistant artist.

In 1975, Willits moved to California and began working for the Occidental Petroleum Company in Los Angeles. Her first position there was as a typesetter and production artist. In 1982, Pat was appointed Staff Photographer, a newly created position. The company then sent her to a four-month course at Brooks Institute of Photography in Santa Barbara.

In 1989, Willits was promoted to the position of Corporate Photographer, a position she presently holds. Pat lives in the San Fernando Valley.

CAREERS IN PHOTOGRAPHY

Index

Photograph by Bob Shell.